the
nordic
kitchen

Claus Meyer

the nordic kitchen

One year of family cooking

Photography by Anders Schønnemann

MITCHELL BEAZLEY

Introduction

I come from a part of the world where ascetic doctors and puritanical priests have led a 300-year-long crusade against sensuality and the pleasure-giving qualities of food. For centuries the idea of preparing wonderful meals for loved ones was considered a sin, in line with theft, wild dancing, incest and masturbation. The philosophy peddled by these fine people was that, if you want to live a long and healthy life and avoid going to hell, just eat something bland and get it over with quickly.

It was in this spirit that I was brought up in a middle-class family in the Sixties – the darkest period in Danish food history. My mother represented the first generation of Danish women to work outside the home. It was an era of canned meatballs, powdered potatoes, sauce colouring and the stock cube. My parents raised me on a diet of chopped fatty meat of the cheapest-possible quality and frozen vegetables pre-boiled years before in Kazakhstan.

Most of the meat was coated in toasted breadcrumbs, three or four times, before it was deep-fried in margarine packed with trans fatty acids – we used the excess margarine for dipping. At the age of 15, I weighed 94kg and was one of the fattest kids in the region. Eating during my childhood was never a matter of reaching out for the beauty of life . It was a matter of economic efficiency; food should cost very little, and be prepared and eaten in less than 30 minutes.

What subsequently changed my life was one transcendent year spent in France after high school. I started out working as an au pair with a dentist in Paris but fell ill. I was sent to recuperate with a French baker and *traiteur*, Guy Sverzut, and his wife Elizabeth in Agen, Gascony. I recovered surprisingly quickly and decided to spend most of my remaining time in France with Elizabeth and Guy, who treated me like the son they never had. Guy quickly realized that I was

obsessed with food and cooking, and he invited me to work at his side. His bakery, Au Petit Marquis, was a time capsule representing the golden age of French culinary craftsmanship. He was a man who always bought the best produce and never challenged a price. He regularly offered free bread and cakes to friends, family, neighbours and loyal clients. In Denmark, our evening meal would take my mother no more than 30 minutes to assemble from semi-prepared food and the three of us a maximum of 10 minutes to eat it. In Agen, every single day we would spend lots of time cooking and would frequently enjoy hours having dinner with friends and family. Coming from divorced parents, I simply felt I had found paradise on earth, and if I had fallen in love with food itself in Paris, in Agen I lost my heart to French food culture. I had also found my calling (or a calling had found me) – I wanted to change the food culture of my country.

During the next 15 years, while I was studying and, later, launching my first food companies, I believed that changing the food culture of my country was pretty much a matter of introducing the virtues of French cooking into Denmark, and, through cookbooks, TV shows and my food school, I did my best to do so. Then, in the late 1990s, I happened to be a contributor to a book about Spanish food and was charged with covering Andalucia and the Basque Country. In San Sebastian I met Pedro Subijana and Juan Marie Arzak, and I was blown away by the food – it was like nothing I had ever eaten before. But it was not just the food, it was also the underlying culture – the tapas bars, the more than 300 food societies (*Cofradias*) established with the sole purpose of honouring and celebrating iconic Basque produce, not to mention the public food clubs (*Las Sociedades Populares*), where men sharing the same profession meet once a week to cook together. During my encounter with San Sebastian, I understood that in 1978

the leading Spanish chefs had met to write a manifesto pronouncing that Spanish cuisine would one day be counted among the greatest in the world, and they went on to launch a process of revitalization deeply rooted in Spanish food history. As we all know, just 25 years later everyone in the sphere of gastronomy was talking about Spanish food, and El Bulli and Arzak were both ranked among the top five restaurants in the world.

In 1998 I watched two Danish movies that made a strong impression on me along with a large number of others in Denmark and internationally. *The Celebration* and *The Idiots* were the concrete result of an avant-garde film-making movement launched in 1995 by the Danish directors Lars von Trier and Thomas Vinterberg. With their *Dogme 95 Manifesto* they sought to define a modern cinematic expression that excluded the use of elaborate special effects or technology and emphasized the traditional values of film-making and storytelling, in the hope that the industry would give power back to the artist as opposed to the studio. It's fair to say that von Trier and Vinterberg, who were soon joined by other Danish film-makers, inspired film-makers around the globe, and today they are regarded as some of the most accomplished and influential directors in world cinema.

Influenced by these experiences, and provoked by the onslaught of the global junk and fast food industry, particularly in countries lacking a strong food culture, I decided in 2003 to open a restaurant that would work solely with Nordic produce and basically restore the link between cooking and nature in our region. I hired René Redzepi, just 25 years old, as head chef and offered him a partnership in the restaurant that we named noma. Had I known the full potential of this young man I may have had even higher ambitions on behalf of the restaurant itself, but initially the idea was not just to build one

of the best restaurants in the world but to spearhead a process of change in the way we cooked in our restaurants as well as in our homes. With noma we wanted to create a restaurant that explored the potential of Nordic produce that would stand out internationally, and we wanted to identify a common regional culinary identity and engage as many stakeholders as possible in the process of change.

We asked ourselves this: If our food culture should not just bring joy and pleasure, but also one day be counted among the most admired and respected on the planet, which values should we lean on down the road? An answer to that question was given when, in 2004, prior to the New Nordic Cuisine Symposium that we arranged, we collaborated with a number of leading chefs from the region to work out a culinary manifesto (see page 255), a sort of belief system if you will, that became a guiding light to most of us, and to a large number of other important stakeholders on the food scene, during the following decade, and beyond.

My dream year of family food

This book is the result of my desire to understand and communicate what the values embedded in the Nordic Cuisine Manifesto could mean to home cooking. It's also a kind of a testimony to the food we have been eating in my family for the past four to six years. And then it reflects my life-long interest of our culinary heritage. Which dishes from Danish food history deserve to be defended in their original state, which ones should be left behind us, and which just need a sensitive update in order to remain relevant for the next generation?

How does this food and the recipes in this book, differ from, for example, classical French food? Well, apart from featuring different produce from a different territory, as a general rule the sauces are less concentrated and contain less fat, sometimes they are even made from other

ingredients than stock – the result is that the food is lighter and more succulent. Vegetables are also treated differently and play a more distinct role in the New Nordic Cuisine – the same goes for fresh herbs, grains and pulses.

Frying, baking, braising, sautéeing, poaching and grilling are cooking techniques widely used throughout this book, just like they would be in an average French cookbook. Having said this, a number of dishes feature fish, shellfish, meat or vegetables that are simply pickled, cured or marinated. From the beginning of this journey the idea of celebrating the ingredient, nature, rather than honouring a complex process or the magic wisdom of the chef has been one of the core culinary principles of The New Nordic Cuisine. Food served raw, I believe, is an expression of that.

Eating with the seasons

I am sure that today most readers of this book value the concept of seasonality and place – something that is also the structural principle of this book. Our priorities have changed in very few years.

In the Nordic region – and generally speaking in the northern hemisphere – we have four distinct seasons and we have a large number of wild and cultivated foods that are unique to each.

With an immense garden, full of wonderful vegetables, berries, fruits, grains, nuts and herbs that are just waiting to be harvested and eaten, it's crazy not to use them. I believe we should eat what is in season, here, now. With few exceptions the crops you buy frozen aren't produced with the highest levels of deliciousness in mind, and there is no reason to use frozen products when the fresh equivalents are in season. Of course, it's nice to have a stash of blackcurrants, beans and peas in the freezer, thus prolonging the summer. But frozen produce can never replace the

freshly harvested, ultimately juicy and aromatic version of the same product – that's just the way it is. Cooking with frozen greens from a random source that have been pre-boiled has a tendency to make the entire cooking process less soulful, when the purpose should be the opposite.

I could have easily compiled a book of recipes with a guarantee that it wouldn't take you more than a maximum of 30 minutes to cook each dish. I did, honestly, give it some thought, but I came to the conclusion that other cookbook authors are better qualified for such a dogmatic exercise. After careful consideration I selected these EXACT recipes because I think the level of deliciousness they represent justifies the little bit of extra work in the kitchen they may involve. I also have a book of recipes that I am proud to hand down to my children.

Sustainable and delicious

In 2003, Harvard University published the result of a large study led by Professor David Cutler, that showed it was difficult to make a clear link between the level of macro nutrients or the content of vitamins and minerals in a diet and personal health. We shouldn't rule out that it may be healthy to eat according to our blood type or sperm quality, or live off raw food or cut out meat – there is just not much evidence to support these dietary approaches. Some people appear to attain excellent health by consuming a very high-protein diet, while others achieve similar results by eating food that is disproportionately high in fat or by eating predominantly carbohydrates. The Harvard study showed that, as far as food is concerned, the single most important factor to indicate whether you will live a long and healthy life is how often you cook your food yourself. From this perspective, I could theoretically dismiss everything we know about food and health. But of course, the study didn't show that what you eat doesn't matter to your health. In a world where Type 2 diabetes is rising in almost epidemic proportions, where 1.4 billion people are suffering from obesity, and where one in three children is likely to die 10 years younger than their parents, when every other Dane between the ages of 30 and 60 is slightly or heavily overweight – other nations being worse off – I think we have a duty to do our best to create a new food culture, where day by day we eat better and eat fewer processed foods.*

Your personal health is one thing, but the health of the planet is quite another. We have long thought that the two have nothing to do with each other. It's a view that is harder and harder to maintain. What we eat has a profound influence on our surroundings. The way most of us in the Western world eat is not sustainable. Livestock production, for example, accounts for 18 per cent of global emissions – a higher emission than the entire transport sector. Other consequences of our food production are less well known: soil erosion, deforestation, overuse of freshwater resources, loss of biodiversity and pesticides and fertilizers that contaminate soil, water and air. Furthermore, we are using enormous amounts of fossil fuel to transport massive quantities of food over long distances. We can easily take greater account of the planet's health without compromising our

quality of life. It's actually more doubtful whether we can sustain that quality of life without changing our eating habits if we think it's important that future generations should also have the opportunity to live a good life on this planet.

If you live in the northern hemisphere in a temperate climate zone, by cooking the recipes from this book a larger proportion of your energy will come from the plant kingdom and less from animal products than is standard. I believe we should all eat fresh, local produce and more whole grains, eat food from the wild, a variety of vegetables and fruits, and avoid endangered fish species. Choose organic when you can, and try to reduce food waste by cooking no more food than you need, and using any leftovers in your next meal. By following these basic principles you will feel closer to nature, and you will find that you enjoy more food that reflects the seasons and connects you to your surrounding landscape.

Bon Appétit
Claus Meyer, 2016

Foraging code of conduct

It's always lovely to take a walk in the woods, and, once you become familiar with how and when things can be eaten, you will rarely come back empty-handed. It's a very special treat to eat a dish made from ingredients you've collected in the wild. Do keep in mind that there are some rules to respect, however.

On public land, you must pick plants, berries, mushrooms and nuts for personal consumption only. Do not dig up plants or cut off branches. Use secateurs or a sharp knife to avoid damaging the plant unnecessarily. Think of the people who will come along after you and take no more than you need.

On private land, you can only pick what you can reach from public roads and paths. If in doubt, ask the owner! As a rule, they will be happy that you are interested, and you get the opportunity to talk about the area you're planning to visit.

It is an offence to uproot any wild plant without the land owner's permission, or to forage on a Site of Special Scientific Interest (SSSI).

And of course before eating any wild ingredient, be absolutely certain that you have identified it correctly and that it is safe to eat.

*Footnote

The recipes in this book are extracted from Claus Meyer's *Almanak*. The recipe compilation represented by *Almanak* follow the nutritional principles of the OPUS research centre project the New Nordic Diet under the leadership of Professor Arne Astrup, MD, PhD, DM.Sc. Department of Nutrition, Exercise and Sports, University of Copenhagen, Denmark:

- Total fat is not a particular concern but is kept in the range 25–40 per cent of calories
- A minimum of 50 per cent of all fat is unsaturated
- On average, more than 15 per cent of total calories comes from proteins

- Carbohydrates predominantly originate from wholegrain products, root vegetables, fruits and berries
- The fibre content exceeds an average of 3g per megajoule /25–35g per day
- The total calorie intake is the responsibility of each individual

It's all about flavour

Our daily bread

I believe you should eat good bread with your meals. It doesn't necessarily have to be freshly baked – bread can be reheated and good bread is great toasted. Let it be the rule rather than the exception that your bread has a high content of whole grains. The dough should be properly risen, with as little yeast as possible and baked at high temperatures. Good bread makes meals better, helps your digestion and strengthens your health. It's also extremely fun to make, and a discipline where everyone – with a little bit of guidance – can become a better baker the more bread you bake.

Season well

Although I have carefully tested the recipes, I have to say that you always need to taste the food during the cooking process. Quite simply, taste the food and add a little of what you think is missing – salt or pepper, sourness or sweetness. You might have to check the seasoning several times until you are satisfied. If you follow the recipes as they are, you will of course end up with a good result, but season the food carefully to get both a satisfying experience in the kitchen and more flavour in the end result. The art of seasoning is about the balance between the four basic tastes: sour, sweet, salty and bitter. It's very easy to correct and will make for a better end result.

I have taught about 10,000 people in cookery classes over the past 10 years, and in general people don't use enough salt. 39 out of 40 agree that the taste is better with the addition of more salt, because salt enhances the flavour of the food. Once you have added the salt, consider whether the balance between, on the one hand, the sweet and rich attributes of the dish, and, on the other, the bitter and sour elements are at the level you would like them to be. The sweetness keeps the sour and bitterness in check and makes the flavour smoother, in, for example, gravies, soups, dressings and dips.

I often find that acidity is missing. For instance, cooked vegetables can taste very plain if there is no sour element. If a dish is sweeter or richer than you would prefer, you can balance that out with some good vinegar or lemon juice. If you are missing bitterness in the dish, the easiest way to adjust it is by adding a little beer and tasting it along the way, or by adding finely chopped raw shallots, chives, parsley, citrus peel, bitter lettuce leaves. In my own kitchen, I always have 'gastrique' at hand. Gastrique is an acidic, bittersweet, caramelized vinegar syrup that you make by caramelizing sugar in a pan and then adding some good vinegar (not balsamic) and letting the caramel dissolve in it. The gastrique adds bitterness to your gravies and dressings and enhances the overall flavours. It is also good to adjust the 'heat' of your dishes, seasoning them with freshly ground pepper, horseradish, ginger juice, chilli or mustard. Select an ingredient that is already a part of the dish but that could also act to balance out the heat. The hot feeling in the mouth is the result of a chemical reaction in the trigeminal nerve. It doesn't actually have anything to do with taste – it just feels like it.

When making gravy, soup or a stew, you need to consider if the aromas are intense enough, otherwise you will have to reduce the liquid – this is always the best way to enhance all the flavours at once. If you don't have time for that, you can add aromatic ingredients. These could be herbs, chilli paste, tomato purée, mustard, spiced salt, elderberries, soy or chopped olives. This was all taken into consideration in these recipes, so I am confident that the end result will be good food. I would recommend that you look back and remind yourself of these tips from time to time until you are completely familiar with the techniques – you will find that it will take the taste of your food to another level.

Using this book

I don't expect you to cook the food in this book recipe by recipe. I do, however, hope that you will use it as a source of inspiration. If your farmers' market happens to have beautiful beetroots one day or if you can get hold of a load of elderflowers, then do look them up in the index to see if there are any recipes you would like to make.

The exact moment when wild garlic is in season or autumn apples are ripe may vary from year to year, so keep an eye on nature and make friends with your local greengrocer or fishmonger so they can advise what is in season.

I am not an overly didactic person, so that is why, for example, I will never say 'turn on the oven', but rather 'bake in a preheated oven at 200°C for 40 minutes'.

All the recipes in this book are designed for 4 people unless I have indicated otherwise. Bread, cakes and drinks recipes are often given in slightly larger quantities. The same is sometimes the case with larger roasts.

Always read a recipe thoroughly. If, in addition to the main recipe, a separate side dish is included, it will be listed after the main recipe. But be aware that it may sometimes be best if you make the side dish first. The combinations reflect the way we eat the dishes in Denmark, but feel free to combine them whichever way works best for you.

At the start of each chapter are two lists of ingredients that define that season. One lists cultivated produce, in alphabetical order. The other lists foraged ingredients chronologically, according to the order in which they can be found in the wild. Some ingredients straddle the seasons, and therefore appear at the end of one season's list and the top of the next.

Spring

Seasonal ingredients

Cultivated produce

asparagus
beetroot
brill
carrots
celeriac
chervil
chicory
chives
cicely
cod roe
dandelion leaves
eggs
flounder
garfish
green strawberries
grey mullet
horseradish
Jerusalem artichokes
kohlrabi
lamb
leeks
lovage
lumpfish roe
morels
mussels
Norwegian lobster
onions
oysters
parsley
parsnip
pointed cabbage
prawns
radish
rhubarb
sparlings
spinach
squid
turnip

In the wild

dandelion leaves
wild garlic
ground elder
rowan sprigs
nettles
sorrel
garlic mustard
beech leaves
St George's mushrooms
bird cherries
venison
woodruff
fjord shrimps
horse mushrooms
sea arrowgrass
broadleaved pepperweed
winkles
sea plantain
bolete mushrooms
elderflower
rosehips

Soups and starters

Nettle soup
with potato pillows and smoked curd cheese

Potato pillows
1kg large baking potatoes
coarse sea salt
200g plain flour, plus extra for dusting
1 organic egg, lightly beaten
sea salt flakes and freshly ground pepper

Soup
2 large baking potatoes, about
    350–400g in total
1 litre water or vegetable stock
1 shallot
½ garlic clove
1 tablespoon cold-pressed rapeseed oil
100g blanched nettles (*see* right)
sea salt flakes and freshly ground pepper

To serve
4 tablespoons Smoked Curd Cheese
    (*see* right) or full-fat quark
35g hard cheese, such as Høost or
    Cheddar, freshly grated

Start with the potato pillows. Put the potatoes in an ovenproof dish lined with coarse salt and bake in the oven at 180°C/Gas Mark 4 for 45–50 minutes or until soft.

Cut the potatoes in half and use a spoon to scrape the flesh out into a bowl. Mix in the flour and egg using a potato masher or a whisk, then season with salt and pepper. The texture of the mixture should be soft, but definitely not sticky.

On a floured work surface, roll the potato mixture out into a thin sausage shape about the same diameter as your thumb. Cut into bite-sized pieces and then stamp lightly with a fork to give them a cute little pattern. Place the potato pillows on a large baking sheet and chill in the refrigerator until the soup is ready.

To prepare the soup, peel and thinly slice the potatoes, then add them to a pan with the water or stock and cook for about 15 minutes or until soft.

Peel the shallot and garlic and slice thinly. Heat the rapeseed oil in a large pan and lightly sauté the shallot and garlic without browning. Add the blanched nettles and cook for a further 30 seconds.

Pour the potatoes and their cooking liquid into the pan with the shallot, garlic and nettles and simmer the soup for 2 minutes before it goes in the blender. Swiftly blend until smooth – it's important not to blend it for too long, as the soup will become sticky in texture. I normally can't be bothered to pass the soup through a sieve back into the pan, especially as I don't mind a lump of potato or a bit of nettle here and there, but if you wish, feel free to do so. Season the soup to taste with salt and pepper.

Cook the potato pillows in a pan of lightly salted water for 2–3 minutes, a few at a time so that they don't stick to each other. Serve the soup in bowls with some potato pillows, a spoonful of smoked curd cheese and a sprinkle of freshly grated hard cheese on top.

Blanching of nettles

Use the small young shoots or only the tops of older plants. Bring a pan of salted water to the boil, add the nettles and cook for about 30 seconds. Remove the nettles and immediately submerge in cold water to stop the cooking process so that the nettles keep their flavour and colour. Wring out all the cold water before cooking the nettles any further.

NETTLES
Look out for the first nettle shoots to sprout in spring.

Smoked curd cheese
MAKES 1 LARGE CHEESE

Pour 3 litres full-fat milk and 250ml buttermilk into a pan and season with salt (about a tablespoon). Heat to 26°C.

Add 10 drops of rennet to the milk mixture while whisking. Pour the milk mixture into a bowl, cover with clingfilm and leave to sit in the kitchen for 24 hours.

Pour the cheese curds into a sieve lined with a piece of clean thin cloth (I would recommend using a fresh muslin or cheesecloth), set over a large bowl. Leave the curds in the refrigerator to drain for 8 hours.

Flip the cheese over and return it to the refrigerator to drain for another 8 hours.

Now the cheese is ready to be smoked. I normally use a barbecue charcoal chimney starter for this purpose. Put some straw into the barbecue starter and pack it down tightly. If you like, you can put some nettles on top of the straw to add flavour. I use a small wooden pallet as a rack on which to sit the cheese for smoking, placing it on top of the starter, but a metal colander would work well or even a barbecue rack. Now light the barbecue starter – from the bottom. I use a weed burner because it is much easier to control the heat and ignition process, but a flame lighter for lighting a barbecue can also be used.

Start smoking the cheese when the smoke is thick and warm – beware of the straw catching fire – and it should be smoked for approximately 3 minutes, depending on the heat of the smoke. Leave the cheese to sit for 1 hour before serving to allow the smoke flavour to mature, if you have the time.

TIP The cheat's shortcut would be simply to take a full-fat fromage blanc or fromage frais and season it with smoked salt!

Potato soup
with wild garlic and parsley

3 large potatoes
1 litre water
1 shallot
½ garlic clove
1 tablespoon cold-pressed rapeseed oil
10–15 wild garlic leaves
1 handful of flat leaf parsley
sea salt flakes and freshly ground pepper

Peel and thinly slice the potatoes, then add them to a large pan with the 1 litre of water and cook for about 15 minutes until soft.

Peel the shallot and garlic and slice thinly. Heat the rapeseed oil in a separate large pan and lightly sauté the shallot and garlic without browning. Add the wild garlic and parsley and sauté for a further 30 seconds.

Pour the potatoes and their cooking water into the pan with the shallot and herbs and leave the soup to simmer for 2 minutes. Then blend the soup swiftly until smooth – it's important that you don't blend it for too long, otherwise the consistency will become sticky, almost like glue. Season to taste with salt and pepper.

Simmer the soup for a little longer, then serve by itself with some good bread or garnish with a spoonful of wild garlic pesto or a dollop of Homemade Mayonnaise (see page 68) or crème fraîche – as this is a lighter version of the traditional soup, a touch of cream will enrich it.

TIP You could fill out the soup by adding some lumpfish caviar, shellfish or fish.

Mussel soup
with spinach, wild garlic and barley

1kg mussels
2–3 shallots
1 carrot
1 small parsnip
1–2 leeks, trimmed and rinsed
¼ red or green chilli
1 tablespoon rapeseed oil
1–2 glasses white wine
100ml whipping cream
50g fresh spinach
8–10 wild garlic leaves
sea salt flakes and freshly ground pepper
**finely grated zest and juice from
   1 organic lemon, or to taste**
100g pearl barley, cooked

Clean the mussels by scrubbing them thoroughly under cold water and removing the beards. Discard any mussels that don't close after lightly tapping on the work surface, and those with damaged shells.

Peel the shallots, carrot and parsnip, and slice them very thinly, along with the leeks. Deseed and thinly slice the chilli. Sauté in the rapeseed oil in a pan for about 2 minutes so that they start to soften and become sweet. Add the mussels and the wine, cover the pan with a lid and steam for 4–5 minutes or until the mussels have opened. Discard any that haven't opened, as they are not safe to eat. Lift the mussels out, remove from their shells and set aside.

Add the cream to the pan and simmer for a few minutes. Rinse the spinach and wild garlic, then add to the soup.

Pour the soup into a blender and blend to a smooth consistency. Pass the soup through a sieve back into the pan and reheat until it is just about to boil. Add salt, pepper and lemon zest and juice to taste. Return the shelled mussels to the soup and add the cooked pearl barley. Leave on the heat for a minute before serving the soup with a hearty slice of good bread.

Chervil soup
with poached eggs

1 shallot
2 carrots
750ml chicken stock
2 handfuls of chervil
50ml whipping cream
sea salt flakes and freshly ground pepper
4–6 Poached Eggs (see below), to serve

Peel the shallot and carrots, and slice thinly. Add to a pan with the stock and bring to the boil, then simmer for 10 minutes over a low heat.

Roughly pluck the chervil leaves from the stems and place in a blender with the cream. Pour the vegetables and stock into the blender as well and blend until smooth.

Pour the soup back into the pan and reheat. Add salt and pepper to taste. Serve the soup in bowls with a poached egg (see below) in the centre of each, and perhaps with some Crispy Croûtons on top (see page 128).

Poached eggs

4–6 very fresh organic eggs
sea salt flakes and freshly ground pepper

Fill a pan with water, add some salt and bring to the boil. Crack the eggs individually into cups, making sure that no bits of shell find their way into the cups. If the eggs are really fresh, the whites should look bouncy and sit tightly around the yolks. Season the eggs with salt and pepper.

Use a spoon to make a whirl in the boiling water in the pan, then carefully drop an egg into the middle of the whirl and poach for 2–3 minutes. When the egg is poached, immediately lift it out into cold water to stop the cooking process. Repeat with the rest of the eggs.

Soup of green asparagus
with prawns and smoked curd cheese

1 handful of green asparagus
2 shallots
1 tablespoon standard rapeseed oil
500ml water or chicken stock
50ml full-fat crème fraîche
sea salt flakes and freshly ground pepper
2 tablespoons cider vinegar, or to taste
100g small cooked, peeled prawns
   (see page 45)
1 tablespoon Smoked Curd Cheese
   (see page 16)
1 tablespoon cold-pressed rapeseed oil

Break off and discard the woody stem ends of the asparagus, then rinse the spears in cold water. Slice the lower two-thirds of the stems finely, reserving the tips for garnishing later.

Peel the shallots and chop them very finely, then sauté lightly in a pan with the sliced asparagus in the standard rapeseed oil.

In another pan, bring the water or stock to the boil, then add to the shallots and asparagus and cook for 2 minutes – it's important to keep the cooking process swift so that the asparagus retains its green colour and fresh taste.

Pour the soup into a blender, add the crème fraîche and blend together. Pass the soup through a sieve back into the pan to get rid of any stringy bits of asparagus that haven't blended. Season to taste with salt, pepper and some of the vinegar.

Cut the asparagus tips in half lengthways and mix with the prawns, smoked curd cheese, cold-pressed rapeseed oil, salt, pepper and the remaining vinegar to taste.

Reheat the soup and serve with a spoonful of the asparagus and prawn mixture in each bowl.

White asparagus
with smoked curd cheese cream

20 white asparagus
sea salt flakes
200g small cooked, peeled prawns
   (see page 45)
freshly ground pepper
a pinch of sugar

To serve
Smoked Curd Cheese Cream (see right)
chopped fresh herbs, such as chervil, chives and parsley

Peel the asparagus and break off the woody stem ends (see the panel on how to prepare asparagus).

Bring a large pan of water to the boil, add a little salt and cook the asparagus for 2–3 minutes, depending on their thickness and to taste: 2–3 minutes will give you crisp asparagus, as I like them, but if you prefer them tender, give them 3–4 minutes, or up to 5–6 minutes if you like your asparagus completely meltingly tender, tending to the overcooked. Lift the asparagus out of the water and let them drain on a clean cloth napkin or tea towel on a platter – or if you wish to serve the asparagus warm, wrap them in the cloth, place on the platter and pour over a little of the warm asparagus cooking water.

Season the prawns with salt and pepper and just a pinch of sugar – the sugar highlights the fine prawn flavour, but be careful not to overdo it. Arrange the asparagus on a platter, adorn with little dollops of the Smoked Curd Cheese Cream (see below) and sprinkle the prawns on top. Finish with a sprinkle of chopped herbs to taste, and serve immediately.

This is one of the most sophisticated spring starters I can think of, and when asparagus and prawns are in season, I do not hesitate to bring the two ingredients together at every given opportunity. It is simply a very happy marriage.

Smoked curd cheese cream

75g Smoked Curd Cheese (see page 16)
200ml semi-skimmed milk
50ml whipping cream
1 grating of nutmeg
finely grated zest of ½ organic lemon
sea salt flakes and freshly ground pepper

Mix the smoked curd cheese with the milk and cream in a bowl to a soft cream. Add a hint of nutmeg, the lemon zest and salt and pepper to taste.

How to prepare asparagus

There are different methods for preparing white and green asparagus. White asparagus should be peeled before cooking, and the easiest way to do this is to lay the spears on a chopping board and use a speed peeler to peel from under the tip down the spear. Once peeled all over, bend the spear at the base and it will naturally snap where the woody part of the stem begins – if you try to trim the end with a knife, you risk not cutting away enough of the woody part and you'll be chewing on unpleasant fibres.

Green asparagus does not require peeling – just snap off the base of the spear to break off the woody part.

Both types of asparagus require only a short cooking time in order to retain their fresh and crisp texture – white asparagus will require a little longer cooking than the green.

Asparagus
and chervil mousseline

8 white asparagus
8 green asparagus
sea salt flakes
1 teaspoon caster sugar
Chervil Mousseline (*see* **below), to serve**

Prepare the asparagus. Peel the white ones and break off the woody stem ends (see the panel on preparing asparagus on page 19). Rinse the green asparagus in cold water.

Bring a pan of water to the boil with salt and the sugar added, but don't cook the asparagus before the mousseline sauce is ready (*see* below) and your guests are seated.

Asparagus varies slightly in girth, and the white usually needs to be cooked a little longer than the green. Boil the white asparagus for 2–3 minutes and then the green for 1–2 minutes.

Transfer the freshly cooked asparagus spears to a bowl of cold water, to keep their colour and freshness, then remove them again immediately to prevent them from losing too much heat. Let them dry briefly on a clean tea towel, then serve the asparagus warm with the Chervil Mousseline (*see* right) and great bread.

- -

TIP If your guests are not ready to eat asparagus the moment you pull them out of the boiling water, place them on a platter covered with a cloth, napkin or clean tea towel, tuck the cloth around them and pour on a little of the hot cooking water – this way they will keep warm until the party is seated.

- -

Chervil mousseline

3 organic egg yolks
2 tablespoons cider vinegar, plus extra
   for seasoning
2 tablespoons water
sea salt flakes
180g butter
1 handful of chervil (save some to garnish),
   chopped
freshly ground pepper
50ml whipping cream

Whisk the egg yolks, vinegar, measured water and a little salt together in a bain-marie (a heatproof bowl set over a pan of barely simmering water) to a creamy consistency and until the whisk leaves a trail when you lift it from the foam.

Melt the butter gently in a saucepan. Some people take the time to remove the whey, which sinks to the bottom, to clarify the butter, but I never do. Mix the butter into the eggs by pouring it in a thin stream and whisking until all of it is incorporated and the sauce is rich and smooth. Season with plenty of chopped chervil, salt, pepper and a little more vinegar.

Whip the cream lightly and fold into the mousseline just before serving – this makes it light, airy and creamy. Serve the chervil mousseline, sprinkled with chervil, with the warm asparagus as a wonderful start to a May dinner.

Toast with mussels
and sweet cicely

8 thin slices of white bread
1 tablespoon olive oil
1 tablespoon Homemade Mayonnaise
   (*see* page 68)
3 tablespoons Greek yogurt (2% fat)
1 teaspoon prepared mustard
finely grated zest and juice of ½ organic
   lemon
a pinch of curry powder
200g steamed and shelled mussels
   (*see* tip)
sea salt and freshly ground pepper
½ handful of sweet cicely, chopped

Drizzle the bread slices with the olive oil toast on a griddle pan for about 1–2 minutes on each side. The toasted slices should be very crisp and golden.

Combine the mayonnaise, yogurt, mustard, lemon zest and juice and curry powder in a bowl to make a dressing. Mix the mussels in the dressing and season with salt, pepper and the chopped sweet cicely.

Serve the mussel salad on the warm toast as a small starter, maybe with a little salad.

- -

TIP You can use canned mussels here, but fresh mussels will elevate the taste to a whole other level, and by spending the few minutes it takes to steam them (*see* page 18), you will also have one of the best stocks around – perfect for the nettle soup on page 16.

- -

Wild garlic

In early April, the forest floors teem with the first 3–6cm-wide, bright green leaves of wild garlic (Allium ursinum), also known as Nordic garlic. They grow to about 15–20cm in length and, later in the season, sprout white star-like flowers in small sphere-shaped clusters atop triangular stems. Wild garlic may be confused with lily of the valley, which is highly toxic, but if you smell the plants, you should be left in no doubt, as wild garlic has a very strong garlicky scent and taste. Good places to look for it are moist, humus-rich, leafy deciduous forests and woodland populated with ash and hazel or damp riverbanks. Place the leaves in a sealed bag with a few drops of water and they will keep fresh for up to a week in the refrigerator.

Using wild garlic

Cut as many leaves as you need, rinse them and use them chopped in a potato salad, soup or stew, or on a slice of rye bread. Mix the shredded leaves with a little oil and some salt to make a paste to use as dip for fish, chicken or smoked meats, for example. You can store the wild garlic paste in small containers in the freezer, which will preserve both its flavour and colour, but it will also keep well in the refrigerator. The white flowers are perfect as a garnish, and have a delicious crunchy texture and a distinct leek flavour. The green buds that appear in June can be sprinkled over dishes or pickled as capers.

Wild garlic pesto

You will need about 20 wild garlic leaves, 1 handful of parsley, 30g fresh crustless bread, 50g skinned hazelnuts (see page 156), 200ml cold-pressed rapeseed oil, sea salt flakes and freshly ground pepper and a little unrefined cane sugar or honey.

Rinse the herbs and leave them to drain thoroughly before you tear them into smaller bouquets – you can include some of the stems too. Add to a blender with the bread, hazelnuts and oil and blend to a coarse paste. Season to taste with salt, pepper and the sugar or honey. The pesto is really good with baked root vegetables or potatoes and a piece of fried fish, meat or poultry.

Pickled wild garlic buds

You will need 200g wild garlic buds, 100g coarse sea salt, 200ml cider vinegar, 100ml water, 100g sugar, 5 whole black peppercorns and 2 bay leaves.

Check that the wild garlic buds are fresh, then rinse them thoroughly, place them in a bowl and sprinkle with the salt. Leave in the kitchen for 12 hours. Wash the buds and put them into sterilized preserving jars. Combine the vinegar, measured water, sugar and spices in a saucepan and bring to the boil. Remove from the heat and leave to cool, then pour the brine over the wild garlic buds, seal the jars tightly and leave them to pickle in the refrigerator for 7 days before you start using them. They will keep fresh for up to 6 months in the refrigerator.

Wild garlic salt

You will need 10 wild garlic leaves and 2 tablespoons coarse sea salt – that's all.

Put the garlic leaves and salt in a food processor and blend to a beautiful, green salt. Store the salt in a glass jar or other airtight container and use it to sprinkle over soft-boiled eggs, scrambled eggs or bread, or to season a steak or a piece of fish.

Meat

Roast leg of lamb
with crust of herbs

1 whole leg of lamb on the bone,
    about 2kg
sea salt flakes and freshly ground pepper
3 garlic cloves
1 tablespoon English mustard
2–3 tablespoons fresh breadcrumbs
200g chopped fresh herbs, such as
    parsley, rosemary and thyme
2 tablespoons softened butter

Rub the leg of lamb thoroughly with salt and pepper. Peel and chop 1 garlic clove and mix it with the mustard, then glaze the lamb with the mixture.

Place the lamb in a roasting tin and cook in a preheated oven at 220°C/Gas Mark 7 for about 10 minutes to glaze, then lower the temperature to 180°C/Gas Mark 4 and roast for a further 30 minutes.

Peel the rest of the garlic cloves, then crush them into a small bowl and mix them with the breadcrumbs, chopped herbs and softened butter until you have a smooth paste. Take the roast out of the oven and spread the butter mixture on top of the leg, then return to the oven for a further 30 minutes. You may wish to use a meat thermometer to check the temperature of the meat by inserting it into the thickest point, but without sticking it all the way into the bone. When it reaches 60°C, the meat should be pink and juicy.

Take the lamb out of the oven and leave to rest for 15 minutes. Cut the meat into thin slices, carefully so that the delicate herby crust doesn't fall off. Serve with cooked grains and a nice green salad.

Pan-fried lamb kidneys
with beetroot and kohlrabi in gastrique

2 tablespoons sugar
5 fennel seeds
5 whole black peppercorns
100ml cherry vinegar
3 early-season beetroot or 1 large one
1 kohlrabi
2 tablespoons cold-pressed rapeseed oil
sea salt flakes and freshly ground pepper
2 lambs' kidneys (order from your butcher)
4 bay leaves
1 tablespoon standard rapeseed oil
1 tablespoon chopped rowan sprigs
    (see right)

Start by making the gastrique. Caramelize the sugar by heating in a pan until it is lightly golden in colour (make sure it doesn't get too dark or burn), then add the fennel seeds, peppercorns and vinegar and simmer until you have a syrup consistency.

Take the pan off the heat and leave the gastrique to cool. Peel the beetroot and kohlrabi and slice very thinly, either with a sharp knife or using a mandoline. Mix the cold-pressed rapeseed oil into the gastrique, then add the vegetables and leave them to soak for about 15 minutes before seasoning with salt and pepper.

While the vegetables are soaking, remove the cores and fat from the kidneys. Rinse the kidneys under cold running water for about 15 minutes until they have no aroma. Dry the kidneys with kitchen paper, then fry them with the bay leaves in a frying pan in the standard rapeseed oil for about 2–3 minutes on each side. Season with salt and pepper.

Prepare a plate with the kidneys, some of the beetroot and kohlrabi and a little of the gastrique. Finish off with a sprinkle of the chopped rowan sprigs and serve with some good bread.

Rowan sprigs

The European rowan (*Sorbus aucuparia*) is typically found in forests and woodland, often growing in slightly poor soils, and also thrives at high altitudes, hence its other name of mountain ash. It is also commonly seen by the side of country roads or in the parks of our cities. The tree can grow to a height of 15 metres, but frequently takes the form of a shrub 3–6 metres tall. The bark of the tree is smooth and shiny and grey in colour. The distinctive compound leaves of the rowan are made up of six to eight serrated leaflets. The white flowers have a sweet scent and grow in clusters. Around August to September, the edible berries, which are 6–8mm in diameter, will start to mature and turn orangey red in colour, although they taste very bitter if not dried or frozen. However, the young tender sprigs that sprout in April are a great delicacy for your salad bowl, their flavour resembling that of bitter almonds. Pick the sprigs while they are still small and use them fresh – whole or chopped up. But don't worry, you won't damage the tree – it will simply grow more new shoots.

Pan-fried lamb kidneys »

Grilled lamb chops
with vegetable mash and green salsa

8 bone-in lamb chops, about
   80–100g each
1 tablespoon olive oil
sea salt flakes and freshly ground pepper

Inspect the lamb chops thoroughly and use a knife to remove any bone fragments from the meat. Oil the chops with the olive oil and season well with salt and pepper.

Cook the chops in a very hot frying pan or on a griddle for about 2 minutes on each side or until their surface is beautifully golden but they are still pink and juicy at the bone.

Serve with Vegetable Mash (see below) and Green Salsa (see right). A nice salad on the side would also be a good accompaniment, for example my White Cabbage Salad (see page 210) with orange and chilli.

Vegetable mash

1kg mixed root vegetables, such as
   celeriac, carrots and parsnips
75g butter
sea salt flakes and freshly ground pepper
finely grated zest and juice of
   ½ organic lemon

Peel and roughly dice the vegetables. Cook in a pan of boiling water for about 20 minutes until very soft. Drain and leave for the steam to rise for a minute.

Start mashing roughly using a whisk. Cut the butter into little cubes and add one cube at a time as you continue mashing. Season to taste with salt, pepper and the lemon zest and juice. Give the vegetables another stir and season with some more salt and pepper if needed.

Green salsa

1 handful of flat leaf parsley
1 handful of basil
6 slices of yesterday's white bread,
   roughly diced
1 garlic clove, peeled
100ml good-quality olive oil
50ml white wine vinegar
sea salt flakes and freshly ground pepper

Pick all the leaves from the herb stems, rinse them and put in a food processor with the diced bread, garlic clove, olive oil, vinegar, salt and pepper. Blend to a thick salsa.

Serve in a bowl to accompany the lamb chops, or with soup, potatoes, as a dip for bread or really with anything that could use a bit of a green kick.

Oven-roasted shoulder of lamb
with potatoes and wild garlic

1 boneless shoulder of lamb, about
   1.5–2kg
1–2 garlic cloves
1.5kg potatoes
4–5 red onions
10 wild garlic leaves or 2 garlic cloves
2 handfuls of flat leaf parsley
1 rosemary sprig
standard rapeseed oil, for oiling
sea salt flakes and freshly ground pepper
500ml water or light stock (chicken, veal
   or vegetable)

Using a sharp knife, score a criss-cross pattern into the meat. Peel the garlic and rub the meat with half a clove (save the piece of garlic). Peel the potatoes and cut into not-so-thin slices. Peel and slice the red onions. Chop the wild garlic (or extra garlic cloves), parsley, rosemary and the rest of the garlic finely and mix with the onions.

In a roasting tray oiled with rapeseed oil, lay out the potato slices in rows slightly overlapping each other. Then cover with a layer of the onion and herb mixture, then a layer of overlapping potatoes and so on, seasoning each layer with salt and pepper as you go. Pour the 500ml of water or stock over the potatoes.

Season the lamb with salt and pepper and place it with the criss-cross pattern down on to the potatoes. Roast in a preheated oven at 200°C/Gas Mark 6 for 15 minutes, then reduce the heat to 160°C/Gas Mark 3 and cook for a further 1½ hours. You can use a meat thermometer to check the temperature at the centre of the roast, which should be about 65°C. Take the meat out of the oven and leave to rest, covered, for 5–8 minutes.

Meanwhile, finish the potatoes under a hot grill until the surface is crispy.

Slice the lamb and serve it on top of the potatoes or in a warmed serving dish with the potatoes on the side. With the potatoes already soaking in the delicious herby broth, there is really no need for a sauce, so this is definitely one of those all-in-one dishes. The only additional item that might accompany the dish to the table would be apple chutney or some onion and horseradish marmalade.

Lamb meatballs
with potato compote, cream cheese and lovage

10 coriander seeds
10 cumin seeds
1 onion, peeled
½ apple, peeled
500g minced lamb, 6–8% fat
2 thyme sprigs, chopped
6–8 mint leaves, chopped
sea salt flakes and freshly ground pepper
1 tablespoon prepared mustard
rapeseed oil, for frying

Toast the coriander and cumin seeds in a dry frying pan until they pop, then grind them using a pestle and mortar.

Peel and grate the onion and apple finely, then mix with the minced lamb and spices, herbs, salt, pepper and mustard. Leave the meat mixture to rest in the refrigerator for 20 minutes or so before starting to cook it.

Heat up a little rapeseed oil in a frying pan and then start forming the meat mixture into meatballs. Fry the balls for about 2–3 minutes on each side or until they are still slightly pink and juicy in the middle.

Serve the lamb meatballs with the Potato Compote, Cream Cheese and Lovage (see below), some good bread and maybe a green salad if you like. Another nice accompaniment would be Baked Turnips with Sorrel and Honey (see page 50).

Potato compote, cream cheese and lovage

1kg new potatoes
sea salt flakes
15g cold butter
40g cream cheese
freshly ground pepper
½ handful of lovage, chopped

Wash the potatoes thoroughly, scrubbing them using a sponge or a brush, but don't remove all the skin. Add the potatoes to a pan of salted water to just cover and bring to the boil, then simmer, covered, for 8 minutes. Turn off the heat completely and leave the potatoes to sit in the hot water for a further 8 minutes.

Drain the potatoes but save some of the cooking water for the compote. Mash the potatoes and mix in the cold butter, cream cheese, salt, pepper and chopped lovage. Thin to the desired consistency with the reserved potato cooking water, but add it little by little to avoid making the compote watery. Serve the potato compote with the lamb meatballs.

Veal stew
with young vegetables, prawns and dill

600g veal blade or chuck
1 litre water
sea salt flakes
3 bay leaves
500g new potatoes
5 turnips
½ young celeriac, about 300g
8 spring onions
1 fennel bulb
15g butter
25g plain flour
2 organic egg yolks
100ml whipping cream
freshly ground pepper
100g small cooked, peeled prawns
  (see page 45)
1 handful of dill, chopped

Cut the veal into 3cm pieces, add to a casserole dish and pour over the 1 litre of water so that it just covers the meat. Bring to the boil and then add some salt as well as the bay leaves. Skim off any foam (impurities) that rises to the surface. Cover the pan with a lid, reduce the heat and leave to cook for about 1½ hours until the meat is nice and tender.

Meanwhile, prepare all the vegetables. Since the vegetables should be very young and fresh, it really isn't necessary to peel them, so just scrub the potatoes, turnips and celeriac thoroughly in the sink. Cut the vegetables into slightly smaller dice than the meat; as the meat shrinks a little during the cooking process, both meat and vegetables will end up bite-sized when the stew is done. Cut off the tips of the spring onions, leaving about 5cm of the green top, then wash them thoroughly. Dice the fennel roughly and rinse it in cold water.

Once the meat is done, remove it from the stew and start blanching the vegetables in the broth, vegetable by vegetable, as they each require a different cooking time:

6–7 minutes for the potatoes, 3–4 minutes for the turnips, 2–3 minutes for the fennel and 1 minute for the celeriac and spring onions. When all the vegetables are cooked and set aside, strain the broth through a sieve to remove any remaining impurities into a bowl.

Melt the butter in the casserole and add the flour while stirring vigorously with a whisk. Slowly add the broth back into the pan, little by little, still stirring vigorously, then simmer for about 5 minutes. Combine the egg yolks and the cream and stir into the sauce so that you have a nice creamy consistency. Return the meat and vegetables to the pan and heat it all up again. (You can leave the stew to simmer for a while if you like; the flour will prevent the egg yolks from coagulating.) Season to taste with salt and pepper. Sprinkle the prawns and the chopped dill on top and serve straight from the pan or in a large bowl with some good bread or cooked grains on the side.

• •

Tip You can serve the stew without prawns, but if using prawns, it is important to use fresh prawns rather than frozen ones or those in brine, otherwise you will end up with an unpleasantly rubbery consistency and you will lose most of their flavour when they are heated through.

• •

Boiled smoked saddle of pork
with spinach in lemon cream sauce

1 onion
1 carrot
2 bay leaves
10 whole black peppercorns
800g smoked saddle of pork (smoked, cured pork joint)

Peel the onion and carrot, add to a large pan of water with the bay leaves and peppercorns and bring to the boil. Add the piece of smoked pork and make sure that the water just covers it. Let the water return to the boil, then lower the heat, cover the pan with a lid and cook for about 45 minutes.

Turn the heat off and leave the pork to sit in the cooking water for a further 15–20 minutes. Take the meat out, remove any string or netting and cut into thin slices. Serve immediately with the Spinach in Lemon Cream Sauce (see below) and boiled potatoes.

Spinach in lemon cream sauce

1.5kg fresh spinach leaves
10g butter
100ml whipping cream
freshly grated nutmeg, to taste
finely grated zest and juice of
    1 organic lemon
sea salt flakes and freshly ground pepper

Rinse the spinach very thoroughly, several times if necessary to make sure all the dirt is washed away. Put in a sieve and leave the water to drip off.

Melt the butter in a pan, add the spinach and sauté for 1–2 minutes until it starts to soften. Add the cream and cook for about 30 seconds, then season to taste with nutmeg, the lemon zest and juice, salt and pepper. Serve immediately.

Parsley-stuffed pork tenderloin
with warm radishes and butterhead lettuce with cream vinaigrette

1 trimmed pork tenderloin
½ handful of flat leaf parsley,
sea salt flakes and freshly ground pepper
10g butter
100ml water or light stock (chicken or veal)

Cut away the large sinews from the tenderloin, then dry the meat with kitchen paper. Slice the tenderloin halfway through lengthways, then place in a double layer of plastic food bags and tenderize it using a meat mallet.

Rinse the parsley, leave it to dry and then chop it roughly. Season the tenderloin on both sides with salt and pepper and then stuff it with the parsley. Roll it up into a tight roll with the parsley inside and tie some kitchen string around the roll to secure it.

Heat the butter in a pan until it turns golden in colour before adding the tenderloin. Fry on all sides, then add the water or stock, cover the pan with a lid and cook over a low heat for 7–8 minutes. Turn the meat over and cook for a further 7–8 minutes so that it cooks for no more than 15 minutes in total.

Take the tenderloin out of the pan, wrap in foil and leave to rest for about 10 minutes. Cooking the meat for a relatively short time and then letting it rest for so long afterwards gives it a perfect, slightly pink and juicy centre. Cut into slices and serve with some of the gravy from the pan, along with Warm Radishes and Butterhead Lettuce with Cream Vinaigrette (see right).

Warm radishes

20 radishes
2 tablespoons cider vinegar
50ml cold-pressed rapeseed oil
1 teaspoon acacia honey
sea salt flakes and freshly ground pepper

Cut off the base of each radish and remove the largest leaves while leaving the smaller ones in place. Cut them in half and add to a pan with the vinegar, rapeseed oil, honey, salt and pepper. Heat up and cook for 1–2 minutes until the radishes are cooked through but still al dente. Serve while they are warm.

Butterhead lettuce with cream vinaigrette

1–2 tablespoons cider vinegar
50ml whipping cream
1–2 tablespoons caster sugar
sea salt flakes and freshly ground pepper
1 butterhead lettuce

Mix the vinegar into the cream in a bowl and leave to stand until it thickens. Add the sugar and stir well. Season to taste with salt and pepper.

Rinse the lettuce well and dry in a salad spinner or a clean tea towel. Rip the leaves into smaller pieces and mix with the cream dressing. Serve immediately so that the lettuce doesn't go soggy.

Pork roast
with herbs, fennel and new potatoes

SERVES 6

1 spring onion
4 rosemary sprigs
5 sage sprigs
5 chervil sprigs
1 organic lemon
1 boneless pork loin, skin on
sea salt flakes and freshly ground pepper
1.2kg new potatoes
2 tablespoons cold-pressed rapeseed oil
100g fresh spinach
1 fennel bulb

Peel the spring onion and slice it thinly. Rinse the herbs and pluck the leaves from the stems, but keep the stems for the roast to sit on in the oven. Finely grate the zest of the lemon.

Cut the pork almost in half, leaving a small portion uncut on one side so that you can open out the meat, and fill it with the herb leaves, lemon zest, salt and pepper. Close it again and tie it tightly together with kitchen string to seal all the goodness inside the meat.

Rinse the potatoes thoroughly and cut in half. Put them into an ovenproof dish together with the zested lemon, cut into quarters. Drizzle the rapeseed oil on top, season with the herb stems, salt and pepper and mix well. Put the pork on top of the potatoes and roast in a preheated oven at 180°C/Gas Mark 4 for 1–1¼ hours until the crackling is nice and crisp and the potatoes are golden and crisp on the outside but soft in the middle. If you like, use a meat thermometer to check the temperature at the centre of the roast, which should be about 65°C.

Take the roast out of the oven and leave to rest for 5–10 minutes. Meanwhile, rinse the spinach several times in cold water and leave in a sieve for the water to drip off. Rinse the fennel and then slice thinly.

Mix the fennel and spinach with the potatoes – enough to warm them a little, but not so much that they become soggy.

Carve the roast and serve with the fried potatoes and all the lovely greens. You don't really need any other accompaniments, as you have everything in one dish. With this recipe, once you have put the meat in the oven, the work is done and dinner is on its way!

Mock chicken

Originally, pork tenderloin wasn't a piece of meat that you would cook by itself. The lean muscle was usually minced together with a fattier part of the pig and used as pork mince or to stuff sausages. In the second half of the 19th century when fresh meat became more abundant, we started frying tenderloin either sliced up or whole, stuffed with, for example, apples and prunes, or parsley as in this recipe. The first time parsley-stuffed tenderloin appeared was in the recipes of Frøken Jensen, called 'mock chicken'. Until well into the 20th century, chicken was considered an expensive food item, and was reserved for Sunday roast, typically stuffed with parsley and butter.

DANDELION LEAVES
These little leaf rosettes are perfect in a salad.

Roasted duck breast
and baked rhubarb with horseradish

2 duck breasts
3 lemon thyme sprigs
1 tablespoon cider vinegar
sea salt flakes and freshly ground pepper

Prepare the duck breasts by cutting away the sinews and removing any remaining bits of feather. Using a sharp knife, lightly score a criss-cross pattern into the skin.

Sauté the breasts in a hot pan, first on the skin side for a couple of minutes so that the fat renders and the skin crisps, then on the other side for about a minute. Don't forget to save the duck fat afterwards – it is great for sautéing potatoes!

Put the breasts into an ovenproof dish and marinate in the lemon thyme, vinegar, salt and pepper – simply shower the ingredients over the duck and massage them into the flesh, then leave to soak into the duck for about 15 minutes.

Cook in a preheated oven at 170°C/ Gas Mark 3½ for 8–10 minutes.

Remove the duck breasts from the oven and leave to rest for 2–3 minutes, then cut them into slices. Serve with Baked Rhubarb with Horseradish (see below) and a large dish of boiled new potatoes.

Baked rhubarb with horseradish

5–6 rhubarb stalks
3 tablespoons unrefined cane sugar
sea salt flakes and freshly ground pepper
2 tablespoons elderflower vinegar
10g freshly grated horseradish
1 tablespoon cold-pressed rapeseed oil
½ handful of chervil

Cut off the tops and bottoms of the rhubarb stalks, but be careful not to remove the white 'foot' of the stalk, which is where the rhubarb flavour is most concentrated and

best. Rinse the stalks in cold water, cut into 7–8cm pieces and put into an ovenproof dish.

Sprinkle the sugar, salt, pepper and the vinegar over the rhubarb and bake in a preheated oven at 160°C/Gas Mark 3½ for 8–10 minutes. The stalks should be soft, yet al dente, but don't worry if you accidentally bake them for too long – it happens, believe me – because then you will simply have a compote instead, which really isn't a bad thing.

Take the dish out of the oven and carefully mix in the grated horseradish and rapeseed oil. (If the rhubarb has turned into a compote, mix in the horseradish first and then drizzle the oil on top.) Pick the chervil leaves from the sprigs and use to garnish the rhubarb. Serve while warm with the roasted duck breast or a classic roast chicken.

Honey-glazed chicken with black pepper
and fennel-asparagus crudités

SERVES 6
1 large organic chicken, about 1.5–2kg
3 rosemary sprigs
3 thyme sprigs
½ organic lemon
1 tablespoon honey
2 tablespoons elderflower vinegar
1 tablespoon olive oil
15 whole black peppercorns, lightly crushed
sea salt flakes

Check the chicken for any feather stumps and pluck them out. Remove any blood or intestine residues from the cavity and wipe with kitchen paper. Stuff the chicken with the whole rosemary and thyme sprigs, then cut the lemon into large cubes and add to the cavity.

Mix the honey, vinegar, oil and crushed peppercorns together in a bowl to make

a marinade, then lubricate the skin of the chicken all over with the marinade.

Season the chicken all over with salt.

Place the chicken in an ovenproof dish and roast in a preheated oven at 180°C/Gas Mark 4 for 1 hour.

Take the chicken out and leave it to rest for 10–15 minutes before you cut it into pieces. Serve the chicken with boiled new potatoes and the Fennel-asparagus Crudités (see below).

Fennel-asparagus crudités

2 fennel bulbs
10 green asparagus
2 tablespoons cold-pressed rapeseed oil
2 tablespoons cider vinegar
sea salt flakes and freshly ground pepper

Cut the fennel bulbs in half, rinse them thoroughly in cold water and drain. Break off the woody stems of the asparagus and discard (or save them to make soup), then rinse the spears in cold water too.

Slice the fennel and asparagus thinly lengthways – use a mandoline if you have one or otherwise a sharp knife – then put them in a bowl.

Add the oil, vinegar, salt and pepper to the raw vegetables and toss to coat, then leave to stand for 2 minutes before serving.

Fish

Steamed mussels
with lovage, chervil and beer

2kg mussels
3 shallots
2 garlic cloves
white part of 1 leek, rinsed
10g butter
240ml cider or tart apple juice
300ml lager or pale ale, plus extra to
    season if you like
500ml whipping cream
½ handful of lovage
½ handful of parsley
½ handful of chervil
sea salt flakes and freshly ground pepper

Prepare the mussels as described on page 18.

Peel and chop the shallots, garlic and leek finely, and put them in a large pan with the butter. Lightly sauté, and before they start to brown, add the mussels and stir well. Pour the cider or apple juice and lager into the pan, cover the pan with a lid and steam the mussels for 4–5 minutes until they have opened up. Discard any that haven't opened, as they are not safe to eat.

Strain the mussel broth into a saucepan, add the cream and bring it to the boil, then simmer for about 5 minutes. Meanwhile, set the mussels aside in their cooking pan with the lid on.

Add the fresh herbs (reserving some for a garnish) to the broth, then pour it into a blender and blend to a smooth green sauce. Season with salt, pepper and little extra fresh lager if you wish. Pour the sauce over the mussels, give them a generous sprinkle of herbs and serve with some good wholemeal bread for soaking up the sauce.

....

TIP If you don't eat all the dish, take the mussels out of their shells and return them to the sauce. Store in the refrigerator, then heat up the next day with small cooked potato cubes or boiled grains to make a nice stew.

....

Pan-fried sparling
with cream-stewed cucumber and dill oil

1 handful of dill
50ml olive oil
12–16 sparlings (*see* tip)
sea salt flakes and freshly ground pepper
1 tablespoon standard rapeseed oil
1 cucumber
100ml whipping cream
2 tablespoons cider vinegar

Start by making the dill oil. Take half the dill and pluck the feathery leaves from the stems into a blender. Add the olive oil and blend to a green oil. Save the oil for later.

Now check the sparlings – they should smell fresh and a bit like cucumber (*see* tip). Clean and debone the sparlings, but leave the tail in place to hold together the 2 small fillets. (Alternatively, get your fishmonger to do the work for you.) Season with salt and pepper, then fry the sparlings in the rapeseed oil in a hot frying pan for about 30 seconds on each side until they are very crispy on the outside but juicy in the middle.

Peel the cucumber, cut it in half lengthways and scrape the seeds out with a teaspoon. Cut the cucumber into chunky pieces.

Heat the cream in a saucepan and leave to simmer for a while. Season with the vinegar, salt and pepper to taste. Add the cucumber pieces and cook for a few minutes until the cream clings to the cucumber. Finely chop the remaining dill and sprinkle into the pan. Give a little stir and serve the cucumber with the fried sparling and a drizzle of the dill oil. Serve as a starter or add some potatoes or cooked grains and serve for dinner.

....

TIP The sparling (also known as smelt) is a small, fjord or freshwater fish that can be caught from February to May. Characteristically it smells of fresh cucumber, so much so that some fishermen call it 'the cucumber fish'! If you can't find any, just use herring instead and cook for 2–3 minutes longer in the pan.

....

ST GEORGE'S MUSHROOMS
In parks and gardens, these precious little mushrooms will start sprouting in spring.

Pan-fried garfish
with rhubarb chutney

2 large garfish, descaled
1 tablespoon mustard
sea salt flakes and freshly ground pepper
rye flour, for dusting
10g butter, plus extra for greasing
1 tablespoon standard rapeseed oil
flat leaf parsley leaves, to garnish

Remove the bones from the garfish to create 4 fillets (or ask your fishmonger to do this for you). Spread the flesh side of the fillets with the mustard, salt and pepper, then cut each fillet into 4 pieces and fold them together skin side out. Dust the fish pieces with rye flour.

Fry the garfish fillets in the butter and rapeseed oil in a hot pan for 2–3 minutes on each side. The skin should be beautifully golden and crisp. Season if necessary with a little extra salt and pepper.

Serve the garfish with Rhubarb Chutney (see below), a little of the frying butter and oil mixture and boiled new potatoes. Sprinkle with flat leaf parsley leaves just before serving.

Rhubarb chutney

8–10 rhubarb stalks, trimmed and cut into 1cm pieces
1 large red onion, chopped
1 whole red chilli
1 teaspoon curry powder
1 teaspoon coriander seeds
3 tablespoons unrefined cane sugar
3 tablespoons cider vinegar
1 handful of sultanas

Cook the rhubarb pieces in a saucepan over a low heat along with the rest of the ingredients, simmering until the rhubarb has offered up all of its flavour, which should take about 15–20 minutes. Remove the chilli from the chutney and discard it, then pour the chutney into sterilized preserving jars and leave to cool. Enjoy immediately or store in the refrigerator for 2–3 weeks.

Skate wings
with pointed cabbage in broth with herbs

1kg skate wing, 600g pure fillet
sea salt flakes and freshly ground pepper
500ml fish stock
½ fennel bulb
½ pointed (sweetheart) cabbage
8 spring onions
2 handfuls of chopped fresh herbs, such as chervil, parsley and tarragon
a little cider vinegar

Remove the skin and bones of the skate wing, or ask your fishmonger to do this – it can be a little difficult. Scrape the fillet free of any slime.

Divide the fillet into 4 pieces, season with salt and pepper and roll them from the thick end to the thin end so that each roll seals itself.

Bring the stock to the boil in a pan and poach the skate wing fillets over a low heat for 6–7 minutes – they should only just tremble in the hot liquid. Remove the skate from the stock, place on a plate and cover with a clean tea towel.

Rinse the vegetables in cold water. Slice the fennel thinly, then cut the cabbage and spring onions into larger chunks. Add the vegetables to the stock and cook for a few minutes until tender, but still with plenty of crunch. Add the chopped fresh herbs and season with salt, pepper and vinegar to taste.

Place each skate wing fillet in a soup plate and pour the stock and vegetables over. Serve immediately with some good bread.

Potato salad
with green asparagus, dill and crispy fried prawns

500g new potatoes
sea salt flakes
8 green asparagus
6 radishes
2 tablespoons cider vinegar
2 tablespoons cold-pressed rapeseed oil
1 teaspoon honey
freshly ground pepper
1 handful of dill
200g raw small prawns
2 tablespoons standard rapeseed oil

Wash and scrub the potatoes, put them in a pan with water to just cover and add salt. Bring to the boil then lower the heat and simmer the potatoes, covered, for 8 minutes. Turn off the heat and leave the potatoes to sit in the hot water for a further 8 minutes. This way, they will be tender but not overcooked – I always cook new potatoes this way.

Drain the potatoes and leave to cool slightly, then dice them roughly and place in a bowl. Prepare the asparagus by breaking off the woody stem ends, and prepare the radishes by cutting off the tops and roots, then rinse both vegetables in cold water. Slice the asparagus and radishes thinly and add them to the potatoes.

Mix the vinegar, cold-pressed rapeseed oil, honey, salt and pepper together in a bowl to make a dressing. Pour over the potatoes, stir well and add the dill, freshly chopped.

Now it is time for the prawns. Snip the heads off the prawns. Heat up a frying pan with the standard rapeseed oil, add the prawns and fry them over a very high heat for 1–2 minutes until the shells become completely golden and crisp, then season with salt.

Serve the crisp, hot prawns with the potato salad and some great bread on the side for a quick and easy main dish. I know that there are people who will refuse to eat the prawns in all their glory (that is, in all their shell!), but the intense frying makes the shells crispy and quite delicious. Sometimes I even fry the prawns whole and eat them with their heads intact, but that is where my family draws the line.

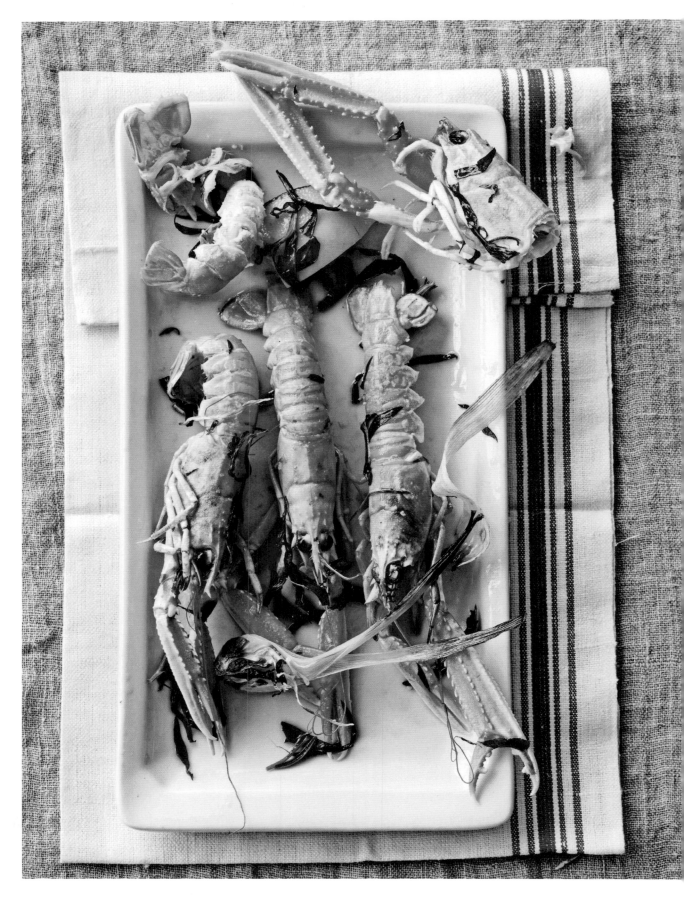

Boiled red king crab
with tomato mayonnaise

2 raw red king crab legs
½ handful of dill
10 whole black peppercorns
1 tablespoon coarse sea salt
2 tablespoons cider vinegar
sea salt and freshly ground pepper
2 tablespoons cold-pressed rapeseed oil

Cut the crab legs into sections at the joints and put them in a saucepan with the stems from the dill, the peppercorns, coarse salt and 1 tablespoon of the vinegar. Cover the crab with water and bring the water to the boil, then skim off the foam (impurities) and lower the heat.

Cook the crab legs for 5 minutes, then turn off the heat completely and leave to sit in the hot broth for about 10–15 minutes.

Remove the meat from the crab legs by cutting the shells open with a pair of kitchen scissors. The meat can then be lifted out in whole pieces or prised out with the end of a teaspoon. Put the crabmeat in a bowl and season with salt, pepper, the remaining 1 tablespoon vinegar and the rapeseed oil.

Serve the crabmeat with Tomato Mayonnaise (see below), a green salad and toasted bread. Depending on how hungry you are and the composition of the rest of the meal, the dish may be served either as a starter or a main course.

Tomato mayonnaise

2 pasteurized egg yolks (available from online suppliers)
sea salt flakes
1 tablespoon prepared Dijon mustard
2–3 tablespoons cider vinegar
150ml cold-pressed rapeseed oil
2 tablespoons tomato purée
freshly ground black pepper

Using an electric whisk or balloon whisk, whisk the egg yolks, salt, mustard and vinegar together in a bowl until thick and white. Whisk in the oil in a thin stream – it is important to do this slowly to avoid the mayo splitting. If it begins to curdle, you can try to save it by adding a few drops of cold water while whisking vigorously. Add the tomato sauce (or purée) and possibly a little extra salt and pepper to taste, then serve.

Lumpfish roe
with potato rösti and buttermilk dressing

300g fresh lumpfish roe (see page 188)
sea salt flakes and freshly ground pepper

Rösti
4–5 baking potatoes
1 small garlic clove, chopped
2–4 thyme sprigs, leaves chopped
2 tablespoons standard rapeseed oil

Dressing
200ml buttermilk
2 tablespoons cider vinegar
1 tablespoon caster sugar
1 pack growing salad cress, chopped

Remove any membranes from the roe and taste it – you might need to add salt or it may have already been salted. Store it in the refrigerator until serving.

To make the rösti, peel the potatoes and grate them on the coarse side of the grater. Press all the liquid out of the potatoes and put them in a bowl. Season well with salt, pepper and the chopped garlic and thyme.

Heat a small frying pan, about 15–18cm in diameter, and make sure it is nonstick so that the rösti comes off easily. Oil the pan with the rapeseed oil. Press the grated potato into a firm pancake and fry in the pan over a medium heat for about 5 minutes on one side until it becomes golden and crisp. Place a plate or lid over the pan, turn the whole lot upside down and slide the rösti back into the pan, then cook for 5 minutes on the other side.

Transfer the rösti to a baking sheet and roast in a preheated oven at 200°C/Gas Mark 6 for about 10–15 minutes until it is completely cooked through. Take it out of the oven and cut it into 4 neat pieces.

For the dressing, mix the buttermilk, vinegar, sugar, salt and pepper together in a bowl, add the chopped cress and whisk until well combined.

Serve the warm potato rösti on individual plates with a dollop of the roe on top. Drizzle with some of the dressing before enjoying the crispy goodness.

Langoustines with tarragon and garlic

1kg langoustines (12–16)
1 very fresh whole garlic bulb
1 handful of tarragon
sea salt flakes
50ml olive oil
½ organic lemon
freshly ground pepper

Check that the langoustines are fresh – they should smell of the sea. Place them in a large ovenproof dish. Chop the whole fresh garlic bulb and the tarragon roughly, and sprinkle both over the langoustines. Season with salt and drizzle with the olive oil. Squeeze most of the juice from the lemon half over the langoustines, then cut it into chunks and add to the langoustines so that the rind provides extra citrus flavour.

Place the dish in the preheated oven at 250°C/Gas Mark 10 (or your highest Gas Mark setting) and bake the langoustines for 8–10 minutes. Of course, you can also cook them outside on the barbecue if you like, and they will cook in no time. Remove the langoustines from the oven and serve immediately, with good bread to dip in the juices in the bottom of the dish.

Light dishes

Warm brioches
with smoked salmon and wild garlic spread

MAKES 20 BRIOCHES

Pre-dough
300ml cold water
20g fresh yeast
250g wheat flour

Brioche dough
100ml full-fat milk
750g plain flour, plus extra for dusting
10g sea salt flakes
12 organic eggs
300g softened butter
100g caster sugar
1 beaten organic egg, for glazing

Filling
10 wild garlic leaves
250g Greek yogurt, 2% fat
1 teaspoon acacia honey
finely grated zest of ½ organic lemon
sea salt flakes and freshly ground pepper
1 red onion
1 Little Gem lettuce
200g smoked salmon

Day 1
Pour the 300ml cold water into a bowl and stir in the yeast. Add the flour and knead the dough well. Cover with clingfilm and keep in the refrigerator for 12 hours.

Day 2
Take the pre-dough out of the refrigerator a few hours before using and leave in the kitchen to reach room temperature. Meanwhile, mix the milk, flour, salt and eggs for the brioche dough together in a large bowl and knead until smooth. Knead in the softened butter, and continue kneading until the dough is smooth again, then knead in the sugar until completely combined. Add the pre-dough and knead until smooth and supple. If kneading by hand, you should expect to spend 8–10 minutes; if using a stand mixer fitted with a dough hook, kneading should take 6–8 minutes.

Leave the dough to rise in the bowl, covered with a damp tea towel, in the kitchen for 2 hours.

Hand knead the dough on a floured work surface, then cover it and let it rest on the work surface for 30 minutes. Split the dough into 2 pieces, roll each into a sausage shape and divide each sausage into 10 pieces. Roll the pieces into buns, place them on 2 baking trays covered with baking paper and leave to rise for a few hours until doubled in size.

Glaze the brioches with the beaten egg and bake in a preheated oven at 220°C/ Gas Mark 7 for about 10–12 minutes until golden and fluffy. Remove from the oven and leave to cool on a wire rack.

While the brioches are cooling, make the filling. Rinse the wild garlic leaves, then chop roughly and blend them with the yogurt, honey, lemon zest, salt and pepper in a blender or food processor, or using a stick blender, to a smooth green cream. Season with additional salt and pepper if necessary.

Peel the red onion and cut it into very thin slices. Pick and rinse the lettuce, then dry the leaves well. Cut the warm brioches in half, spread over the wild garlic cream and add the slices of smoked salmon, lettuce and red onion. Eat the brioches as part of a brunch or as lunch sandwiches – or pack a picnic basket and enjoy them in the spring countryside.

· ·

TIP Instead of wild garlic you can use chives with a little garlic, a similar combination to wild garlic.

· ·

Pan-fried chicken livers
with nettles and pickled onions

200g fresh chicken livers
2 red onions
2 tablespoons acacia honey
50ml cider vinegar
sea salt flakes and freshly ground pepper
1 tablespoon olive oil
2 handfuls of nettle shoots
½ frisée lettuce
1 tablespoon cold-pressed rapeseed oil

Check the chicken livers for freshness – they must have a beautiful dark red colour, smell of flesh and blood and have a smooth, shiny surface. Remove any sinews or membranes, and place the livers in the refrigerator until it is time to fry them.

Peel the red onions, cut them into thin wedges and put them in a bowl. Add the honey, vinegar, salt and pepper, and leave to marinate for 20–30 minutes, stirring a few times at regular intervals.

Heat a frying pan with the olive oil and fry the chicken livers for 1–2 minutes on each side over a high heat so that they have a nice fried surface but remain pale pink in the middle.

Rinse the nettle shoots, chop them roughly and add them to the pan with the chicken livers to fry for the last 10 seconds of cooking time, softening them a little but keeping their structure and beautiful green colour intact. Season with salt and pepper.

Rinse and tear the lettuce, then dry it using a salad spinner or a clean tea towel. Remove the livers from the pan and serve immediately with the pickled onions, lettuce and some good bread, drizzling the cold-pressed rapeseed oil over the plate. Serve either as a starter or a light lunch.

Pan-fried chicken livers »

Fried porridge

300ml chicken stock or water
200ml beer
5g sea salt flakes
60g wholegrain rye flour
60g wholegrain barley flour
35g hard cheese, such as Høost or
    Cheddar, freshly grated
10g butter
1 tablespoon standard rapeseed oil,
    plus extra for greasing

To serve
600g good-quality fresh sausages
    straight from your butcher's
1 handful of ground elder, garlic mustard
    or other fresh herb of your choice
Onion Compote (see below)

Bring the stock or water, beer and salt to
the boil in a pan, add the flours and stir
vigorously. Reduce the heat and simmer for
20–25 minutes, stirring frequently, until the
mixture no longer tastes of flour. Add the
grated cheese and butter and stir until you
have a smooth mixture.

Pour into an oiled baking tray. Cover with
clingfilm and chill in the refrigerator to set
until firm.

Cut the cold porridge into thin slices and fry
them in the rapeseed oil in a frying pan.

If your sausages aren't pre-cooked, it might
be a good idea to fry them before the
porridge; if they are, just quickly fry them in
the same pan after frying the porridge.

Serve the crispy porridge slices warm with
the fried sausages, sprinkled with the fresh
herbs and with a dollop of Onion Compote.

Onion Compote

150g red onions
50ml cider vinegar
50g sugar
50ml water
1 tablespoon mustard
sea salt flakes and freshly ground pepper

Peel the onions and chop them finely.
Add to a pan with the vinegar, sugar and
measured water, bring to the boil and then
simmer for about 20 minutes or until you
have a compote consistency. Remove from
the heat and add the mustard, salt and
pepper until seasoned to perfection.

Raw salmon
with lime, horseradish and garlic mustard

200g very fresh skinless salmon fillet
2 tablespoons water
finely grated zest and juice
    of 1 organic lime
2 tablespoons freshly grated
    horseradish
1 tablespoon cold-pressed rapeseed oil
1 tablespoon unrefined cane sugar
1 tablespoon sea salt flakes
freshly ground pepper
10 garlic mustard leaves or chives,
    finely chopped

Check that the salmon is really fresh and
appetizing – it is supposed to smell of the
sea, not the harbour! Slice the salmon thinly
and divide between 4 plates.

Whisk together the water, lime zest and
juice, horseradish, rapeseed oil, sugar, salt
and pepper to taste in a bowl until smooth.
Pour over the salmon and leave to stand for
5 minutes.

Sprinkle the garlic mustard leaves (or finely
chopped chives) over the salmon and serve
immediately before the acid 'overcooks'
the fish. The acid from the lime doesn't only
give flavour but acts as a cooking agent,
changing the structure and colour of the
fish. The method could be referred to as
'cold cooking' and is used in the South
American dish ceviche. I like to stop the
process at the stage where the salmon still
remains slightly raw.

Serve the salmon with some good bread,
preferably toasted.

TIP Garlic mustard is a garlic-flavoured
herb found in deciduous forests,
woodland, parks and hedgerows.
The leaves are heart shaped with barbed
edges, somewhat like nettles, and the
herb is often found growing next to
nettles. Later in spring the plant bears
white flowers, which, as with the leaves,
make an excellent condiment and garnish
for anything from a salad to a sandwich.
If you can't find garlic mustard, you can
replace it with finely chopped chives.

GARLIC MUSTARD
The first tender shoots of garlic mustard
are particularly good sprinkled on an
egg sandwich.

Prawns
with crispy potatoes and smoked curd cheese

200g small potatoes
1 litre grapeseed oil, for frying
1kg small cooked, peeled prawns (see above)
80g Smoked Curd Cheese (see page 16)
a little dill, for sprinkling
sea salt flakes and freshly ground pepper
1 tablespoon cold-pressed rapeseed oil

Wash the potatoes thoroughly – peeling isn't necessary – and cut into very thin slices using a mandoline or a potato peeler. Soak the potato slices in a bowl of water for 10 minutes, then drain.

Gently heat the oil for frying in a pan to about 160°C – it should sizzle when you dip the wooden end of a match in the oil. Meanwhile, leave the potato slices to dry on kitchen paper. Fry the potato slices in the hot oil until lightly golden and crisp – approximately 1–2 minutes. Be careful that the oil doesn't become too hot and overbrown the potatoes. Serve the crisp potatoes with the peeled prawns and smoked curd cheese, sprinkled with a little dill, salt and pepper, and with the rapeseed oil drizzled over the dish. Serve as a small appetizer or a snack with a glass of bubbly on the terrace.

Open rye bread sandwich
with new potatoes, smoked curd cheese dressing, radishes, wild garlic and cress

4 slices of rye bread
400g boiled new potatoes (see method on page 36)
4 tablespoons Smoked Curd Cheese Dressing (see right)
4 wild garlic leaves, rinsed
4 radishes, rinsed
½ pack or tray growing salad cress
sea salt flakes and freshly ground pepper

Place the bread slices on a platter. Slice the potatoes, lay them out on the bread slices and add a tablespoonful of Smoked Curd Cheese Dressing to the top of each slice.

Cut the wild garlic leaves into very thin strips. Cut the radishes into thin slices too. Sprinkle the wild garlic and cut cress and then the radishes on top of each sandwich. Season with salt and pepper, then serve.

Smoked curd cheese dressing

3 tablespoons Smoked Curd Cheese (see page 16)
100ml semi-skimmed milk
1 teaspoon acacia honey
sea salt flakes and freshly ground pepper

Put the smoked curd cheese in a bowl, add the milk and mix to a smooth cream. Add the honey and salt and pepper to taste.

Omelette
with peppered mackerel, potatoes and spring onion

1 smoked peppered mackerel fillet
1 spring onion
400g boiled new potatoes (see method on page 36)
10g butter
sea salt flakes and freshly ground pepper
6 organic eggs
200ml semi-skimmed milk
½ handful of chives

Remove any skin and bones from the mackerel fillet. Chop the spring onion finely and cut the boiled potatoes into large cubes.

Sauté the spring onion and potatoes in the butter in an ovenproof frying pan, and season with salt and pepper. Mix in the mackerel.

Beat the eggs and milk in a bowl and season with a little salt and pepper. Pour the egg mixture into the pan and put the pan in a preheated oven at 180°C/Gas Mark 4. Bake the omelette for 8–10 minutes until the egg mixture is firm and slightly golden on top. If the omelette lacks a little colour, turn on the grill for the final few minutes.

Finely chop the chives and sprinkle over the omelette. Serve immediately with rye bread, mustard and a green salad or green asparagus with a vinaigrette of Parsley, Anchovies and Cider Vinegar (see page 50).

Crispy onion rings

250g plain flour
1 small organic egg
200ml beer
150ml warm water
25ml standard rapeseed oil
fine salt
a little caster sugar
3 onions
sea salt flakes
2 organic egg whites
1–2 litres grapeseed oil, for frying

First make the batter. Mix together the flour, egg, beer, measured warm water, rapeseed oil, some fine salt and a little sugar in a bowl with a whisk and leave to rest in the refrigerator for about an hour. (The egg whites are not added until immediately before use.)

Peel the onions and cut into rings. Put the onion rings into a bowl, sprinkle with sea salt flakes and leave them to stand for 10 minutes so that they soften and release some of their liquid.

Heat the oil in a pan to 160–180°C – it should sizzle when you dip the wooden end of a match in the oil. Whisk the egg whites until stiff and then fold them gently into the batter (the trick is to mix the first spoonful of whites in vigorously, then fold the rest of them in gently). Dip the onion rings into the batter, then fry them in the hot oil until golden and crisp. Lift them out with a skimmer and place them on a piece of kitchen paper, then give them a sprinkle of salt.

Serve the crispy onion rings while they are still warm, with a portion of Sweet and Sour Dip with Dill and Horseradish (see right) or Green Salsa (see page 26) for dipping. The onion rings are a great snack to accompany a pint of cold beer and can also be served on top of a piece of boiled or braised meat.

Spinach tart
with cottage cheese

Pastry
100g Öland or organic wholegrain wheat flour, plus extra for dusting
50g oat flour
50g rye flour
1 teaspoon baking powder
5 tablespoons standard rapeseed oil, plus extra for greasing
2 tablespoons water
1 teaspoon salt
250g low-fat natural yogurt

Filling
350g cottage cheese
200ml semi-skimmed milk
3 organic eggs
3 gratings of nutmeg
sea salt flakes and freshly ground pepper
10g butter
500g fresh spinach leaves, washed and drained
1 shallot
35g hard cheese, grated

To finish
1 shallot
1 handful of fresh herbs, such as sweet woodruff, chervil and sweet cicely
a few drops of cider vinegar
a few drops of cold-pressed rapeseed oil

First make the pastry. Mix all the ingredients together in a bowl to make a dough. Wrap the dough in clingfilm and leave to rest in the refrigerator for 30 minutes.

Meanwhile, prepare the filling. Mix the cottage cheese, milk, eggs, nutmeg, salt and pepper together in a bowl to a smooth paste.

Melt the butter in a saucepan and briefly sauté the spinach, just until it starts to collapse and releases its liquid. Season with salt and pepper. Pour the spinach into a sieve and strain off the liquid.

Roll the pastry dough out into a thin layer on a floured work surface, then transfer it to a 24–26cm diameter, 3cm deep, tart dish oiled with rapeseed oil. Press the dough firmly into the dish and trim the excess dough from around the edges.

Put the drained spinach into the pastry case and cover with the cottage cheese paste. Peel and slice the shallot into very thin rings, then spread over the top of the paste. Lastly, sprinkle the grated cheese over the tart.

Bake the tart on the bottom shelf of a preheated oven at 170–180°C/Gas Mark 3½–4 for 30–35 minutes until the filling has set. The tart should be light golden on the top and the pastry baked through.

Just before serving, peel and cut the other shallot into thin rings, then toss with the freshly torn herbs in the vinegar and rapeseed oil, just to give them a bit of shine. Arrange the shallot and herb mixture on top of the tart and serve warm. If you want more greenery, serve with a small salad on the side. You can also choose to make the tart a day ahead and serve it cold for lunch or as an accompaniment to a main course.

Sweet and sour dip
with dill and horseradish

50g sugar
2 teaspoons dill seeds
3 slices of peeled fresh horseradish, 2mm thick
1 garlic clove, peeled
200ml cider vinegar
sea salt flakes

Caramelize the sugar by heating in a pan until it is lightly golden in colour (make sure it doesn't get too dark or burn), then add the dill seeds, horseradish, the whole garlic clove and finally the vinegar. Bring to the boil and then reduce the heat and cook until reduced by half. Season with a few grains of sea salt and leave to cool before serving.

Vegetable accompaniments

Boiled leeks
with vinaigrette of parsley, anchovies and cider vinegar

6 winter leeks
sea salt flakes
4 anchovy fillets, chopped
2 tablespoons capers or elderberry capers
1 tablespoon prepared mustard
½ handful of parsley, torn
3 tablespoons cider vinegar
1 teaspoon honey
2 tablespoons cold-pressed rapeseed oil
freshly ground pepper

Cut off the roots and tops of the leeks and rinse them thoroughly in cold water. Drain, then cut them into 4–5cm chunks.

Bring a pan of lightly salted water to the boil, add the leeks and when the water returns to the boil continue boiling them until they are tender – about 5–7 minutes, depending on thickness.

Make a rustic vinaigrette by mixing together the chopped anchovies, capers or elderberry capers, mustard, parsley, vinegar, honey and rapeseed oil in a bowl until well combined.

Lift the tender leeks from their cooking water and add them directly to the vinaigrette so that they absorb the flavours. Give them a stir and season to taste with salt and pepper.

Serve the leeks immediately while still warm, either as a small vegetable dish on its own or as a side for fish or meat.

••••••••••••••••••••••••••••••••••••

TIP For a little luxury, I sometimes replace the anchovies with 3–4 roughly chopped Limfjord oysters.

••••••••••••••••••••••••••••••••••••

Baked turnips
with sorrel and honey

500g turnips
2 tablespoons cider vinegar
2 tablespoons cold-pressed rapeseed oil
1 tablespoon honey
sea salt flakes and freshly ground pepper
25g sorrel (you can use any type of sorrel or even lemon balm)

Wash the turnips well in cold water and cut the tops and bottoms off, as if they were large radishes. Slice the turnips very thinly using a mandoline or a sharp knife.

Mix the turnips with vinegar, rapeseed oil, honey, salt and pepper, then place them in an ovenproof dish and bake in a preheated oven at 170°C/Gas Mark 3½ for 6–7 minutes until they are just becoming tender and start absorbing the marinade but still remain crisp. Stir and leave them to cool slightly.

Roughly chop the sorrel and toss it into the turnips at the last minute, otherwise it will lose its colour and freshness due to the acid in the vinegar. Serve with fish or meat.

Potato salad
with ground elder and shallots

1kg large potatoes
sea salt flakes
50ml cider vinegar, plus extra if needed
1 tablespoon acacia honey
2 tablespoons cold-pressed rapeseed oil
freshly ground pepper
3 shallots
2 handfuls of ground elder or flat leaf parsley or chervil

Peel the potatoes, cut them into 2cm cubes and rinse them under cold water. Bring a pan of salted water to the boil, pop the potatoes in and cook for 6–7 minutes or until they are cooked but al dente. Drain and put the potatoes in a bowl.

For the marinade, whisk together the vinegar, honey, rapeseed oil, salt and pepper in a bowl. Add to the potatoes while they are still warm to allow them to absorb the marinade.

Peel the shallots and cut them into thin rings. Rinse the ground elder and pick off all the leaves, or chop it roughly. Add the shallots and elder to the potatoes and mix well. If needed, season with extra salt, pepper and vinegar. The salad is delicious warm as well as cold, but remember that the elder will lose its beautiful dark green colour if in contact with heat or acid for too long.

SORREL
This plant hibernates during winter, but you'll find it in abundance growing wild in spring.

Baking and sweet things

Swedish syrup bread
MAKES 2 LOAVES

150g Swedish dark syrup
150g prunes, pitted and chopped
80g whole blanched almonds, coarsely
    chopped
100g rye flour
1.5kg Dark Rye Bread dough
    (*see* page 55)
butter, for greasing

Mix the syrup, prunes, almonds and rye
flour into the Dark Rye Bread Dough and stir
to create a compact, slightly sticky texture.

Pour the dough equally into 2 loaf tins that
can hold about 2 litres each, buttered well.
Leave the dough to rise in a warm kitchen
for 1 hour. Bake in a preheated oven at
160°C/Gas Mark 3 for 1¼ hours–1 hour
25 minutes, or until a skewer inserted comes
out clean. Turn the loaves out of the tins,
place directly on the oven shelf and bake for
a further 10 minutes.

Remove the loaves from the oven and
transfer to a wire rack. Eat the bread warm
with cold butter and a little Danish blue
cheese – this is a serious grown-ups' treat!
The bread is also great for toasting and if
being enjoyed in this way it will keep for
several days after baking.

Barley bread
MAKES 2 LOAVES

500ml cold water
3g fresh yeast (the size of a small pea)
100ml Sourdough Starter (*see* right)
300g barley flour
300g plain flour
10g sea salt flakes
50g honey
cold-pressed rapeseed oil, for greasing

Day 1
Pour the measured cold water into a bowl
and stir in yeast and Sourdough Starter.
Mix in the barley flour, plain flour, salt and

honey, and knead until the dough almost
stops sticking to the sides of the bowl.
Barley dough is very soft and requires a
long kneading time to become smooth
and elastic, so knead the dough for about
20 minutes to obtain the right texture. If
you do not have a stand mixer with a dough
hook, you can use a hand mixer fitted with
a dough hook or simply work the dough
with a wooden spoon and plenty of elbow
grease. Pour the dough into a plastic bowl
oiled with cold-pressed rapeseed oil, cover
it with clingfilm and place in the refrigerator
for 24 hours.

Day 2
Pour the dough equally into 2 wooden
moulds (metal moulds can also be used)
that can hold 1.5 litres dough each, oiled
with rapeseed oil. Leave the dough to rise
until it reaches the top edges of the moulds,
which will take about 2–3 hours at room
temperature. Bake in a preheated oven
at 180°C/Gas Mark 4 for 45 minutes until
golden and baked through. Remove from
the oven and turn the hot bread out of the
moulds to cool on a wire rack.

Sourdough starter

If you bake regularly, you should always
have a sourdough starter in your kitchen. It
is by no means complicated, and will make
your bread more individual, complex and
healthy. This starter, among experts also
called a *biga*, is almost as thin as water, but
it adds a wonderful flavour to the bread.

900ml cold water
150g organic wheat flour
75g organic wholemeal flour
75g organic rye flour

Place all the ingredients in a bowl and whisk
together well. Pour the dough into a pan
or a glass or ceramic bowl, partially cover
the container so that the dough can still
breathe and keep it at room temperature.
Whisk the sourdough once a day. After
about 10 days the starter should smell like a

good, strong dark beer – and foam like one.
If that is the case, it is ready for use.

Subsequently stir the starter regularly –
once a day is preferable, but every second
day will be sufficient. Always make sure
that you stir to the very bottom, as the
sourdough starter will form a sediment
that will simply rot if not mixed regularly
with the liquid.

Each time you use the sourdough it needs
a 'refreshment', and the rule is: refresh with
the same amount of flour and water that you
have removed for baking. Store the starter
at room temperature, in a kitchen cupboard
for example, and nourish it with fresh flour
and water at least once a week.

TIP If you don't have a sourdough starter,
you can replace the starter in a sourdough
recipe with a corresponding amount of
crème fraîche, buttermilk, soured milk
(*see* page 16) or other fermented milk
product and a slightly larger amount of
yeast. It will obviously reduce the quality
of the final outcome, but the method can
be used if you are short of time.

Dark rye bread

MAKES 3 LOAVES

Day 1
1.6 litres cold water
500g cracked rye kernels
250g sunflower seeds
250g linseeds
15g fresh yeast
800g rye flour

Day 2
50g sea salt flakes
5g dark malt flour (optional)
sunflower oil, for greasing

Day 1
Mix 1 litre of the measured cold water with the rye kernels, sunflower seeds and linseed in a bowl, cover with a cloth or lid and leave to soak at room temperature for 24 hours.

Pour the remaining 600ml measured cold water into another bowl and dissolve the yeast in it. Mix the rye flour into the liquid and cover the dough with a cloth or lid. Leave this to stand at room temperature for 24 hours. The 2 mixtures should not be combined until the next day, otherwise the dough will be too sour, and too much acetic acid will make it difficult to bake the bread through.

Day 2
Mix the 2 mixtures together and add the salt and roasted malt flour, if using (it makes the bread dark), and knead it all together for about 10 minutes.

Divide the dough into 3 tins that can hold about 2 litres each, greased well with sunflower oil. Leave the dough to rise in a warm kitchen for about 2–3 hours or until it reaches the top edges of the tins. Bake in a preheated oven at 180°C/Gas Mark 4 for about 1 hour 20 minutes. Remove the tins from the oven, turn the loaves out of the tins on to a wire rack and leave them to cool. The bread will keep for 8–10 days stored in a bag. Do not store in the refrigerator, as it will quickly dry out.

This bread is one of the best-selling br in Meyers Deli and one of the tastiest r breads I know. Unlike most other rye b it is made entirely with rye flour, withou any wheat flour added. This creates a r deep rye flavour and a great moistnes:

TIP You can save a few hundred gram of the dough for making the next batch of rye bread for baking – it will keep in the refrigerator for up to 3 weeks. Add the dough to the day 1 mixture on day 2, reducing the quantity of fresh yeast in the day 1 mixture to 10g.

Rye bread

Rye was the most common grain for bread until the end of the 1800s, when white bread began to be cheaper and slowly took over. In the first millennium of rye bread consumption, the loaves were small, since the Iron Age and Viking ovens did not have enough heat or capacity to bake larger bread. But with 12–13th-century stone-building techniques, big masonry *cupola* furnaces were able to accommodate many large oval breads, as they were called then. They were possibly based on sourdough, with the addition of barley flour or similar and seasoning such as aniseed or caraway, coriander or dill seeds when available. These seasonings are not as commonly used with rye bread today, but they complement the rye flavour perfectly.

Focaccia
with wild garlic pesto

650ml lukewarm water
100ml standard rapeseed oil
20g fresh yeast
1kg protein-rich wheat flour, such as Italian '00' flour or Öland or organic wholegrain flour, or a mixture (see tip)
20g sea salt flakes

then turn to full speed for 6 minutes. Leave the dough to rise in the bowl covered with a clean tea towel at room temperature for about 3 hours.

Oil a large roasting tin with standard rapeseed oil. Transfer the dough to the tin and gently spread it out by hand until it covers the entire pan. Pour the cold-pressed rapeseed oil on to the dough and spread it out with your fingers. Drizzle the wild garlic pesto on the dough and gently press it with your fingers, creating small indentations all over the dough, pressing the pesto into them. Leave the dough to rise at room temperature for about an hour.

Bake the bread in a preheated oven at 220°C/Gas Mark 7 for about 25 minutes until it is crisp and golden. Remove from the oven and leave to cool in the tin. Remove from the tin and serve as an entire loaf of bread – not cutting it, but breaking off servings.

TIP You will produce a healthier and tastier bread with the same fine texture as an original focaccia if you bake it using a slightly coarser flour from a stone grinder or a mixture of slightly coarser plain flour and wholegrain flour. Just make sure that the flour has more than 12% protein and a good gluten structure.

All about rhubarb

The appearance of rhubarb marks the departure of the cold winter months, during which we have had to resort to almonds and other nuts, citrus fruits, chocolate and old apples and pears for making desserts. The first rhubarb shoots out of the ground as frozen blue fists in April. If you are very eager, you can put a bell jar over the plant. These young stalks are harbingers of spring and are a taste of heaven in the first fresh fruit desserts of the year or as an accompaniment to roast chicken or a pork chop.

Wild rhubarb

Wild rhubarb is very rare in Denmark, but you will quite often be able to find stray rhubarb in urban areas and in places where garden waste has been disposed. With its 70–80cm-wide smooth leaves and strong green or red stalks, it is easily recognized. The edible stalks have a characteristic sour taste due to their oxalic acid. The inflorescence can grow up to 1.5 metres in length, with a hollow stem and a tuft of white flowers. Varieties of *Rheum rhaponticum*, also known by the misleading name of false rhubarb, are red through the stalk and are the most delicious varieties. When you harvest rhubarb, pull the stalk up with a firm grip at the bottom, close to the root, otherwise it breaks easily and this would be particularly unfortunate because the lower whitish pieces are the most delicious parts of the plant. Never follow rhubarb recipes blindly, as the content of natural sugar in rhubarb varies from variety to variety, from time to time and almost from plant to plant, so you should always taste as you go. And remember that cooked fruit often becomes slightly more acidic in flavour when it has cooled.

Rhubarb soup

Start the rhubarb season by bringing 1 litre water and 400g sugar to the boil in a pan. While the syrup is approaching boiling point, cut about 500g rhubarb stalks into small pieces and put into a bowl, pour the boiling syrup over the fruit and seal the bowl with clingfilm. After an hour, the rhubarb pieces should be crisp and tender, unless they were cut too thickly.

In that case, give the mixture a brief boil. Keep the cooled mixture in the refrigerator for later in the day or the day after, when you can serve it as a cold dessert soup with whipped cream, vanilla ice cream or vanilla cream. While you are enjoying the soup, consider whether you fancy adding any rhubarb-friendly flavourings to the syrup the next time you make it, such as vanilla, mint, rosemary, cinnamon, thyme or lemon or orange rind.

Rhubarb in baking

Cooked rhubarb pieces can also be used as a filling for pies or trifles, or served with ice cream and cakes. Cook the rhubarb with a little water and sugar until completely tender, like a compote, and when it has cooled completely, fold in a portion of whipped cream. Refrigerate until the next day, when the oxalic acid will have firmed-up the whipped cream.

Rhubarb syrup

The juice that forms while boiling rhubarb can be used to make a syrup. Boil 200ml of the liquid to a thick syrup. Boil 100–200ml white wine vinegar (or other mild vinegar) until reduced to a fifth of its original volume. Then mix the rhubarb syrup and vinegar reduction together to taste, carefully adjusting the proportions, adding a little cooked rhubarb if you wish. Serve, for example, with fried flounder, fried chicken or roast lamb. Rhubarb is also highly suitable for chutney (*see* page 36), and it can used in place of plums, tomatoes, apples or any of your other favourite chutney ingredients.

Rhubarb cordial

I recommend this delicious rhubarb cordial. You will need 1kg rhubarb stalks, 300g unrefined cane sugar, 100ml cider vinegar and 2 litres water. Cut off the tops and bottoms of the rhubarb stalks, rinse the stalks in cold water and cut into small pieces. Put into a saucepan along with the sugar, vinegar and water and bring to the boil, then simmer for 5 minutes. Remove the pan from the heat and leave to steep for 20–25 minutes. Pour it into bottles or a jug and store in the refrigerator for up to 2–3 weeks. Leaving the pulp in gives you a thicker squash, but if you want a thinner cordial, you can strain out the pulp.

Rhubarb compote
with ymer and honey

500g rhubarb stalks
½ vanilla pod
150g unrefined cane sugar
finely grated zest and juice
of ½ organic lemon

To serve
ymer (available from Danish food
suppliers) or natural full-fat
Greek yogurt
honey

Cut off the tops and bottoms of the rhubarb stalks, but be careful not to remove the white 'foot' of the stalk, which is where the rhubarb flavour is most concentrated and best. Rinse the stalks in cold water, cut into 2–3cm pieces and put in an ovenproof dish. Split the vanilla pod lengthways and scrape out the seeds into the rhubarb, then add the pod along with the sugar and lemon zest and juice. Toss together.

Bake in a preheated oven at 150°C/Gas Mark 2 for 15–20 minutes. Keep an eye on the dish during the cooking time so that you can retrieve it the moment the rhubarb is tender but not mushy.

Leave the baked rhubarb to cool and serve with a portion of ymer or Greek yogurt and a few drops of honey on top. You can also add some Toasted Oat Flakes (see page 121), nuts or rye bread crumbs if you want to add a crunchy element. Serve the compote as a luxury breakfast or as a small, fresh dessert.

You can make a batch of the compote to store. Once cooled, decant into sterilized preserving jars or an airtight container and keep in the refrigerator for up to 20–30 days.

Rhubarb cake

SERVES 8

Cake layers
4 organic eggs
125g sugar
150g plain flour
1 teaspoon baking powder
butter, for greasing

Rhubarb compote
300g rhubarb stalks
150g unrefined cane sugar
1 handful of lemon balm
½ vanilla pod

To assemble
50g blanched almonds
50g white chocolate, plus extra shavings
to decorate
500ml whipping cream
1 rhubarb stalk
a little sugar, for sprinkling

First make the cake layers. Beat the eggs and sugar together in a bowl until pale and foamy. Mix the flour and baking powder together and sift into the batter, then fold in gently with a spatula.

Grease a springform cake tin, about 22cm in diameter, with butter and pour in the cake batter. Bake the cake in the centre of a preheated oven at 200°C/Gas Mark 6 for about 30 minutes. Remove the cake from the oven and leave to cool in the tin on a wire rack. When the cake is completely cool, carefully cut horizontally into 3 equal layers with a sharp knife.

Now cook the compote. Cut off the tops and bottoms of the rhubarb stalks, but be careful not to remove the white 'foot' of the stalk, which is where the rhubarb flavour is most concentrated and best. Rinse the stalks in cold water, cut into 1–2cm pieces and put in an ovenproof dish with the lemon balm. Split the vanilla pod lengthways, scrape out the seeds and mix with a little of the sugar, making them easier to distribute in the dish. Mix the vanilla sugar into the rest

of the sugar, then sprinkle over the rhubarb. Stir well and add the pod to the dish.

Bake in a preheated oven at 150°C/Gas Mark 2 for 15–20 minutes until the rhubarb is tender but still has a firm bite. Remove the dish from the oven and leave the compote to cool completely.

Chop the almonds and white chocolate roughly. Whip the cream, set half aside for decoration and gently fold the almonds and chocolate into the other half. Add the rhubarb compote and fold in.

Assemble the cake with the flavoured whipped cream between each layer, and finish by decorating it with the pure whipped cream – for the best effect, use a piping bag. Another decorative trick is to create rhubarb shavings by running a vegetable peeler lengthways along a rhubarb stalk. Toss the shavings with a little sugar before scattering over the cake and finish with shavings of white chocolate.

Rhubarb sorbet
with crispy crumbles

SERVES 10–12

500g rhubarb stalks
½ vanilla pod
1 litre water
200g unrefined cane sugar
10 whole black peppercorns
2–3 tablespoons cider vinegar
**1 organic egg white and 30g icing sugar
    (optional)**

Cut off the tops and bottoms of the rhubarb stalks, but be careful not to remove the white 'foot', which is where the rhubarb flavour is most concentrated and best. Rinse the stalks in cold water, cut into chunks and put into a saucepan. Split the vanilla pod lengthways and scrape out the seeds into the rhubarb, then add the pod along with the measured water, sugar and peppercorns – it may sound strange, but the pepper gives a wonderful kick to all that sweetness.

Bring to the boil and cook for 3–4 minutes. Remove the pan from the heat and season to taste with the cider vinegar. Leave the rhubarb mixture to infuse for 20 minutes. Remove the vanilla pod and peppercorns and blend in a blender or with a stick blender. Now strain the blended syrup through a coarse sieve, allowing a little of the rhubarb pulp to pass through.

Place the syrup in the refrigerator to cool completely, then churn it in an ice-cream maker until frozen. Transfer the frozen sorbet to a plastic container with a lid and place in the freezer, where it can stay for 3–4 days and it will keep its creamy texture.

If you don't have an ice-cream maker, pour the rhubarb syrup directly into a plastic container and freeze it. When the syrup is completely frozen, place the block of rhubarb ice on a chopping board and chop it up roughly. Whizz the cubes of rhubarb ice in a food processor until smooth and creamy, then pour back into the container

and return to the freezer. Stir the mixture 2–3 times at 30-minute intervals, then the sorbet is ready to be served.

Another great way to obtain a creamy sorbet without the use of an ice-cream maker is to create a meringue by whisking the egg white with the sugar until stiff, then mixing it into the sorbet after you have whizzed up the frozen syrup in the food processor. Sorbet with meringue still requires a little freezer time before serving.

Regardless of how you have created your rhubarb sorbet, serve it with Crispy Crumbles (see below) on top.

TIP If the sorbet has been in the freezer for longer than 3–4 days and large ice crystals have formed and the texture is hard, you can resuscitate your dessert by melting it and then churning it in the ice-cream maker again. However, this isn't an option if you have mixed meringue into the sorbet, as the mixture won't stand up to the treatment.

Crispy crumbles

20g spelt grains
20g wheat grains
20g rye grains
20g sunflower seeds
10g linseeds
1 tablespoon honey
1 teaspoon sea salt flakes

Day 1
Cover the grains and seeds with cold water and leave to soak at room temperature for 12 hours.

Day 2
Drain the contents in a sieve. Pour the grains into a dry frying pan and toast them gently over a low heat for about 8–10 minutes until golden and crisp. Add the honey and salt and mix well to evenly caramelize the grains. Cool the grains on a plate, then they are ready for crunching.

TIP These crispy crumbles are great as a topping for yogurt, so make a little extra for your Saturday breakfast.

Liquorice parfait
with white chocolate, green strawberries and sweet cicely

50g caster sugar
25ml water
75g pasteurized egg yolks
50ml semi-skimmed milk
25g liquorice root powder
**225g good-quality white chocolate, such
    as Valrhona Ivoire (35% cocoa solids),
    finely chopped**
200ml whipping cream
10–15 green strawberries
½ handful of sweet cicely

Bring the sugar and measured water to the boil in a pan until the temperature reaches about 120°C and it has a syrupy consistency.

Place the egg yolks in a bowl and add the hot syrup by pouring it in a thin stream while whisking vigorously. Continue whisking until the yolks have become creamy and white.

Bring the milk and liquorice root powder to the boil in a saucepan and pour over the finely chopped white chocolate in a bowl to melt it. Stir the milk and chocolate until it comes together into a homogeneous cream.

Whip the cream lightly until it has the consistency of soured cream. Gently combine the egg mixture and chocolate mixture, then fold in the lightly whipped cream. Pour the mixture into 4–6 small ramekins and store in the freezer until the next day.

Take the parfait out of the freezer 10 minutes before serving. Turn the parfaits out of the ramekins directly into soup plates and top with the fresh green strawberries, cut into small cubes and tossed with the cicely, freshly chopped. The fresh green strawberries and the light aniseed flavour of the sweet cicely is an exceptionally good match for the subtle taste of liquorice in the parfait.

•••••••••••••••••••••••••••••••••••

TIP You can also freeze the parfait in a loaf shape, and slice it before serving. Remember to take the parfait out of the freezer about 15–20 minutes before serving.

•••••••••••••••••••••••••••••••••••

Buttermilk ice cream
with lemon and vanilla

SERVES 8–10

100g unrefined cane sugar
80g glucose syrup (*see* tip)
475ml full-fat milk
½ vanilla pod
1 litre buttermilk
finely grated zest of 1 organic lemon

Bring the sugar, glucose and milk to the boil in a saucepan to dissolve the sugar and glucose. Split the vanilla pod lengthways, scrape out the seeds and add both the seeds and pod to the milk mixture.

Pour the buttermilk into a bowl and whisk in the boiling sweetened milk. Add the lemon zest and mix thoroughly. Leave the mixture to cool, then pour into an ice-cream maker. Churn the mixture until frozen, airy and creamy – this should take about 15–20 minutes. Transfer the ice cream to a tightly sealed plastic box and freeze for a couple of hours.

The ice cream will keep its creamy consistency for 2–3 days in the freezer, then the texture will turn hard and crystallized. As with sorbets, you can defrost the hardened buttermilk ice cream and churn it again in the ice-cream maker, but this trick will work only once.

Enjoy the ice cream on its own or serve it with warm rhubarb pie. This ice cream flavour is usually a big hit with Danish children – it tastes exactly like the dessert koldskål, made from buttermilk with lemon and vanilla, and I can recommend serving the ice cream with a buttery biscuit.

•••••••••••••••••••••••••••••••••••

TIP Glucose syrup or liquid glucose contributes to the delicious and creamy texture of this dessert. You will find glucose in shops or from online suppliers specializing in baking and confectionery-making products. If you are unable to get hold of glucose, replace it with an equal quantity of acacia honey, but bear in mind that your ice cream will have a distinct honey flavour.

•••••••••••••••••••••••••••••••••••

LEAVES FROM YOUR FRUIT TREES
Decorate your food with the tender leaves from currant or gooseberry bushes.

Summer

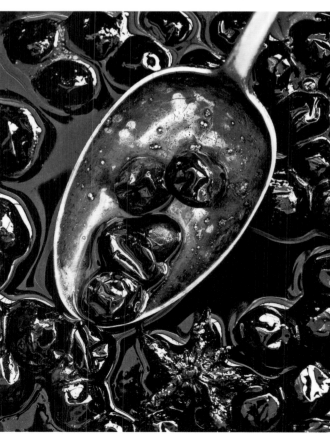

Seasonal ingredients

Cultivated produce

apples
asparagus
aubergines
blackberries
blackcurrants
blueberries
cabbage
carrots
cauliflower
chanterelles
cherries
crabs
crayfish
cucumber
dill

fennel
flounder
goseberries
green beans
grey mullet
herring
horseradish
lovage
mackerel
maize
Norwegian lobster
onions
parsley
peas
pointed cabbage

potatoes
prawns
raspberries
redcurrants
rose petals
rhubarb
salsify
spearmint
spinach
squash
strawberries
summer leeks
tomatoes
venison
wood pigeon

In the wild

rosehips
shore crabs
wild strawberries
marsh samphire
forest raspberries
blueberries
mirabelles
wild berries
wild cherries
bog bilberries
wild apples

woodruff
leaves from berry bushes
   (use them for tea and in salads)
wild thyme
lingonberries
chanterelles
elderberries
sea buckthorn
crowberries
shaggy inkcaps
partridge

Soups and starters

Cold cucumber soup
with mint and salt and sugar-cured mullet

2 cucumbers, peeled and cut into chunks
sea salt flakes
1 spring onion
½ handful of mint, leaves picked,
    plus extra to serve
1 litre low-fat natural yogurt
250ml water
freshly ground pepper

Sprinkle the cucumbers with 1 teaspoon salt flakes and leave them to stand in the kitchen for 10–15 minutes.

Chop the spring onion and put it in a blender or food processor along with the cucumber, mint, yogurt and 250ml water. Blend until evenly combined and smooth.
Season to taste with salt and pepper.

Refrigerate the soup for 30–60 minutes until well chilled and all the flavours have developed.

Serve the soup ice cold with the Salt and Sugar-cured Mullet (see below), cut into thin slices, some mint leaves and good bread.

Salt and sugar-cured mullet

100g very fresh skinless grey mullet fillet
1 teaspoon sugar
1 teaspoon coarse sea salt
freshly ground pepper

Check that the mullet is really fresh and smells of the sea, not of the harbour. Check the fish for bones and scrape off any stray scales with a knife. Place in a dish and sprinkle evenly with the sugar and salt. Cover the dish with clingfilm and leave in the refrigerator for 12 hours – or give it 24 hours if you like. Cut the fillet into very thin slices and season with freshly ground pepper.

White asparagus soup
with pearl barley and smoked curd cheese

1 handful of white asparagus
2 shallots
standard rapeseed oil
500ml chicken stock or water
50ml full-fat crème fraîche
sea salt flakes and freshly ground pepper
cider vinegar, to taste
100g cooked grains, such as pearl barley,
    pearled spelt or pearled rye
1 tablespoon Smoked Curd Cheese
    (see page 16)

Place the asparagus on a chopping board and, using a fine peeler, peel the spears from just below the tip downwards. You may need to go over them with the peeler a second time to make sure you remove every last bit of skin. Break off the woody stem ends of the spears, just where they naturally give way. Throw the peelings and stem ends away, or save them for use in other soups or broths – they are too bitter to use in a pure asparagus soup like this. Cut off the bottom two-thirds of the asparagus and save the last third, the tips, for the garnish.

Peel and chop the shallots very finely, then lightly sauté them with the asparagus slices in a little rapeseed oil in a saucepan. Add the chicken stock or water and simmer for 2 minutes only – if you cook the asparagus for too long, they will lose their beautiful fresh asparagus flavour and be overcooked, tasting like canned ones.

Pour the soup into a blender and blend it with the crème fraîche. You can pass the soup through a sieve back into the pan if you like, to remove the stringiest asparagus bits. Season with salt, pepper and cider vinegar to taste just before serving.

Cut the asparagus tips lengthways finely and mix them with the cooked grains, smoked curd cheese, a little rapeseed oil and some salt, pepper and cider vinegar to taste.

Use this small 'asparagus salad' as a garnish – serve the soup in bowls with a spoonful of the 'salad' on top.

Tip It is also nice to give the soup some extra substance in the form of chicken meatballs – see page 186.

Cold pea soup
with mint and skyr

sea salt flakes
250g podded peas
3 mint sprigs, leaves picked
finely grated zest of 1 organic lemon
1 teaspoon acacia honey
freshly ground pepper
250ml skyr or Greek yogurt

Bring a pan of salted water to the boil and blanch the peas for 1–2 minutes. Remove the peas and immediately immerse them in cold water, reserving the cooking water. This way they will be tender but keep fresh and beautifully green.

Drain the peas and add to a blender with the mint, saving some peas and a few mint leaves to sprinkle over the soup. Add the lemon zest, honey, salt, pepper and finally 300ml of the reserved cooking water, then blend all the ingredients for about a minute to make a smooth green soup.

Pour the soup into a bowl and place it in the refrigerator to cool. Serve the cold soup topped with the reserved peas and mint and a spoonful of skyr or yogurt, along with some good bread.

Tip This soup makes a refreshing small summer starter, and can also be served with a piece of fried fish, a little seafood or some smoked fish added to the serving bowl. If serving the soup as a main course, double the quantity and preferably include one of the aforementioned additions.

Cold cucumber soup »

Crab claws
with fennel mayonnaise

1kg raw crab claws
sea salt flakes
1 lemon
10 whole black peppercorns, plus
  pepper mill for serving
½ handful of dill

Put the crab claws in a saucepan, cover with water and add 1 tablespoon sea salt flakes, 2 slices of the lemon, the peppercorns and dill. Bring to the boil and skim off the foam. Reduce the heat and leave the claws to cook for 5–7 minutes. Turn off the heat and leave the claws to sit in the hot broth for about 20 minutes or until cooked.

When the claws have cooled slightly, gently crush them with a hammer, just enough for the meat to be accessible with a fork. Serve the claws whole so that your guests can enjoy digging out the good crabmeat, and place sea salt, a pepper mill, the rest of the lemon cut into wedges and a bowl of Fennel Mayonnaise (see below) on the table. And don't forget the toast. Since I usually season the mayonnaise with the French aniseed apéritif pastis, I also serve this with the claws instead of white wine, diluted with water and with lots of ice cubes of course.

Fennel mayonnaise

Homemade mayonnaise
2 pasteurized egg yolks
sea salt flakes
1 tablespoon Dijon mustard
1–2 tablespoons cider vinegar
150ml cold-pressed rapeseed oil

To finish
1 fennel bulb
½ handful of chervil or sweet
  cicely, chopped
2 tablespoons pastis, or to taste

First make the mayonnaise. Using an electric whisk or balloon whisk, whisk the egg yolks, salt, mustard and vinegar together in a bowl until thick and white. Whisk in the oil in a thin stream – it is important to do this slowly to avoid the mayo splitting. If it begins to curdle, you can try to save it by adding a few drops of cold water while whisking vigorously.

Cut the fennel in half and rinse it thoroughly in cold water. Drain and then slice it very finely before mixing it into the mayo along with the chopped chervil or sweet cicely.

Finish off the fennel mayonnaise by adding the pastis to taste.

Tip This mayonnaise also makes an uncannily good base for a seafood salad. Mixing the remaining crabmeat and some cooked prawns or lobster tails, and piled generously on top of a piece of toasted rye bread as a late night snack makes me close to being a happy man. Some leftover boiled potatoes to dip in isn't a bad idea either.

Boiled crayfish
with dill mayonnaise

2–3 litres water
1 tablespoon sea salt flakes
1 teaspoon sugar
5 dill sprigs
2–3 slices of lemon, plus lemon wedges
  to serve
1kg live crayfish

Bring the water to the boil in a saucepan with the salt, sugar, dill and lemon slices added. Throw in the crayfish and boil for 6 minutes.

Remove the pan from the heat and leave the crayfish to cool in their broth. The cooling-down process must be fairly quick, so either stand the pan in a bowl of water with ice cubes or directly in the refrigerator and leave it to sit there for about 20–25 minutes.

Lift the cold crayfish out of the broth and serve them with the Dill Mayonnaise (see right), toast and lemon wedges as a starter or a summer lunch. The tails are good, but the most delicious part, in my opinion, is biting into the head and sucking out all the luscious juices.

TIP On the rare occasion when any crayfish is left over, I always make a salad with the meat, cold new potatoes and dill mayonnaise. I save the heads from which the juices have not been sucked out as well as the shells for making shellfish bouillon. I am amazed time after time at just how much flavour they add.

Dill mayonnaise

1 quantity Homemade Mayonnaise
  (see left)
1 handful of dill, chopped
sea salt flakes and freshly ground
  pepper, if necessary

Season the prepared mayo with the chopped dill and a little extra salt and pepper if you think it needs it, then serve.

Shore crabs

When the sea warms up in late summer, the shore crabs venture into the shallow waters. The pentagonal shell or carapace of a shore crab is about 10–12cm wide, and they vary in colour from shades of brown to green. During the day they hide under rocks or seaweed, but they are easy to lure out and catch from a bathing jetty or dock.

How to catch crabs

Put a plastic clothes peg on the end of a length of string and attach a lightly crushed mussel to the clothes peg – you can also use a small piece of fish or meat. Lower the bait to the sea floor, and soon the crabs will come out and begin to bite. Now, ever so gently, start hoisting up the clothes peg with the crab holding onto it and dump it into a bucket. Even more fun is catching crabs at night. Shine the light from a torch into the water and simply snatch the crabs out of the water using your hands – grasp them where the shell is at its widest and drop them into your bucket. You can wear a pair of gardening gloves for protection. In the summer in Smålandshavet or Nordsjælland, my family and I often amuse ourselves by swimming around in shallow water equipped with goggles, the top half of an empty 1.5-litre plastic fizzy drink bottle in one hand and a glove on the other hand. We then fill the bottle with crabs as we catch them – with one hand gripped around the bottle neck, an adult can manoeuvre it around in the water without the crabs escaping.

Soup and stew of shore crabs

Shore crabs make a very tasty soup or stew. Quickly kill the crabs by plunging them in boiling water, or by cutting them lengthways with a sharp knife, as follows:

Place a crab on a chopping board top (back) shell down, underside facing upwards. Using your best kitchen knife, pin the blade against the breast shell, then press down and cut through its head. Continue in the same way with the rest of the crabs, every now and then scraping the prepared crabs and juices from the chopping board into a bowl.

Now you are ready to make your shore crab soup or stew. For the latter, fry your crabs with onion and garlic in butter or oil. Add cider or a mixture of apple juice and cider vinegar to the pan, then reduce over a high heat until it is almost gone. Next, add chopped tomatoes and lots of parsley or dill – preferably fresh dill rather than dill seeds. Heat up, add a knob of butter and season to taste with salt and pepper. Serve with boiled new potatoes, pearl barley, rice or pasta. It is mandatory to bite into the crab shells so that all the lovely juices flow into your mouth.

Meat

Roast chicken
and braised peas with baby onions, bacon and lettuce heart

SERVES 4–6

1 large organic chicken, about 1.5kg
1 handful of flat leaf parsley
1 lemon
20g butter
sea salt flakes and freshly ground pepper

Check the chicken for any feather stumps and pluck them out. Remove any blood or intestine residues from the cavity and wipe with kitchen paper.

Pick off the leaves from the parsley sprigs and rinse them, and cut the lemon into quarters. Stuff the chicken with the parsley and lemon, along with the butter, salt and pepper. Tie the chicken up with kitchen string so that the thighs are hugging the breast – that way the chicken will be juicier. Place the chicken on a roasting rack set over a roasting pan to catch the juices. Roast in a preheated oven at 170°C/Gas Mark 3½ for 1 hour, then turn off the oven and leave the chicken in the oven for a further 10 minutes.

Take the chicken out of the oven and leave to rest for 10 minutes before starting to carve it. Serve the chicken with Braised Peas with Baby Onions, Bacon and Lettuce Heart (see below), boiled new potatoes and some good bread.

Braised peas with baby onions, bacon and lettuce heart

1kg peas in the pod (about 250–300g
**   podded weight)**
15g cold butter
150g baby onions
30g bacon, cut into small cubes
1 Little Gem lettuce heart
½ handful of flat leaf parsley, chopped
sea salt flakes and freshly ground pepper
juice of ½ lemon

Pod the peas, peel the baby onions but keep them whole.

Place the butter and bacon in a sauté pan and sizzle the bacon over a low heat until lightly golden. Add the whole baby onions and sauté with the bacon for a few minutes so that they soften and absorb some of the fat.

Meanwhile, rinse the lettuce and parsley and leave both to drain thoroughly. Cut the lettuce into large chunks.

Check that the onions are soft inside before adding the peas and sauté them for about 30 seconds, then add the lettuce and parsley. Mix well and season with salt, pepper and the lemon juice to finish off. Serve immediately to retain the beautiful colour, crispness and flavour of the peas.

• •

TIP Braised peas with baby onions, bacon and salad (or peas *bonne femme*), is a French classic that I love; it is no crime to replace the baby onions with any other onion. The braised green peas are wonderful with chicken, and I cannot eat a steak béarnaise without them. You can also omit the bacon if you like, to give you peas Française instead.

• •

Poached chicken
with salad of peas, summer cabbage and dill

SERVES 4–6

1 organic chicken, about 1.2–1.4kg
1 onion, peeled and halved
1 garlic clove, peeled
5 thyme sprigs
5 whole black peppercorns
sea salt flakes and freshly ground pepper

Check the chicken for any feather stumps and pluck them out. Remove any blood or intestine residues from the cavity and wipe with kitchen paper.

Place the chicken in a large pan, cover with water and add the halved onion, garlic, thyme and peppercorns. Bring to the boil and skim off any foam (impurities) that rises to the surface. Lower the heat and simmer for 30 minutes.

Turn off the heat and leave the chicken to sit in the hot broth until done – it will take about 15–20 minutes.

Remove the chicken and carve off the breast meat in large pieces. Season with a little salt and pepper. Serve the warm breast meat with the Salad of Peas, Summer Cabbage and Dill (see below) and possibly some cooked grains or potatoes and good bread.

• •

TIP Store the broth from the chicken, either in the refrigerator or in the freezer – it is always good to have at hand when making soup or risotto, or to use as a braising liquid.

• •

Salad of peas, summer cabbage and dill

½ summer cabbage
500g peas in the pod (about 200g podded)
1 new-season onion
100ml Greek yogurt
1 tablespoon honey
2–3 tablespoons cider vinegar
sea salt flakes and freshly ground pepper
1 handful of dill, roughly chopped

Rinse the cabbage and drain thoroughly. Slice very finely and place in a bowl. Pod the peas, and peel and slice the onion very finely. Throw both in with the cabbage.

Mix the yogurt with the honey, vinegar, salt and pepper in a bowl to make a dressing. Add to the salad bowl and toss around.

To finish, fold the dill into the salad.

Serve immediately while it is crisp and delicious. I like to serve this salad with poached chicken, but it is also an excellent accompaniment to meatballs, kebabs or patties as a kind of fresh, summery coleslaw.

Roast chicken »

Barbecued venison
and green potato salad with rocket, peas, radishes and dill
SERVES 6

1 haunch (hind leg) of venison, about 1.5kg
2 tablespoons honey
4 tablespoons cider vinegar
10 thyme sprigs, leaves picked
sea salt flakes and freshly ground pepper

Cut off the muscles from the leg bone, dividing the meat into the topside (top portion), silverside (middle portion) and thick flank (lower portion above the shin). Remove the shin and any other trimmings and save for mince. You can ask your butcher to prepare the meat for you.

Cut away the tendons from the muscles. Combine the honey, vinegar, thyme leaves, salt and pepper in a dish with the pieces of venison and leave to marinate in the refrigerator for 30–60 minutes.

Throw the meat on a barbecue or cook in a grill pan over a medium heat for about 30–35 minutes so that it is still slightly pink in the middle.

Remove the meat from the barbecue and leave to rest for 10 minutes before cutting into slices. Serve with the Green Potato Salad (see right) and some good bread.

. . . .

TIP Run the shin meat and trimmings through a mincer or food processor and enjoy some venison meatballs the following day.

. . . .

Green potato salad

1kg new potatoes
sea salt flakes
500g peas in the pod (about 200g podded weight)
10 radishes
2 tablespoons white wine vinegar
2 tablespoons cold-pressed rapeseed oil
1 tablespoon honey
freshly ground pepper
1 handful of chervil, roughly chopped
1 handful of dill, roughly chopped

Cook the new potatoes as in the Potato Salad recipe on page 36, which gives a perfect result every time. Once drained and slightly cooled, cut them into quarters and put in a bowl.

Pod the peas. Rinse the radishes and cut into thin slices, then add to the bowl of potatoes with the peas.

Mix the vinegar, oil, honey, salt and pepper together in a bowl to make a vinaigrette and add the chopped chervil and dill.

Pour the vinaigrette over the still-warm potatoes and mix carefully – the vinaigrette will be absorbed much more effectively while the potatoes are warm, and they will even thicken it.

Season with more salt and pepper if necessary and serve warm or cold – this makes an ideal side for all kinds of barbecue and summer food.

Seared hanger steak
with frisée lettuce

600g hanger steak (see tip)
10 thyme sprigs, chopped
2 tablespoons olive oil
sea salt flakes and freshly ground pepper
1 frisée lettuce
½ handful of parsley
1 small red onion
2 tablespoons cider vinegar
2 tablespoons cold-pressed rapeseed oil

Remove the largest tendons and membranes from the hanger steak and rub the meat with the chopped thyme, olive oil, salt and pepper.

Heat up a griddle pan and fry the steak for a short time over a very high heat – give it about 2–3 minutes on each side so that it is still quite pink and juicy in the middle.

Meanwhile, cut off the root of the lettuce and divide it into large leaves. Wash the leaves and dry in a salad spinner or a clean tea towel. Pick off the leaves from the parsley and wash and dry them as well. Peel and finely slice the red onion, then mix with the frisée and parsley. Toss with the vinegar, rapeseed oil, salt and pepper.

Remove the meat from the pan and leave it to rest for 1 minute before cutting it into thin slices and serving with the salad. This makes a lunch for 4 people, but you can stretch it to 6 people if serving as a starter.

. . . .

Tip Hanger steak, also known as butcher's steak and what the French call onglet, is so called because it hangs from the diaphragm, and is located just above the kidneys. You can order hanger steak at your butcher's, or just replace it with flank steak.

. . . .

Beef patties
with baked new-season onions, parsley and pearl barley

600g minced beef, 6–8% fat
sea salt flakes and freshly ground pepper
1 tablespoon standard rapeseed oil
10g butter

Shape the meat into 4 patties of 150g each and give them a little squeeze so that they are flat. Then use a knife to score the surface of each patty in a criss-cross pattern. Season with salt and pepper.

Heat up a frying pan with the oil and add the butter. When the butter is sizzling, start frying the beef patties over a medium heat – they should be cooked for about 3 minutes on each side so that they are still pink in the middle. At least, that's how I like my beef patties, provided that the beef is freshly ground from the butcher's, otherwise in the interests of food safety you should cook the meat all the way through. Serve with Baked New-season Onions, Parsley and Pearl Barley (*see* below).

Baked new-season onions, parsley and pearl barley

2 large handfuls of coarse sea salt
18 new-season red onions
5 thyme sprigs
10g butter
½ handful of flat leaf parsley, chopped
2–3 tablespoons cider vinegar
100g cooked pearl barley
sea salt flakes and freshly ground pepper
15g freshly grated horseradish,
**   or to taste**

Cover the base of an ovenproof dish with the coarse salt and place the whole unpeeled onions and thyme sprigs on top.

Bake the onions in a preheated oven at 170°C/Gas Mark 3½ for 20–25 minutes until they are soft and sweet. Remove from the oven and leave them to cool slightly, then cut the root off each onion and squeeze the baked onion flesh out of the skin.

Melt the butter in a saucepan, add the baked onion flesh, chopped parsley, vinegar and pearl barley and sauté for about 1–2 minutes over a low heat or until heated up thoroughly.

Season the onion compote with salt, pepper and horseradish to taste. Serve with the beef patties and some rye bread.

Sweet and sour lamb fricassee
with summer cabbage and dill

600g boneless shoulder of lamb
**   or breast**
2 litres water or potato stock (*see* Tip)
**   and water**
100g whole black peppercorns
50g allspice berries
20 bay leaves
1 handful of thyme
1 garlic clove, peeled
small handful (about 15) dill stems
4 carrots
2 onions
4 parsley roots
sea salt flakes
100ml aged white wine vinegar
2 tablespoons unrefined cane sugar
50ml whipping cream
100ml full-fat milk
freshly ground pepper
2–3 tablespoons cornflour mixed with a
**   little cold water**
½ handful of finely chopped dill
½ summer cabbage, finely chopped

Cut the meat into 3cm cubes and blanch them in a saucepan of boiling water for 4–5 minutes. Strain and place in another saucepan with the 2 litres water or potato stock and water. Bring to the boil and skim off any foam (impurities) that rises to the surface.

Make a bouquet garni by placing the peppercorns, allspice, bay leaves, thyme, garlic and dill stems in the centre of a square of gauze, or fill an empty tea bag, and tie with a piece of cotton string to seal. Peel the carrots, onions and parsley roots and throw into the pan. Season with 1 tablespoon salt and add the bouquet garni.

Cook the meat and vegetables over a low heat for about 25 minutes until the vegetables are tender and have given off some flavour, then remove the vegetables and save them for the garnish.

Continue cooking the meat with the bouquet garni for about 1½ hours until very tender.

Pour about 1 litre of the broth through a sieve into another pan. Season with the vinegar, sugar, cream, milk, salt and pepper. Stir in the cornflour paste and simmer until thickened while you cut the reserved vegetables into large cubes. Add the meat and vegetables to the thickened sauce and heat through before seasoning once again.

Finally, add the finely chopped dill and summer cabbage and swiftly mix it all up so that the cabbage just warms through but is still quite raw and crunchy.

Serve immediately with some boiled potatoes and wholegrain bread.

. . . .

TIP The potato stock that I use in this recipe is good old-fashioned water from boiling potatoes but of the more flavourful kind. When you cook new potatoes, just add lots of parsley to the boiling water, and when the water comes to the boil, skim off any foam (impurities). Once the potatoes are cooked, you can use the cooking water as a lightly parsley flavoured stock in, for example, soups or stews.

. . . .

Roast pork belly

with parsley sauce and refrigerator-pickled cucumbers

750g pork belly, sliced
sea salt flakes and freshly ground pepper
30g butter
3 tablespoons plain flour
500ml semi-skimmed milk
freshly grated nutmeg, to taste
1 large handful of parsley, chopped

If the pork belly slices are thick, wrap them in a double layer of plastic bags and tenderize them a little using a meat mallet. Season the slices well with salt and pepper.

Place on a roasting rack set over a roasting pan to catch the fat and juices and roast in a preheated oven at 180°C/Gas Mark 4 for 10–15 minutes or until very crisp and brown.

Melt the butter in a small saucepan and gradually add the flour, stirring, to make a smooth roux. Add the milk while stirring vigorously. Simmer for 5–10 minutes to cook out the flour, stirring occasionally. Season the sauce to taste with grated nutmeg, salt and pepper, and then add lots of chopped parsley – you can't really add too much. At this point my mother would add the fat from the pork belly to the sauce, but you really shouldn't, as it would smother the distinct but lovely flavour of the parsley and would not enhance the sauce as a companion to the pork belly. Serve the pork belly and parsley sauce with some boiled new potatoes and Refrigerator-pickled Cucumbers (see below).

Refrigerator-pickled cucumbers

200ml white wine vinegar
200ml sugar
200ml water
10 whole black peppercorns
4 bay leaves
1 teaspoon dill seeds
2 cucumbers
sea salt flakes

Combine the vinegar, sugar, water, peppercorns, bay leaves and dill seeds in a saucepan and bring to the boil. As soon as it reaches boiling point, remove from the heat and leave to cool.

Wash the cucumbers and cut them into very thin slices – use a mandoline if you wish. Place the cucumber slices in a bowl, sprinkle with salt and leave to

stand for 10–15 minutes so that they give off a little liquid. Wring out as much liquid as possible from the cucumbers using your hands and then throw them into the cooled pickling vinegar. Leave the cucumbers to pickle for at least a few hours before serving them.

The cucumbers can be stored in sterilized preserving jars in the refrigerator and will keep fresh for about 20–30 days.

Barley porridge

with a stew of chanterelles, baby onions and pork sausages

300ml chicken stock or water
200ml beer
5g sea salt flakes
60g coarse rye flour
60g coarse barley flour
35g hard cheese, such as Høost, or ripe Gouda or Grana Padano, freshly grated
10g butter

Bring the chicken stock or water, beer and salt to the boil in a saucepan and then add the flours in a steady stream while stirring. Cook for 20–25 minutes until all the flour taste has cooked away, stirring occasionally. While the porridge boils, you can make the Stew of Chanterelles, Baby Onions and Pork Sausage (see right).

When the porridge is done, add the grated cheese and butter, and stir until smooth.

Scoop a bit of porridge on to a plate and top with some of the stew, then serve immediately. This can be eaten as a lunch dish, starter, side or garnish for poultry or light meat (veal or rabbit).

I am aware that serving porridge as a savoury dish will be a novelty to many, but in reality it is no different from the polenta widely used in southern Mediterranean cuisine. In the Nordic countries, since ancient times we have eaten lots of porridge and other spoon-friendly foods based on grains and flour – before we fed on bread, we fed on porridge, so to speak. In fact, porridge has been on the menu for the past 6,000 years!

Stew of chanterelles, baby onions and pork sausage

100g chanterelles
50g baby onions
2 pork sausages
10g cold butter
50ml water
sea salt flakes and freshly ground pepper
1 tablespoon olive oil
2 tablespoons cider vinegar
½ handful of flat leaf parsley, chopped

Clean the chanterelles with a brush or a small vegetable knife. Peel the baby onions and cut the sausages into large chunks.

Put the onions in a small saucepan with the butter, the 50 ml water, salt and pepper and sauté over a low heat for 4–5 minutes or until tender.

Add the sausages and chanterelles to a hot pan with the olive oil and fry over a high heat for 1–2 minutes until they are well done. Transfer to the pan of onions and sauté together for a few minutes. Season the stew with the vinegar, salt and pepper. Finish off the stew with the chopped parsley.

Tip Serve a bowl of tender, ripe plums for dessert.

Making your own sausages

✳

Wash your hands. Hygiene is of the utmost importance when making sausages. Once the casing is stuffed and sealed, it is a closed system where aggressive bacteria can spread and thrive.

✳

Buy sausage casings (skins) made from animal intestines at your butcher's or from online stores. Hog casings are the cheapest and will make a sausage the thickness of medister, a traditional Danish pork sausage flavoured with allspice and cloves (about 2.5cm). Lamb casings have a smaller diameter, are thinner and will therefore result in a crisper sausage. Beef casings will give you 'ølpølse', a long, spicy Scandinavian sausage slightly resembling a salami in texture and taste, but usually the diameter of a middle finger. The casings are usually stored in brine, so make sure you rinse them in plenty of cold water before using them.

✳

Use good meat and fat. Choose the type of meat you like the best and add about 200g hard pork back fat to 800g meat. Sausages are usually made with fat, but if you don't add enough fat you will end up with a dry sausage with little flavour.

✳

Buy yourself a meat mincer with a sausage-making attachment from a kitchenware shop or supplier.

✳

Find yourself some exciting recipes, and season well to taste. For example, hot and spicy: finely grated lemon zest, chilli, garlic, cumin, fresh coriander (to take away some of the spiciness), ground ginger, salt and pepper; for traditional: fresh mint, sage, white wine vinegar, garlic, beer, prunes, nutmeg, salt and pepper.

✳

Always use meat that is as cold as possible – it will be easier to mince, and will bind with the liquid and spices more easily. If the meat becomes too warm, the fat will split from the mince and form little 'grains', and this will impair the flavour and result in a dry sausage. So make sure you store your sausage ingredients in the refrigerator or freezer during the process. It is also a good idea to store your mincer and other utensils in the freezer before and during the process.

✳

Always let the filling sit for an hour or so for the flavours to meld and reach optimal taste and texture.

✳

Make a small test meatball. No matter how sure you are of your seasoning, when dealing with spices it is always a good idea to fry a small amount of the filling so that you can sample exactly how the sausage will taste when it is made.

✳

It is important not to seal the end of the casing when you begin to stuff the filling into it because then the air won't have anywhere to escape. Wait until the casing is fully stuffed before you seal both ends. Follow these steps:

1 Fit the casing over the sausage-making nozzle attachment.

2 Fill the casing by running the finished filling through the feed tube of your mincer.

3 Make a knot in each end of the casing once it is full, but be careful not to fill it too much. You will need some room to divide it into smaller sausages, and when frying the sausages the casing will contract and may burst more easily if you have stuffed it too firmly.

4 Divide into smaller sausages by twisting the casing at equal intervals. This process is a bit like making balloon animals, alternating the direction of the twisting each time by making one twist to the left and then the next twist to the right.

✳

Pre-boil your sausages if you wish. Regardless of whether you want to fry, barbecue or smoke your sausages, it may be a good idea to pre-boil them for 10–15 minutes to reassure yourself that they are cooked through. Boiling also reduces the risk of the sausages bursting when you fry them. However, there are types of sausage that you normally wouldn't pre-boil, such as medister for example (see left).

✳

Enjoy your homemade sausages while they are still warm. Sausages are more delicious when the fat is soft, so make sure your dinner guests are gathered round the table as soon as the sausages are cooked.

✳

Enjoy a good beer with your sausages. This last piece of advice is definitely worth remembering. Serve a stout beer with a stout sausage – a decent bitter ale to match the fatty sausage!

Homemade sausages

100g potatoes
1 onion
1 garlic clove
500g mixed minced pork and beef,
**   8–10% fat (or 400g minced meat and**
**   100g hard pork back fat that you**
**   mince yourself)**
sea salt flakes
300ml semi-skimmed milk
1–2 organic eggs
3 rosemary sprigs, chopped
1 teaspoon ground fennel
1 teaspoon ground allspice
freshly ground pepper
2–3 metres hog or lamb casings
**   (sausage skins)**

Peel the potatoes, onion and garlic, and chop roughly. Add to a pan of water and cook for 20–25 minutes until they are soft.

Drain the vegetables, then mash thoroughly in a large bowl with a potato masher or whisk. Mix in the minced meat and salt. Continue mixing, adding the milk, eggs, rosemary, spices and pepper.

Fry a small meatball of the filling until cooked through and taste to check the seasoning before proceeding. Now let the stuffing begin! The process in itself isn't difficult, but it requires some explanation for a first-time sausage maker. Therefore I suggest you take a look at Making Your Own Sausages (see page 79) where I explain in detail how to stuff your sausages. When you have finished stuffing the sausages and used up all the filling, put the sausages in the refrigerator to rest for 30–60 minutes to give the filling time to set.

Fry or barbecue the sausages for 3–4 minutes on each side until they have a beautiful crisp outside and are cooked through, but still juicy in the middle. If you like, you can pre-boil the sausages – this will help keep their shape when you fry them and won't burst as easily.

You will soon discover that making your own sausages is surprisingly easy and fun, and I bet you will start making your very own variety of sausages with anything from pork and beef to lamb and duck.

....

TIP If you don't have a mincer with a sausage-making attachment, you can wrap the filling in caul fat and still enjoy the homemade sausage experience. Caul fat is a thin membrane which surrounds a pig's stomach and can be ordered from your butcher. Soak the caul fat before using it, then wrap it in a thin layer around the filling that you have shaped into a sausage. Make sure the caul fat fits really tightly around the filling and is well sealed so that the juices won't leak out during the cooking process. As the sausage cooks, the caul fat is supposed to melt away, but this will only happen if the layer is thin enough. If there is a lot left, you may need to strip it off before eating the sausage. Now that you have engaged with the sausage-making process, why not make double or triple the quantity and divide into portions to bag up and store in the freezer. They will make the perfect dinner and the kids will love them! Be sure to pre-boil the sausages before freezing them in the interests of food safety. Serve with a Classic Potato Salad (see page 36).

....

Homemade hotdogs

2 small baguettes
2 tablespoons olive oil
2 tablespoons prepared mustard
4 Homemade Sausages (see left)
Homemade Tomato Ketchup (see right)
1 shallot, peeled and finely sliced
**   into rings**
½ handful of chives, finely chopped

Cut the baguettes in half. Slice each piece of bread lengthways, making sure not to cut it all the way through. Oil the cut sides with the olive oil and toast on a hot griddle pan or in a dry frying pan until they become crisp and slightly golden.

Take the breads off the heat and spread the mustard in them before placing a sausage in each. Finish off with some Homemade Tomato Ketchup (see below) and sprinkle the shallot rings and chives on top. Serve immediately while the breads and sausages are still warm and crisp. You can comfortably serve a luxurious hotdog such as this as a main, or enjoy for lunch or as a royal midnight snack.

Homemade tomato ketchup

1 onion
1 garlic clove
1 tablespoon olive oil
40g unrefined cane sugar
1 star anise
1 teaspoon curry powder
sea salt flakes and freshly ground pepper
500g tomatoes
50ml cider vinegar

Peel and chop the onion and garlic – it doesn't matter how finely, as the ketchup will be blended later. Sauté lightly in the olive oil in a saucepan. Add the sugar, star anise, curry powder, salt and pepper to the pan and let the onion caramelize in the sugar.

Dice the tomatoes roughly and add to the pan with the vinegar. Leave to simmer over a low heat for about 45 minutes until a compote consistency.

Transfer the tomato mixture to a blender and blend to a smooth purée. Pass through a very fine sieve, using a spoon to facilitate the process if necessary. Pour the ketchup into a bowl ,then refrigerate.

If you are not planning on using it straight-away, pour the ketchup into a sterilized preserving jar and store in the refrigerator. Unopened it will keep well for 50–60 days and opened for about 10–15 days.

Pork chops
marinated in elderflower and cider vinegar

**4 bone-in pork chops with fat, about
    200g each**
**2 tablespoons elderflower concentrate
    or cordial**
1 tablespoon cider vinegar
1 tablespoon cold-pressed rapeseed oil
sea salt flakes and freshly ground pepper

Score the fat of the chops a few times so
that it doesn't contract too much during the
cooking process. Place the chops in a dish,
add the elderflower concentrate or cordial,
cider vinegar, rapeseed oil, salt and pepper
and marinate at room temperature for
10–15 minutes.

Cook the chops on a very hot barbecue or in
griddle pan for 3–4 minutes on each side so
that they have a beautiful crust but are still
juicy in the middle. Remove the chops from
the barbecue or griddle pan and season
with some more salt and pepper. Serve with
the Crispy Salad of Cauliflower, Hazelnuts
and Celery (see page 100), some good
bread and boiled new potatoes.

Barbecued veal chops
with 'burnt' summer leeks

**4 bone-in veal chops with fat, about
    250g each**
5 thyme sprigs, chopped
1 tablespoon olive oil
sea salt flakes and freshly ground pepper

Scrape the chops with a knife to remove
any bone fragments and score the fat a
few times so that it doesn't contract too
much during the cooking process. Place
the chops in a dish, add the thyme, oil,
salt and pepper and turn the chops to
coat in the marinade.

Cook the chops on a very hot barbecue or
griddle pan for 2 minutes on each side or
until well browned on the outside but still
juicy inside. Serve with 'Burnt' Summer
Leeks (see below).

'Burnt' Summer Leeks

8 young leeks
2 tablespoons cider vinegar
2 tablespoons cold-pressed rapeseed oil
1 tablespoon unrefined cane sugar
sea salt flakes and freshly ground pepper
1 handful of flat leaf parsley, chopped
10 mint leaves, chopped

Cut off the root and tops of the leeks, then
rinse them thoroughly in cold water.

Drain them and place on a medium-hot
barbecue or griddle pan. Cook the leeks
for 3–5 minutes on each side so that they
are completely black and charred on the
outside – you should eat the 'burnt' bits as
well, which bring a pleasing smoky flavour
to the otherwise sweet summer leeks.

Mix the vinegar, oil, sugar, salt, pepper,
parsley and mint together in a bowl to make
a dressing.

Slice the leeks open lengthways and place
them on a platter with the soft and tender
insides upwards. Pour the dressing on top
of the leeks and serve them while they are
still warm with the veal chops.

Chargrilled liver
with warm salad of beetroot, horseradish and dill

300g lambs' or veal or venison liver
4 thyme sprigs, chopped
2 garlic cloves, very finely chopped
2 tablespoons olive oil
sea salt flakes and freshly ground pepper
8 beetroot
50g unrefined cane sugar
5 whole black peppercorns
15 fennel seeds

200ml cherry vinegar
½ fennel bulb, finely sliced
10g freshly grated horseradish
½ handful of dill, chopped

Remove any outer membrane from the liver
and wipe it lightly with kitchen paper. Cut
the liver into thick strips and put them in a
bowl. Add the thyme, garlic, oil, salt and
pepper and leave the liver to marinate in the
refrigerator for 30–45 minutes.

Meanwhile, wash and place the beetroot
whole in a saucepan of salted water. Cook
over a low heat, with the lid on, for about
15–20 minutes until tender, but al dente.

Drain and rinse the beetroot in cold water,
then gently rub off the skins with your hands
– put on a pair of plastic gloves if necessary
so that your hands are not completely
stained red. Cut the beetroot into wedges
and place them in a bowl.

Combine the sugar, peppercorns, fennel
seeds and cherry vinegar in a saucepan
and cook until the mixture has reduced by half
and begun to turn syrupy in consistency.
Remove the peppercorns and fennel seeds.
Throw the beetroot into the hot syrup and
cook for 1–2 minutes, stirring to make sure
they are glazed on all sides. Remove from
the heat, throw in the finely sliced fennel,
horseradish and dill and toss around
thoroughly. Season with salt and pepper,
and sprinkle extra salt on top if needed.

Cook the marinated liver on a hot barbecue
or griddle pan for about 2 minutes on each
side and still pink and juicy in the middle.

Cut the liver into thin slices and serve
immediately with the warm beetroot and
some good bread.

• •

Tip This dish can also be made with beef
heart or, if you are able to get it, venison
heart. If using heart, cut it in half and rinse
thoroughly under cold running water, then
leave to soak in cold water for 2–3 hours,
then follow the method for the liver.
• •

Chargrilled liver »

Fish

Pan-fried mackerel
with pickled tomatoes and thin and crunchy rye bread toasts

2 large mackerel
1 tablespoon standard rapeseed oil
sea salt and freshly ground pepper

Check that the mackerel are fresh – they should have glossy, bulging eyes, red gills and smell of the sea, not of the harbour. Clean the mackerel, scrape any scales off the skin with a knife and wash in cold water. Remove the bones to create 4 fillets, using a pair of tweezers for the small ones if necessary, or just get your fishmonger to do the work for you.

Heat the oil up in a frying pan and start frying the mackerel fillets – first on the skin side for 2–3 minutes or until the skin is crisp and golden, then flip them over and fry for 1 minute on the other side, seasoning with salt and pepper as you go. You will only fit 2 fillets in the pan at a time, so if you have an extra frying pan, fire that one up as well and you will have all the fillets done at the same time.

Serve the warm mackerel fillets with Pickled Tomatoes and Thin and Crunchy Rye Bread Toasts (see right). This is a glorious combination – oil-rich fried mackerel and crispy toasts, with the sour-sweet tomatoes balancing the richness of the fish. The dish is as good for lunch as it is for dinner.

· ·

TIP You can replace the crispy toasts with cooked potatoes to serve with the mackerel and pickled tomatoes.

· ·

Pickled tomatoes

12 cherry tomatoes
50ml olive oil
50ml cider vinegar or other white vinegar
2 shallots
10 fennel seeds
1 garlic clove, peeled
sea salt flakes and freshly ground pepper
sugar, to taste

Wash the tomatoes but keep the stalks on, as they give off a lovely fresh tomato flavour when cooked. Put them in an ovenproof pan and add the oil, vinegar, shallots, peeled and cut into fine wedges, and fennel seeds and garlic clove, lightly crushed to get more flavour out of them, with salt, pepper and sugar to taste.

Gently heat up the tomato mixture, then transfer the pan to a preheated oven at 100°C/lowest Gas Mark setting and cook for about 30–45 minutes or until the tomatoes start to burst.

Take the dish out of the oven and leave the tomatoes to sit for at least 1–2 hours before you eat them. They are even better if you prepare them a few days in advance so that they have more time to sit and mature in the pickling juice.

Thin and crunchy rye bread toasts

8–12 very thin slices of rye bread (see tip)
2 tablespoons cold-pressed rapeseed oil
sea salt flakes

Place the bread slices on a baking sheet lined with baking paper – press them flat to the sheet by hand if needed. Drizzle with the rapeseed oil and sprinkle some salt on top. Bake the bread slices in a preheated oven at 160°C/Gas Mark 3 for 10–12 minutes or until they are very crisp.

Take them out of the oven and leave on a wire rack to cool, when they will become even crispier.

· ·

Tip In order to slice the rye bread as thinly as possible, use bread that is a few days old and chill it in the refrigerator beforehand so that it is firmer and therefore easier to slice.

· ·

MARSH SAMPHIRE
On salt marshes and tidal flats, samphire (salt water baby asparagus) are at their best in summer and stand tall ready for harvest.

Barbecued mackerel
with warm gooseberry compote

4 small mackerel, about 250g each,
   or 2 large, about 400–500g each
1 organic lemon
5 dill stems, chopped
2 tablespoons mustard
1 tablespoon standard rapeseed oil
sea salt flakes and freshly ground pepper

Check that the mackerel are fresh – they should have glossy, bulging eyes, red gills and smell of the sea, not of the harbour. Clean the mackerel, scrape any scales off the skin with a knife and wash in cold water (or get the fishmonger to do the work for you). Cut the lemon into slices and place them in the cavity of the mackerel along with the chopped dill stems and mustard. Close up the cavity using a trussing needle if you wish.

Score the skin of the mackerel a few times, rub it with the rapeseed oil and sprinkle with salt and pepper.

Cook the mackerel on a very hot barbecue for 3–5 minutes on each side, depending on the size. Ensure that you don't move the mackerel around or turn them ahead of time, as the skin easily breaks. If you have a little patience, both the skin and the fish will loosen from the rack after the requisite length of cooking time.

Eat the freshly cooked mackerel with Warm Gooseberry Compote (see below) and boiled new potatoes.

Warm gooseberry compote

300g green gooseberries
2 shallots
100g unrefined cane sugar
10 fennel seeds
5 whole black peppercorns
100ml cider vinegar or other light
   fruit vinegar
sea salt flakes and freshly ground pepper

Snip off the stems and flower ends from the gooseberries with a pair of kitchen scissors and rinse the fruit in cold water. Peel the shallots and cut into thin rings.

Put the sugar, fennel seeds and peppercorns in a saucepan and warm up. When the sugar begins to bubble and caramelize, add the shallots, gooseberries and vinegar and season with a pinch of salt. Simmer for 10–15 minutes with the lid on until you have a dense compote. Season if you wish with some extra sugar, vinegar, salt or pepper.

Remove the peppercorns from the compote before serving if you prefer, or make your diners aware of them at least, as they are not very pleasant to chew on.

Barbecued sea trout
with cauliflower and asparagus in yogurt dressing

600g sea trout fillet, skin on
sea salt flakes
½ cauliflower
12 green asparagus
200ml low-fat natural yogurt
50ml cider vinegar
2 tablespoons cold-pressed rapeseed oil
1 teaspoon acacia honey
freshly ground pepper
10 caraway seeds

Check that sea trout is fresh and smells of the sea, not of the harbour. Use a knife to scrape the scales off the skin of the fish and remove any bones, then divide into 4 pieces approximately 150g each. Season the sea trout pieces with a little salt and leave to sit at room temperature for 10 minutes before cooking them.

Meanwhile, start making the salad. Cut the cauliflower into large florets and break off the woody ends of the asparagus. Cut both the cauliflower florets and asparagus into small pieces, then rinse and let the vegetables drain well in a colander.

Mix the yogurt with the vinegar, oil, honey, salt and pepper in a bowl to make a dressing. Toast the caraway seeds in a dry frying pan until they pop, then crush them using a pestle and mortar and add to the dressing.

Pour the dressing over the vegetables and mix well. If necessary, season with more salt, pepper, vinegar and honey to taste.

Cook the sea trout pieces on a hot barbecue for 2–3 minutes on each side – first on the skin side, until the skin is crisp and golden, then flip over and cook until done. Turn the fish pieces over once only to avoid them breaking or sticking. Serve with the cauliflower and asparagus salad, boiled new potatoes and some good bread.

Barbecued herring
with vinaigrette of mustard seeds, green strawberries and cold-pressed rapeseed oil

6 herrings
2 tablespoons prepared mustard
finely grated zest of 1 organic lemon
sea salt flakes and freshly ground pepper
½ handful of dill, chopped
2 tablespoons cold-pressed rapeseed oil

Vinaigrette
1 tablespoon yellow mustard seeds
1 shallot
10 green strawberries
2 tablespoons elderflower vinegar
2 tablespoons cold-pressed rapeseed oil
½ bunch of dill, chopped
sea salt flakes and freshly ground pepper

Check that the herrings are fresh – they should have glossy, bulging eyes, red gills and smell of the sea, not of the harbour. Clean the herrings, scrape the scales off the skin with a knife and remove the bones to create 12 individual fillets (or ask the fishmonger do the work for you).

Place the herring fillets, skin side down, in a dish, spread the mustard on to the flesh side and sprinkle with the lemon zest, salt, pepper and chopped dill. Leave the herrings to marinate in the refrigerator for 20–25 minutes before grilling them.

Meanwhile, prepare the vinaigrette. Toast the mustard seeds lightly in a dry frying pan, just until they start to release their wonderful aroma. Peel the shallot and chop it very finely, and cut the green strawberries into thin slices.

Drizzle the rapeseed oil over the herrings and cook them on a very hot barbecue, first on the skin side for about a minute, then for a minute on the other side.

Transfer the herring fillets to a deep dish and sprinkle over the mustard seeds, shallot and strawberries. Finish off by drizzling over the elderflower vinegar, rapeseed oil and chopped dill, and season to taste with salt and pepper.

This is a summery, playful way of preparing fried herring and I am absolutely nuts about it. Serve the herring warm and fresh from the barbecue with some good wholegrain bread and a green salad for lunch, or with some boiled new potatoes for dinner – both combinations are utterly delicious.

Do put the elderflower vinegar and rapeseed oil on the table so that your guests can help themselves to some extra dressing if they so wish.

Pan-fried herring
with stewed leeks

8 double herring fillets
2 tablespoons prepared mustard
15g freshly grated horseradish
1 handful of dill, chopped
sea salt flakes and freshly ground pepper
100g rye flour
3 tablespoons standard rapeseed oil
10g butter

Check that the herring fillets are fresh and smell of the sea, not of the harbour. Clean the herrings and scrape the scales off the skin with a knife. Place in a dish, skin side down, spread the flesh side with the mustard and sprinkle with the grated horseradish, chopped dill, salt and pepper. Fold the fillets together and dip them in the rye flour.

Heat a frying pan and add the oil, and when that is hot, add the butter and leave it to bubble. Fry the herring fillets for about 3 minutes on each side until they are golden and crisp. It may be necessary to press down a little on the folded herring fillets with a fish slice when you first add them to the pan so that they don't unfold.

Serve the freshly fried herring with Stewed Leeks (see right) and a pot of cooked potatoes.

• •

Tip I love fried herring, and should there be leftovers after dinner, I cook up some pickling brine in just 5 minutes (see page 94) and let the fried herring spend the night in it. Then at lunchtime the next day I can enjoy pickled and fried herring with rye bread and raw onions, but the herring only gets better over the following days. I also tend to fry extra herrings deliberately, since I have the frying pan going anyway.

• •

Stewed leeks

6 large leeks
200–300ml water
sea salt flakes
3 tablespoons plain flour
950ml skimmed milk
juice of ½ lemon
freshly ground pepper
a little sugar, if needed
freshly grated nutmeg, to taste
½ handful of parsley, chopped

Cut off the root and tops of the leeks, then cut them into 2cm-thick rings. Rinse them thoroughly in cold water so that all the soil is washed away.

Put the leeks in a saucepan with the water and some salt and cook for 2–3 minutes over a low heat. Mix the flour with 200ml of the milk until smooth and stir into the leeks and boiling water, then add the rest of the milk. Let the stew cook for 4–5 minutes so that it thickens and the flour taste is cooked away.

Taste the stew and add lemon juice, salt, pepper, a little sugar if necessary and grated nutmeg – as much as you like. Sprinkle the stew with the chopped parsley and it is ready to be served.

Besides being perfect with fried herring, these stewed leeks are also lovely with other classics such as fried eel, meatballs and sausages.

Steamed mussels
with wheat beer, young leeks and dill

2kg mussels
3 shallots
2 garlic cloves
white part of 1 large leek, rinsed
15g butter
100ml cider or tart apple juice
300ml wheat beer, plus extra to season
50ml whipping cream
12–16 small young leeks
sea salt flakes
½ handful of dill, chopped
1 tablespoon cider vinegar
2 tablespoons cold-pressed rapeseed oil
freshly ground pepper

Follow the first three steps of the recipe for Steamed Mussels with Lovage, Chervil and Beer on page 34 to prepare and steam the mussels, and to make the sauce with the mussel broth and cream.

Cut off the root and the tops of the small young leeks, then rinse them thoroughly in cold water. Blanch the leeks in salted boiling water for about 4–5 minutes, drain, then mix them with the chopped dill, vinegar, oil, salt and pepper to make a fresh 'salad'. Pour on to the mussels.

Season the sauce with salt, pepper and a little extra fresh beer. Pour it over the mussels as well and serve the dish immediately with some good wholegrain bread to soak up the delicious sauce.

Gravad turbot
and fennel crudités with mustard vinaigrette

200g very fresh skinless turbot fillets
10 coriander seeds
5 juniper berries
10 fennel seeds
5 whole black peppercorns
1 teaspoon sea salt
1 teaspoon unrefined cane sugar

Check that the turbot is really fresh and smells of the sea, not of the harbour. Remove any remaining bones and skin fragments, and scrape away any stray scales and membranes if necessary.

Toast the spices in a dry frying pan until they start to release their lovely aromas, then crush them using a pestle and mortar. Place the turbot in a dish and sprinkle with the salt, sugar and spices. Cover the dish tightly with clingfilm and leave the turbot to marinate in the refrigerator for 36–48 hours. Flip the fillets over a few times during the process, but remember to re-cover it with the clingfilm afterwards so that the fish doesn't dry out.

Once the marinating time has elapsed, take the turbot out of the dish and lightly pat dry with kitchen paper while trying not to dislodge the spices. Cut the fish into thin slices and serve with some toasted rye bread and the Fennel Crudités with Mustard Vinaigrette (see right) – it makes a great Sunday lunch.

Fennel crudités with mustard vinaigrette

1 fennel bulb
1 shallot
2 tablespoons cider vinegar
1 tablespoon prepared coarsely ground mustard
1 teaspoon honey
sea salt flakes and freshly ground pepper
2 tablespoons cold-pressed rapeseed oil

Rinse the fennel thoroughly in cold water and slice it very finely, using a mandoline if you wish.

Peel the shallot and cut it into chunks. Put in a blender with the vinegar, mustard, honey, salt and pepper and blend into a smooth dressing. Then add the oil in a very thin stream with the blender running so that the dressing retains its consistency.

Toss the fennel with the vinaigrette and season with some more salt and pepper. Serve immediately while the fennel is fresh and crisp.

WILD THYME
The bright pink flowers of wild thyme are both decorative and taste nice.

Steamed mussels »

Pan-fried plaice
with browned butter, parsley and new potatoes

4 plaice
plain flour, for dusting
sea salt flakes and freshly ground pepper
100g butter
2 tablespoons elderflower vinegar
1 handful of flat leaf parsley, chopped
1kg new potatoes, boiled (*see* method on page 36), to serve

Check that plaice is fresh, with beautiful clear, bulging eyes and a smell of the sea, not of the harbour. Clean the plaice, cutting off the head and fins, and remove the skin, then rinse the fish thoroughly in cold water, cleaning off all the blood and guts (or get your fishmonger to do all the work for you).

Cut an incision all the way down the line that the plaice naturally has down the middle, which will prevent the super-fresh fish from contracting too much and arching during cooking. This cut has a second important function – while frying, you can spoon some of the hot butter from the pan on to the thick end of the plaice (where the head was) so that it penetrates the flesh and enables both the thick and thin parts to be cooked evenly in the same time rather than the thinner part drying out before the thicker part is properly cooked.

Dust the plaice with flour and season with salt and pepper. Melt the butter in a hot frying pan and let it bubble, then fry the plaice for about 3–4 minutes on each side or until they are beautifully golden on both sides. You can probably only fit a single plaice in the pan at a time, unless you have a very large frying pan, so it may be a good idea to use 2 pans at a time. A good trick to check whether the plaice are done is to find the pointed bone that sits just below where the head has been cut off. If it can be pulled out effortlessly, the plaice are finished; if not, they need a little more time in the pan.

Serve the plaice with the butter from the pan flavoured with the vinegar and chopped parsley, along with the boiled potatoes. This dish is simple and exceptionally good.

A long history

Pan-fried plaice has been a constant feature of Danish food culture for centuries. In the first published recipe for the dish, which appeared in Marcus Loofts' cookbook in 1766, the flounder, as the fish was called, is skinned, dusted in flour and fried at a high temperature, then served with browned butter, lemon juice and a sprinkle of parsley. By the early 1800s, the fish was fully coated – C. Jacobsen recommends in his cookbook of 1815 that the fish be first dipped in beaten egg and then in breadcrumbs mixed with flour before frying over a high heat in browned butter.

Pan-fried mullet
with cucumber and peas in dill butter with aquavit

600g grey mullet fillets, skin on
sea salt flakes
1 tablespoon olive oil
1 cucumber
15g butter
200g podded peas
1 shallot
freshly ground pepper
grated zest of ½ organic lemon
½ handful of dill
1 tablespoon aquavit

Check that the mullet is fresh and smells of the sea, not of the harbour. Use a knife to scrape the scales off the skin of the fish and remove any bones, then divide into 4 pieces approximately 150g each and score the skin lightly a few times. Sprinkle salt on both sides and leave to stand for 5 minutes.

Heat up a frying pan with the oil and fry the mullet first on the skin side for 2–3 minutes or until the skin becomes beautifully crisp and golden, then flip the fish over and cook for 1–2 minutes on the other side.

Meanwhile, peel the cucumber, cut it in half lengthways and scrape out the seeds with a teaspoon, then slice it into 1cm-thick wedges. Melt the butter in a pan, add the cucumber and peas and sauté for about 2 minutes over a low heat.

Peel and chop the shallot finely, then add to the pan with the cucumber and peas. Season with salt, pepper and the lemon zest. Chop the dill and add to the pan along with the aquavit and mix well. Serve immediately with the fried mullet fillets, with some boiled new potatoes and a green salad as side dishes.

TIP Buy 100g extra mullet fillet, but ask your fishmonger to remove the skin, and use for the Salt and Sugar-cured Mullet to serve the following day with the Cold Cucumber Soup – see page 66.

Light dishes

Omelette
with new potatoes, spinach and hot-smoked salmon

1 onion
400g new potatoes, boiled (see method on page 36)
10g butter
sea salt flakes and freshly ground pepper
50g fresh spinach
100g hot-smoked salmon
6 organic eggs
200ml low-fat milk

Peel and slice the onion finely, and cut the boiled potatoes into large cubes. Sauté the onion and potatoes in the butter in an ovenproof frying pan (see tip), then season to taste with salt and pepper. Rinse the spinach well, drain and add it to the pan.

Divide the hot-smoked salmon into smaller pieces, add to the pan and mix well. Crack the eggs into a bowl – one at a time so that you can check that they are fresh. Add the milk and whisk together, then pour the mixture into the pan. Fry the omelette for a few minutes in the pan so that it just sets before transferring it to a preheated oven at 200°C/Gas Mark 6.

Bake the omelette for 8–10 minutes or until it has set fully and is slightly golden on top. Serve while it is warm with some wholegrain rye bread. Pickled beetroot (see page 195) is also a good accompaniment, and I personally have a weakness for mustard whenever there is an egg dish on the table.

· ·

Tip If you don't have an ovenproof frying pan, you can make the omelette on the hob and cover with a lid from a large saucepan so that the eggs get a little heat from above as well.

· ·

Lightly salted sea trout
with cucumber and dill in smoked curd cheese dressing

200g very fresh skinless sea trout fillet
1 teaspoon sugar
2 tablespoons sea salt flakes
1 cucumber
10g Smoked Curd Cheese (see page 14)
1 tablespoon cider vinegar
1 tablespoon standard rapeseed oil
50ml Greek yogurt, 2% fat
sea salt and freshly ground pepper
½ handful of dill

Day 1
Check that the sea trout is really fresh and smells of the sea, not of the harbour. Check the fish for bones and scrape off any remaining scales with a knife so that the fillet is nice and clean, then place it in a small dish.

Mix the sugar and salt together and sprinkle the mixture evenly over the sea trout fillet. Cover the dish with clingfilm and leave in the refrigerator for 12 hours.

Day 2
Peel the cucumber, cut it in half lengthways and scrape out the seeds with a teaspoon, then cut it into cubes. Mix the smoked curd cheese with the vinegar, oil, yogurt, salt and pepper in a bowl to make a dressing. Toss the cucumber pieces in the dressing. Rinse and chop the dill finely, and add it to the cucumber mixture. Season with more salt and pepper if necessary.

Take the sea trout out of the dish and pat dry with kitchen paper. Cut into thin slices and serve with the cucumber and dill mixture, along with some good white bread. Serve the dish as a light meal or as part of a Sunday lunch.

Salad of white and green asparagus
with prawns

6 white asparagus
6 green asparagus
sea salt flakes and freshly ground pepper
½ fennel bulb
2 tablespoons elderflower vinegar or light fruit vinegar
1 tablespoon unrefined cane sugar
1 hard-boiled organic egg, shelled and chopped
1 tablespoon prepared mustard
2 tablespoons cold-pressed rapeseed oil
100g small cooked, peeled prawns (see page 45)
½ handful of chervil, chopped

Peel the white asparagus and break off the woody stem ends, but simply rinse the green ones in cold water before breaking off the stem ends.

Cook the white asparagus in a saucepan of boiling salted water for 2–3 minutes, depending on thickness, then immediately transfer them to cold water to stop the cooking process. They should be tender but still quite crisp.

Cut the white asparagus on a slight diagonal into 3–4cm lengths and slice the raw green asparagus quite finely, then add both to a bowl. Slice the fennel very finely with a sharp knife or a mandoline, rinse it in cold water and then let it drain for a while before adding it to the asparagus.

Mix the vinegar, sugar, hard-boiled egg, mustard, salt, pepper and oil together in a bowl to make a dressing. Pour on to the salad and toss well. Sprinkle the peeled prawns and chopped chervil on top, and eat the salad with some good bread.

Mackerel pickled in cider vinegar
with sweet cicely

4 mackerel, about 300–400g each
2 tablespoons sea salt flakes
½ organic lemon, cut into wedges
4 carrots
2 red onions
2 garlic cloves
500ml water
300ml cider vinegar
10 fennel seeds
2 star anise
10 whole black peppercorns
2 tablespoons sugar
1 handful of sweet cicely

Day 1
Clean and fillet the mackerel as in the Pan-fried Mackerel recipe on page 84. Make a few diagonal cuts in the skin, then place the fillets in a deep dish, scatter them with the salt and lemon wedges and leave in the refrigerator for 30 minutes.

Meanwhile, peel the vegetables and garlic cloves, then cut the carrots into slices and the onions into wedges but leave the garlic cloves whole.

Put the vegetables in a pan with the 500ml water, vinegar, spices, sugar and the stems from the sweet cicely (save the leaves for later). Bring to the boil, and as soon as the liquid reaches boiling point, pour it over the mackerel fillets. Remove the sweet cicely stems, as they have already added their flavour. Cover the dish with clingfilm and leave the fillets in the refrigerator until the following day.

Day 2
Take the dish out of the refrigerator and serve the mackerel fillets and vegetables just as they are, with the cicely leaves, freshly boiled potatoes and rye bread. The dish can be served as both a lunch and a dinner.

Tip You can also heat the mackerel and vegetables in the dish in a preheated oven at 160°C/Gas Mark 3 for 8–10 minutes and eat them warm.

Rye salad
with blackberries, beetroot and horseradish

300ml pearled rye
600ml water
3 tablespoons cherry vinegar, or to taste
3 tablespoons cold-pressed rapeseed oil
1 teaspoon acacia honey
sea salt flakes and freshly ground pepper
6–8 small beetroot
20g freshly grated horseradish, or more to taste
½ handful of chervil, chopped
100g fresh blackberries

Rinse the rye grains in cold water and place in a saucepan with the water, or enough to cover them. Bring the water to the boil, skim off any foam (impurities), then lower the heat. Cook the rye for 20 minutes or until it is tender, but al dente. Leave to stand, covered, for 5–10 minutes.

Strain off any excess water from the rye grains and add the vinegar, oil, honey and salt and pepper to taste so that they absorb all the flavours, then leave them to cool slightly.

Take the skin off the beetroot, cut them in half and then slice them very thinly – use a coarse grater if you have one. Add the rye to the beetroot, horseradish, chervil and blackberries in a bowl and gently toss the salad around. Season with more salt, pepper and vinegar if needed. This grain salad with a piece of cheese and some good bread would easily fill me up. You could also serve the dish as a side for *steak à la Lindström* or a piece of pink-roasted veal liver, for example.

Stew of chanterelles on toast

400g chanterelles
20g butter
50ml cider or sherry
100ml whipping cream
sea salt flakes and freshly ground pepper
1 shallot
finely grated zest and juice of ½ organic lemon
8 slices of white bread
1 tablespoon olive oil

Cut off the root end of the chanterelles and clean the mushrooms with a brush or a small vegetable knife. If they are very dirty, you can wash them gently. Cut the chanterelles into smaller pieces and leave them on kitchen paper to dry if necessary.

Melt the butter in a saucepan, add the chanterelles and sauté over a medium heat for 3–5 minutes. Add the cider or sherry and cream and cook the chanterelles until they have absorbed the liquid and the mixture has begun to thicken. Season with salt and pepper. Peel and chop the shallot very finely, then add it to the chanterelles towards the end of cooking – it makes them firmer and adds a sharp contrast to the cream. Season with the lemon zest and juice.

Drizzle the bread slices with the olive oil and toast them under the grill, in a griddle pan or in the oven.

Spoon the stewed chanterelles on to the crisp bread and serve as a small starter or a lunch with a good salad. I think this is terrific food!

Tip You can of course use other wild or cultivated mushrooms in the stew.

Eggs in pots
with chanterelles and grated cheese

4 organic eggs
1 tablespoon olive oil
sea salt flakes and freshly ground pepper
10g butter
100g cleaned chanterelles (*see* left)
20g Comté cheese
2 chervil sprigs, chopped

Crack the eggs – one at a time into individual cups to check them for freshness. Oil 4 ovenproof glasses or small bowls with the olive oil and then put one egg into each. Season the eggs with salt and pepper and bake them in a preheated oven at 170°C/ Gas Mark 3½ for about 10–12 minutes or until the eggs are firm but still soft in the middle.

Melt the butter in a pan and fry the chanterelles for 2–3 minutes over a high heat, then season with salt and pepper.

Place the fried chanterelles on top of the baked eggs. Grate the cheese on top and sprinkle with the chervil. Serve the eggs while they are warm. This works wonderfully as a brunch dish or as a different kind of lunch.

Chicken salad
with baked shallots and chanterelles

6 shallots
sea salt flakes
1 teaspoon prepared mustard
1 teaspoon honey
2 tablespoons cider vinegar
2 tablespoons cold-pressed rapeseed oil
freshly ground pepper
about 150g poached chicken (*see* Tip)
100g cleaned chanterelles (*see* left)
2 tablespoons standard rapeseed oil
½ handful of parsley, chopped

Place the whole unpeeled shallots in an ovenproof dish, sprinkle them with a little salt and bake them in a preheated oven at 180°C/Gas Mark 4 for 15–20 minutes or until they are fully cooked.

Then remove from the oven and leave the shallots to cool. Cut the root off the onions and slip them out of their skins. Cut the shallots into chunks and put them in a bowl.

Mix the mustard, honey, vinegar, cold-pressed rapeseed oil, salt and pepper together in a bowl to make a dressing and pour it over the shallots. Place the chicken on top of the shallots.

Heat up a pan and fry the chanterelles in the rapeseed oil over a medium heat for 3–4 minutes or until they have shrunk a little. Season with salt and pepper, remove the mushrooms from the heat and leave them to cool slightly.

Add the chanterelles and chopped parsley to the salad, toss around well and season with more salt and pepper. Serve on a slice of toasted rye bread or white bread as a starter, or as a small lunch dish with a good salad.

Tip If you don't have any cooked chicken lying around, then cook 2 chicken legs according to the instructions for Poached Chicken on page 72, leave them to cool and then pick the meat off them – this should yield the equivalent of the 150g chicken meat you need for the salad.

WILD BLUEBERRIES
On heaths and in well-lit pine forests, wild blueberries will be starting to sprout.

Stew of chanterelles »

Tartlets
with summer vegetables in béchamel sauce

20g butter
20g plain flour
500ml warm chicken stock
1 organic egg yolk
50ml whipping cream
sea salt flakes and freshly ground pepper
finely grated zest and juice of
    1 organic lemon
4 white asparagus
4 green asparagus
½ summer cabbage
500g peas in the pod (100–150g podded
    weight)
½ handful of sweet cicely or chervil,
    freshly torn
12 Tartlet Cases (*see right*)

Melt the butter in a saucepan and add the flour, stirring, to make a smooth roux. Add the warm chicken stock and stir vigorously while it comes to the boil to avoid any lumps forming. Leave to simmer for 7–8 minutes.

Mix the egg yolk and cream together, then whisk into the sauce and simmer for a further 2–3 minutes. Pass the sauce through a sieve and season to taste with salt, pepper and lemon zest and juice. The sauce should be light, creamy and velvety.

Peel the white asparagus and break off the woody stem ends, but simply rinse the green ones in cold water before breaking off the stem ends. Slice the asparagus and cabbage finely, shell the peas and add all the vegetables to the sauce, then cook for 1–2 minutes. Remove from the heat and mix the freshly torn sweet cicely or chervil into the stewed vegetables.

Warm the tartlet cases in a preheated oven at 200°C/Gas Mark 6 for 2 minutes, then fill them with the stewed vegetables. Serve the tartlets as a starter or a light main, depending on the number of diners.

Tartlet cases
MAKES 12 TARTLET CASES

2–3 tablespoons standard rapeseed oil
300g puff pastry (defrosted if frozen)
plain flour, for dusting

You will need 24 tartlet moulds, each about 10–12cm in diameter. Oil 12 on the inside and 12 on the outside thoroughly with the rapeseed oil.

Roll the puff pastry out thinly on a floured work surface. Cut out 12 circles about 12–14cm in diameter and use to line the internally oiled moulds. Make sure the pastry is pressed firmly into the moulds, with no air bubbles caught under the dough, then place the externally oiled moulds on top of the pastry cases, to keep the dough pressed against the bottom moulds. Leave them to rest in the refrigerator for 20–25 minutes.

Bake the tartlet cases in a preheated oven at 200°C/Gas Mark 6 for 12–14 minutes. Leave them to cool slightly in the moulds before gently turning them out.

Tip The tartlet cases can also be made with 'dull pastry' – puff pastry that has been kneaded so that the butter layers have been removed, typically the rekneaded trimmings left over from cutting out the dough. Pastry cases made with 'dull pastry' will keep their shape a little better, but they are not quite as crisp and flaky.

Tartlet traditions

Pies or small cups of pastry served with stews or sweet fillings have been popular for centuries in Europe. With the birth of classic French cuisine in the 18th century, these dishes were refined with the use of puff pastry or shortcrust pastry. In the 1700s, the term 'tartlets' referred only to sweet dishes, and it was not until the subsequent century that savoury recipes were introduced. The tartlets had their heyday in the 20th century where they were served between the starter and main course at the great dinners of the bourgeoisie, but soon they became a beloved part of menus at festive occasions at all levels of society. As a child, I had enough margarine-based industrial tartlets to last a lifetime, so if you don't have the opportunity to make croustades or tartlet cases using proper butter-based pastry, I would recommend toasted bread instead.

Vegetable accompaniments

Pea purée
with almonds and mint

200g podded peas (500–600g unpodded
    weight)
20g whole blanched almonds
2 tablespoons olive oil
2 tablespoons fresh cheese, such as
    cream cheese or ricotta
20g Parmesan cheese, freshly grated
4 mint leaves, chopped
sea salt flakes and freshly ground pepper
juice of ½ lemon or a little cider vinegar,
    or a little finely grated lemon zest

Blanch the peas in a saucepan of boiling
water for 30 seconds and then immediately
drain and plunge them into cold water to
stop the cooking process.

Roast the almonds in a dry frying pan until
they are slightly golden.

Put the peas in a food processor with
the roasted almonds, oil, fresh cheese,
Parmesan and chopped mint and process
to a coarse purée. Season with salt, pepper
and the lemon juice or cider vinegar. You
can also use a little grated lemon zest
instead if you want to avoid the purée
turning a more khaki-coloured green
from the acid of the lemon juice or vinegar.
Eat the purée with a piece of toasted bread
or some crackers as a snack, or as a side for
barbecued or grilled meat.

Cauliflower purée
with a crispy salad of cauliflower, hazelnuts and celery

1 cauliflower, green leaves discarded
3 celery sticks
25g hazelnuts
2 tablespoons standard rapeseed oil
sea salt flakes and freshly ground pepper
finely grated zest and juice of
    ½ organic lemon
10g butter
some mixed herbs, such as chervil and
    flat leaf parsley, rinsed

Cut off the outermost small florets of
the cauliflower and put them in a bowl.
Cut the rest of the cauliflower into large
chunks and place in a saucepan with a
little water. Steam the cauliflower, with
the lid on, for about 10–12 minutes. The
cauliflower should be tender, but not
overcooked as it might start to smell and
taste a little 'soggy' – that lingering smell
of cauliflower filled the air in every staircase
in my childhood!

Meanwhile, make the salad. Wash the
celery and cut it into very fine strips, and
crush or chop the hazelnuts lightly. Add
the celery and hazelnuts to the small
cauliflower florets in the bowl and marinate
them in half the oil, salt, pepper and a little
of the lemon juice.

Put the steamed cauliflower and 100ml of
the cooking water in a blender, add the
butter, the remaining oil and lemon juice
and the zest and blend to a smooth purée.
Season with salt and pepper.

Serve the warm purée sprinkled with the
crisp salad and garnished with the herbs on
top as a starter with some good bread, or
use it as a side. The creamy purée is almost
like a mayonnaise, and I am absolutely nuts
about combining it with fish and shellfish,
for example as an accompaniment to boiled
langoustines, prawns or squid.

Griddled vegetables
with sprinkle of smoked pork fat, dill seeds and sorrel

10 freshly harvested carrots with tops
8 freshly harvested onions
1 handful of green asparagus
1 courgette
2 tablespoons olive oil
sea salt flakes and freshly ground pepper
30g smoked pork fat (lard)
finely grated zest and juice of
    1 organic lemon
1 teaspoon dill seeds
a little parsley and chervil, chopped
1 small handful of sorrel (wood sorrel or
    lemon balm can also be used)

Wash and peel the carrots and onions, and
chop the carrots in half lengthways and the
onions into quarters. Break off the woody
stem ends of the asparagus and cut the
courgette into 1cm-thick slices.

Turn all the vegetables in the oil, salt and
pepper, then cook on a hot griddle or
griddle pan for a few minutes on each side
until they begin to colour and are lightly
cooked – they should still be crunchy.
Arrange the vegetables on a serving platter.

Cut the smoked pork fat into thin slices
and fry them in a dry frying pan for about
2–4 minutes on each side so that they
become golden and crisp. Remove from the
pan and leave to drain on kitchen paper to
absorb the excess fat.

Add 1 tablespoon of the rendered fat from
the pan to a bowl with the lemon zest and
juice, salt and pepper. Toast the dill seeds
in a dry frying pan until they begin to pop,
then remove from the pan and crush them
lightly with the flat side of a chef's knife.
Add to the dressing and pour it over the
vegetables. Sprinkle the crispy fat on top
along with the chopped herbs and sorrel.
Eat the vegetables as a starter or as a side
to fish, meat or poultry.

Salt-baked potatoes

1kg new potatoes
4 tablespoons sea salt flakes

Rinse the potatoes in cold water. Put the potatoes in a heavy-based pan and pour over water to barely cover them. Add salt and bring to the boil. Cook the potatoes, with the lid on, for about 10 minutes or until they still have a little bite.

Pour almost all the water out, leaving 5mm water in the base of the pan, and steam the potatoes, without the lid on, while constantly shaking the pan to keep the potatoes moving in the salt water. When the water has evaporated, a thin layer of salt will have formed on the outside of the potatoes. Put the lid back on and leave the potatoes to sit for 10 minutes off the heat. Take the lid off and place the pan back on the heat for 1–2 minutes, shaking the pan again.

This method of cooking potatoes makes them wrinkly and gives them a unique texture with a chewy exterior and a lovely taste from the salt layer. Eat the wrinkled potatoes with the Lovage Dip and Cream Cheese with Chervil and Lemon (see below) as a snack or small starter before dinner. You can also use them as an accompaniment to shellfish and fish dishes – create a wonderful and easy summer meal by simply adding some smoked herring from your fishmonger and serving with a crisp green salad.

Lovage Dip

½ handful of lovage
1 handful of parsley
100ml standard rapeseed oil
1 shallot, peeled
50ml cider vinegar
30g fresh wheat bread, crust removed
sea salt flakes and freshly ground pepper
a little unrefined cane sugar or honey

Wash and tear the lovage and parsley, then add with the oil, shallot, vinegar and bread to a food processor and blend to a coarse dip.

Season with salt, pepper and sugar or honey so that the balance is just right and serve with the Salt-baked Potatoes.

This dip is also great with ordinary boiled new potatoes or as a green sauce for crisply cooked summer vegetables.

Cream cheese with chervil and lemon

40g cream cheese
1 teaspoon prepared mustard
finely grated zest and juice of
**   ½ organic lemon**
sea salt flakes and freshly ground pepper
1 tablespoon olive oil
½ handful of chervil, chopped

Mix the cream cheese and mustard together in a bowl, then stir in the lemon zest and juice, salt, pepper, oil and, lastly, the chopped chervil.

In addition to being a lovely dip for potatoes and other summer vegetables, this is excellent in a sandwich or on a slice of rye bread.

Barbecued new potatoes
with two kinds of herb butter

1kg new potatoes
sea salt flakes
1–2 tablespoons olive oil

Soak 8–10 wooden skewers in cold water for about 30 minutes to prevent them burning on the barbecue.

Scrub the potatoes in cold water to remove all the soil. Put the potatoes in a saucepan of salted water so that it just covers them, bring to the boil and cook for 6–8 minutes over a low heat until soft but al dente. Drain and plunge them into cold water to stop the cooking process.

Drain the potatoes again and thread 4–6 on to each skewer. Brush with the olive oil and sprinkle with salt. Cook on a hot barbecue for a total of 3–5 minutes, remembering to turn them occasionally so that they get some colour and are crisp on all sides.

Eat the hot potatoes with some herb butter (see below) – select the butter you like the best, or make a little of each kind. Serve as an accompaniment to barbecued food, such as the Barbecued Veal Chops with 'Burnt' Summer Leeks on page 82, or as a small barbecue snack or starter.

Herb butter with parsley, garlic and lemon

100g softened butter
1 handful of flat leaf parsley
1 garlic clove, very finely chopped
finely grated zest and juice of
**   ½ organic lemon**
1 tablespoon soy sauce
sea salt flakes and freshly ground pepper

Put all the ingredients in a bowl and mix together well so that all the flavourings are evenly distributed in the butter. Transfer the herb butter to a clean bowl, or wrap it in clingfilm and form it into a small roll, and place in the refrigerator until it is completely cold. The butter will keep fresh for 2 months in the freezer or 1 week in the refrigerator.

Herb butter with Parmesan cheese and sweet basil

100g softened butter
2 tablespoons freshly grated
**   Parmesan cheese**
1 handful of basil
1 tablespoon cider vinegar
sea salt flakes and freshly ground pepper

Make, chill and store the herb butter as above.

Barbecued new potatoes »

Stuffed tomatoes
with wheat berries, herbs and fresh goat's cheese

8 tomatoes
1 onion
4 celery sticks
2 tablespoons olive oil
200g cooked grains, such as pearl barley
½ handful of parsley, chopped
½ handful of chervil, chopped
½ handful of basil, chopped
sea salt flakes and freshly ground pepper
50g fresh goat's cheese

Cut a lid off the top of each tomato and scrape the flesh out with a teaspoon. Push the tomato flesh through a sieve over a bowl to extract the juice and remove the seeds. Peel and chop the onion, slice the celery finely and sauté both vegetables briefly in 1 tablespoon of the oil. Remove from the heat, mix in the cooked grains and add a little of the tomato juice as well as the chopped herbs – the grain filling should not be swimming in the juice, so add just enough to be absorbed. Season with salt and pepper.

Place a small dollop of goat's cheese in each tomato, then the grain filling on top and finish with a little more goat's cheese. Put the tomatoes in an oiled ovenproof dish, drizzle with the remaining oil and season with salt and pepper. Bake the tomatoes in a preheated oven at 220°C/Gas Mark 7 for 15–20 minutes or until they are baked through and beautifully 'au gratin' on top.

Serve the tomatoes immediately. With a rich salad and some good bread, they will make a great main course, but you can also serve them as an accompaniment to a main course, especially lamb.

Crispy salad of summer cabbage
with peas and spring onions

½ summer cabbage
2 tablespoons prepared mustard
2 tablespoons cider vinegar
sea salt flakes and freshly ground pepper
3 tablespoons cold-pressed rapeseed oil
1 teaspoon sugar
4 spring onions
100g podded peas
1 handful of dill, roughly chopped

Remove the stalk and if necessary the outer leaves of the cabbage and discard them. Slice the cabbage as finely as possible and place in cold water so that it becomes even crispier.

Mix the mustard, vinegar, salt and pepper together in a bowl. Whisk in the oil until the mixture is smooth and adjust the flavour with the sugar.

Slice the spring onions very finely. Drain and dry the cabbage in a salad spinner, then place in a salad bowl and toss it with the spring onions, peas, the vinaigrette and the chopped dill. Finally, season with more salt and a little more pepper if you wish.

Young summer beetroot
with cottage cheese, smoked pork fat and tarragon

12 small young beetroot
sea salt flakes
1 tablespoon cherry vinegar or other fruit vinegar
1 tablespoon cold-pressed rapeseed oil
1 teaspoon acacia honey
freshly ground pepper
30g smoked pork fat (lard)
100g cottage cheese
½ handful of tarragon, chopped

Cut off the 3–4cm-long green leafy tops from the beetroot as well as the roots. Wash them thoroughly in cold water so that you get all the soil off. Put them in a pan of salted water so that the water just covers them and bring to the boil, then boil for 7–8 minutes until soft but al dente. Drain and plunge them into cold water to stop the cooking process.

Rub off the skin of the beetroot to uncover their silky interior – put on a pair of plastic gloves if necessary so that your hands are not completely stained red. Add the whole beetroot to a bowl with the vinegar, oil, honey, salt and pepper and leave them to marinate for 10–15 minutes.

Cut the smoked pork fat into 1cm cubes. Put the fat cubes in a cold pan and fry them gently until they are crisp and the fat has rendered. Drain them in a sieve to remove the excess fat.

Serve the beetroot with a scoop of cottage cheese, and sprinkle some crispy fat cubes and freshly chopped tarragon on top. Season finally with a little salt and pepper. Eat with bread as a small lunch dish, a juicy starter or as part of a main dish.

Baking and sweet things

Quick and easy rye bread

MAKES 1 LOAF

200ml buttermilk
600ml cold water
150ml beer
15g sea salt flakes
10g fresh yeast
300g chopped rye kernels
225g linseed
150g sunflower seeds
115g sesame seeds
250g wholemeal flour
300g rye flour
rapeseed oil, for oiling

Put all the ingredients into the bowl of a stand mixer fitted with a dough hook and knead the dough for 10 minutes. Alternatively, give your arms a workout and hand-knead the dough in a large bowl.

Pour the dough into an oiled rye bread tin that can hold 3.3 litres, cover the tin with clingfilm and place in the refrigerator for at least 12 hours before baking, preferably longer. The longer the dough sits, the more flavour the bread develops, but the maximum you can leave it is 6 days, otherwise the acidity of the finished bread will be too high.

Bake in a preheated oven at 180°C/Gas Mark 4 for 1½ hours. Turn the bread out on to a wire rack to cool thoroughly before you slice it.

Almond and chocolate cake
with strawberries and lightly whipped cream

SERVES 6

Meringue layers
130g whole blanched almonds
2 organic egg whites, about 70–80g
130g icing sugar
100g good-quality dark chocolate, such as Valrhona Manjari 64%

Filling
300g fresh strawberries
20ml whipping cream, lightly whipped
a few lemon balm tips

For the meringue, spread the almonds on a baking sheet lined with baking paper and roast them in a preheated oven at 160°C/Gas Mark 3 for 8–10 minutes or until golden and fragrant. Leave the almonds to cool, then chop them in a food processor or with a knife.

Whisk the egg whites until stiff, then whisk in the icing sugar a little at a time and beat until you have a glossy and smooth meringue mixture. Chop the chocolate roughly and fold into the meringue along with the chopped almonds.

Draw 2 circles, each about 26cm in diameter, on a piece of baking paper on a baking tray and spread the meringue mixture over them using a spatula for a neat result. Bake in a preheated oven at 170°C/Gas Mark 3½ for about 15 minutes until crisp and golden on the outside but still slightly soft in the centre.

Leave the meringue layers to cool, then carefully remove them from the baking paper and place them on a cake plate.

For the filling, rinse the strawberries only if necessary and then hull (see page 114).

Cut them in half and spread them out on the meringue layers, decorating with lightly whipped cream and a lemon balm tips. You can either make 2 open cakes or place the layers on top of each other so that you have a single cake. Serve immediately while the meringue is still lovely and crisp.

WILD STRAWBERRIES
Commonly found in the wild and woodlands in summer – you'll need to hunt for a secret spot to find them!

Mirabelles

Mirabelle is the common name for small, early-ripening red and yellow plums, which are often found in the wild or planted in thickets, hedgerows and cottage gardens. Mirabelles grow on robust bushes or up to 10-metre-tall trees with clear thorns at the ends of the branches and 4–8cm-wide leaves that have a smooth, glossy surface. The white blossom appears at the earliest time for fruit trees, in April–May. The individual trees cross-pollinate each other and produce a wealth of varying flavours.

Where to find mirabelles

Research your hunting ground for wild mirabelles in April–May when you should be able to see the first tiny fruits on the trees so that you can just go out and collect the fruit once they ripen in August.

Occasionally you will find trees with fruits so sweet and juicy that they resemble grapes. Mark their location on your GPS! Other mirabelles may not be so exciting in flavour, but they can still be used in marmalades or for pickling. As some mirabelles lack acidity, you should always add a little cider vinegar or lemon juice to taste when cooking with the fruit, regardless of what the recipe prescribes. Mirabelles can replace plums in most recipes.

Mirabelle marmalade

For this easy marmalade recipe, you will need 1kg mirabelles, 500g sugar, 200ml water and 100ml plum vinegar or other dark fruit vinegar.

Wash the mirabelles and remove the stalks. Add the fruits to a saucepan with the sugar and measured water and bring to the boil with the lid on. Once boiling point is reached, remove the lid and simmer over a low heat for 20–25 minutes until you have a dense compote, giving the mixture the occasional light stir. Add the vinegar and leave the marmalade to cook for another 10–15 minutes. Once the mirabelles are tender and blending together, the stones will float up to the surface and you can then skim them off effortlessly. This way, you can avoid the tedious task of removing all the stones beforehand and they also contribute both flavour (bitterness) and pectin to the marmalade. Pour the marmalade into sterilized glass jars and seal tightly. It will keep fresh in the refrigerator for 4–6 weeks. You can vary the flavour by adding different herbs, for example rosemary, thyme, mint or tarragon.

Almond cake
with blackberries and white chocolate

SERVES 8

5 organic egg yolks
200g sugar
½ vanilla pod, split lengthways and
    seeds scraped out
150g butter, plus extra for greasing
100g good-quality white chocolate, such
    as Valrhona Ivoire 35%, chopped
200g fresh blackberries
250g whole blanched almonds
2 tablespoons plain flour
2 organic egg whites

Beat the egg yolks, sugar and vanilla seeds together until it turns white and creamy with an egg nog-like consistency.

Melt the butter and white chocolate gently in a bain-marie or a heatproof bowl set over a pan of barely simmering water. Stir the blackberries into the egg mixture and add the chocolate mixture. Chop the almonds finely – you can use a food processor for a finer texture – and fold into the batter with the flour.

Whisk the egg whites in another bowl until completely stiff and fold them into the batter.

Grease a springform cake tin, 24–26cm in diameter, with butter and pour the batter into it. Bake in a preheated oven at 180°C/Gas Mark 4 for 30–35 minutes or until golden brown on the top and firm in the centre. Remove the cake from the oven and leave it to cool on a wire rack before serving.

This is one of my favourite almond cakes. It is very moist and stays delicious for several days if you store it in a cool place. You can warm it before serving, but it is not necessary. In spring and early summer I make it with rhubarb and gooseberries, then later in summer with raspberries or as here with blackberries. It is not a light cake,
so even though vanilla ice cream pairs well with just about everything, I actually prefer Yogurt Ice Cream with this (*see* page 246) or Homemade Soured Milk (*see* page 116).

Plum muffins
MAKES 12–15 MUFFINS

100g softened butter, plus extra
    for greasing
200g unrefined cane sugar
2 large organic eggs
125g plain flour
25g walnuts, finely chopped
10 ripe plums

Grease 12–15 cups of 1–2 muffin tins with butter.

Beat the butter and sugar together thoroughly until pale and fluffy, then add the eggs one at a time – don't add the second egg until the batter has absorbed the first one completely, to prevent the batter from splitting. Finally, add the flour and the walnuts and mix until well combined.

Cut the plums in half, remove the stones and cut into large cubes, then mix them into the batter.

Pour the batter evenly into the muffin cups and bake in a preheated oven at 200°C/Gas Mark 6 for about 15 minutes or until the muffins are completely golden and crispy on top. Serve warm.

Gooseberry trifle

Compote
500g green or red gooseberries
150g unrefined cane sugar
½ vanilla pod, split lengthways and
    seeds scraped out, pod reserved
finely grated zest and juice of
    ½ organic lemon

Custard
3 pasteurized egg yolks
50g icing sugar
½ vanilla pod, split lengthways and
    seeds scraped out
50ml whipping cream

To finish
100g Almond Macaroons (*see* page 114)
50ml sherry

For the compote, snip off the stems and flower ends from the gooseberries with a pair of kitchen scissors and rinse the fruit in cold water. Place the gooseberries in an ovenproof dish and toss them with sugar, vanilla seeds and pod and lemon zest and lemon juice. Bake in a preheated oven at 150°C/Gas Mark 2 for 20–25 minutes, tossing them around during the baking time so that the berries are well mixed with the vanilla and lemon. Leave the baked gooseberries to cool and then they are ready to join the trifle.

To make the custard, beat the egg yolks, sugar and vanilla seeds together to a white and creamy egg nog-like consistency. Whip the cream to soft peaks, then fold it gently into the egg mixture so that both the whipped cream and the egg mixture retain their airiness. I usually add a single spoon of the whipped cream first and give it a proper stir, to completely mix it with the egg mixture, then it will be easier to fold in the rest of the whipped cream carefully to create an airy and well-blended custard.

Assemble the trifle in 4 glasses in layers, alternating between the compote, custard and macaroons, sprinkling the macaroons with a little sherry along the way. It is now up to you whether you serve the trifle immediately or leave it to rest in the refrigerator so that the macaroons soften and combine with the compote. Personally, I prefer the latter method, but as with other classics, there are different schools of thought within the field of trifles.

Almond macaroons

MAKES ABOUT 25–30 MACAROONS

100g whole blanched almonds
2 organic egg whites
100g sugar

Spread the almonds on a baking sheet lined with baking paper and roast them in a preheated oven at 160°C/Gas Mark 3 for 10–12 minutes. Leave the almonds to cool, then grind them as finely as possible in a food processor. Lower the oven temperature to 150°C/Gas Mark 2.

Whisk the egg whites until stiff, adding 2 tablespoons of the sugar while whisking. Then fold the remaining sugar and the ground almonds gently into the egg whites.

Place the mixture in a wide, heavy-based saucepan and 'roast' it over a low heat until it is smooth. Leave the batter to cool slightly, then pour it into a piping bag and pipe small blobs on to a baking sheet lined with baking paper, keeping an ample distance between them, since they will spread significantly. Bake the macaroons for about 15 minutes or until crisp on the outside and still slightly soft in the centre. Transfer them to a wire rack to cool and then store them in a cake tin until it is empty!

Elderflower granita
with strawberries

200ml elderflower concentrate
  or cordial
200ml water
2 tablespoons unrefined cane sugar
1 tablespoon cider vinegar
6–8 fennel seeds
5 whole black peppercorns
500g fresh strawberries, to serve

Bring all the ingredients except the strawberries to the boil in a saucepan. Once the mixture has reached boiling point, remove from the heat and leave to infuse for 30 minutes.

Pass the mixture through a sieve into a bowl and place the bowl in the freezer. Freeze for at least a few hours prior to use.

Rinse the strawberries only if necessary and then hull (see panel). When you are ready to serve, cut them into quarters and put them in a bowl or glass dish. Remove the granita from the freezer and, working quickly, scrape out the frozen mixture with a spoon to form elderflower 'snow' or granita. scrape as much as you need and serve immediately on top of the prepared strawberries, since the granita melts quickly.

Strawberries
with tarragon sugar and milk

600g fresh strawberries
60g sugar
½ handful of tarragon, leaves picked
400ml cold semi-skimmed milk

Rinse the strawberries as little as possible, and only if they are very dirty, then snip the hulls (calyxes) off (see panel).

Arrange the strawberries in soup plates. Use a stick blender to blend the sugar and tarragon leaves into a delicious green-flavoured sugar and then sprinkle it over the strawberries. Pour the cold milk over the berries and serve immediately.

Tip Sweet cicely also has subtle notes of liquorice like tarragon, so it makes a good substitute, and it grows wild in many places. Mint and lemon balm are also great alternatives to tarragon in this recipe.

Strawberries

Freshly picked strawberries are a delicacy – and they can be just as delicious when they reach the plate. After strawberries are picked, avoiding rinsing them if they look clean, but if they should need washing, always do so with the hull (calyx) on, as the berries easily absorb water and even more so after hulling. As a result, the strawberries will lose some of their flavour and won't keep fresh for long. Strawberries at room temperature taste far superior to cold strawberries, so if you store the berries in the refrigerator, remember to take them out a few hours before they are eaten or, even better, let them sit in the sun for a short time. Best of all is eating the berries directly from the plants while they are fresh and taste of the summer and sun.

I don't only encourage you to do this because of romantic notions of summer holidays, children with berry-stained smiles and endless strawberry fields – it is a fact that the strawberries' natural sugar content is highest at the time they are picked and the sweet strawberry flavour will diminish from that moment onwards.

Homemade soured milk
with strawberries and honey

SERVES 6

1-litre carton fresh organic full-fat milk
100ml fresh organic buttermilk

To serve
200g fresh strawberries
4 tablespoons runny honey, to serve

Day 1
Pour 100ml of the milk from the carton into a glass and drink it or use it for something else. Now replace the milk you have poured out with the buttermilk, close the carton and shake it well so that the milk and buttermilk blend together. Leave the mixture to sit for 18–24 hours in the kitchen so that it thickens and becomes sour. Don't shake the mixture while it is souring; it won't do the fermentation process any good. Once soured, store the milk in the refrigerator so that it is cold and fresh when serving.

Day 2
Rinse the strawberries only if necessary and then hull (see panel on page 114), and cut them into quarters. Pour the soured milk into 6 breakfast bowls or soup plates and eat it with the strawberries and a drizzle of honey. Serve as part of a brunch or as a light summer dessert.

Raspberry sorbet
with vanilla and black pepper

500g fresh raspberries
1 litre water
400g unrefined cane sugar
½ vanilla pod, split lengthways and seeds scraped out, pod reserved
10 whole black peppercorns
finely grated zest of 1 organic lemon and the juice of 2

1 organic egg white and 30g caster sugar (optional)

Put the raspberries in a pan with the 1 litre of water, sugar, vanilla seeds and pod and peppercorns. Bring to the boil and cook for 3–4 minutes. Remove the pan from the heat and season with the lemon zest and juice. Leave to infuse for 20 minutes.

Remove the peppercorns and vanilla pod and blend in a blender or with a stick blender. Strain the blended syrup through a coarse sieve, allowing a little of the raspberry flesh to pass through. Now follow the recipe for Rhubarb Sorbet on page 60 from step 3 to finish making the sorbet.

Enjoy the sorbet with fresh raspberries and maybe a little cold whipping cream.

Rødgrød (red berry compote)

500g fresh mixed berries, such as strawberries, currants, blueberries and blackberries
100g fresh raspberries or blackberries
100ml water
150g sugar, plus extra for sprinkling
½–1 tablespoon potato starch mixed with a little cold water

Rinse the berries in cold water (but see panel on page 114 if using strawberries) and then remove the stems and hulls. Put all the berries except the raspberries or blackberries in a pan with the 100ml water and sugar, stir well and leave to steep for a few hours so that they give off some of their juices.

Place the pan over a low heat and bring to the boil, skim off the foam and cook the berries for 2–3 minutes. Remove the pan from the heat and gently stir in the raspberries so that they remain as whole as possible.

Thicken the compote with the potato starch paste by adding it when the berries are just

below boiling point; it is important that the compote is still warm, but if it boils after the potato starch has been added, the texture will be gooey.

Sprinkle the compote with a thin layer of sugar to prevent a skin from forming and leave to cool in the refrigerator. Serve the berry compote with milk, cream or a scoop of good vanilla ice cream (see page 60)

Rødgrød with milk

Although many Danes today rarely eat *rødgrød*, we all agree that it is truly a national dish, perhaps most of all because it is what we torture foreigners with when we can't resist demonstrating their inability to pronounce our difficult language in the phrase *rødgrød med fløde* – red berry compote with cream. In fact, we have only cooked this type of fruit compote for the past hundred years or so, since it wasn't until the advent of domestic sugar beet production in the late 1800s that sugar became affordable enough for fruit compotes to be a common summer dish on Danish dinner tables. A perfectly cooked, smooth compote with a mix of mild and intensely flavoured berries served with ice-cold milk and crunchy sugar is royal dining indeed.

FOREST RASPBERRIES
If you find yourself in a humid forest glade, you may be lucky enough to find wild raspberries hiding under the leaves!

« Refrigerator preserved redcurrants

Refrigerator preserved redcurrants

500g fresh redcurrants
200g sugar

Rinse the redcurrants in cold water and remove them from their stems. Alternatively, opt for the rustic solution and leave the stems on – and it looks so beautiful too. Let the currants drain well in a colander, then layer them with the sugar in a dish. Be careful not to stir the currants too much, otherwise you risk them bursting. Leave the currants to chill in the refrigerator for an hour.

Serve the preserved currants with ice cream, a cake or just with lightly whipped cream or skyr that has been softened with a little milk.

Blackberry trifle

Custard
½ vanilla pod
2 organic egg yolks
3 tablespoons sugar
1 tablespoon cornflour
300ml semi-skimmed milk

To assemble
100g Almond Macaroons (*see* page 114)
50ml sherry
200g blackberries
100ml whipping cream, lightly whipped
finely grated zest of ½ organic orange

First make the custard. Split the vanilla pod lengthways, scrape the seeds out and crush them with a little of the sugar on the chopping board with the flat side of your knife. Add the vanilla seeds and pod and the remaining ingredients to a pan, stir well and bring to the boil while whisking vigorously. Boil the custard for 2–3 minutes or until it thickens and becomes smooth.

Pour the custard into a small bowl and place in the refrigerator to cool completely.

When the custard is cold, it is time to build your trifle. Crumble the macaroons lightly and place in the base of a serving bowl or individual serving glasses, reserving some for a final sprinkling, then drizzle with the sherry. Place the blackberries on top and then a little custard. Repeat until you have used up the blackberries and custard. Finish with a topping of lightly whipped cream, a sprinkling of crushed macaroons and grated orange zest. Leave the trifle to soften in the refrigerator for 30–60 minutes before serving.

• •

TIP Trifle is easy to vary according to the season – the combination of macaroons, fruit and custard is eternally good, whether it is hot or cold outside (I can always squeeze down a small trifle), and you can make it with all manner of fruits or berries, for example gooseberries (*see* page 113), plums, stewed apples and quinces, pickled cherries, rhubarb in the spring and so on. I alternate between using the cream in the form of a cooked vanilla custard, as here, or an uncooked vanilla cream, as in the aforementioned Gooseberry Trifle recipe.

• •

Blackberry parfait
with aquavit and homemade almond macaroons

SERVES 6–8

100g fresh blackberries
1 tablespoon aquavit
500ml whipping cream
5 pasteurized egg yolks
½ vanilla pod, split lengthways and
  seeds scraped out
75g sugar
3–5 grains of coarse salt
Almond Macaroons (*see* page 114),
  to serve

Make sure all the ingredients are cold – and the bowls as well. Put the blackberries

in a small bowl, drizzle with the aquavit and leave them to steep in the kitchen for 10 minutes.

Whisk the remaining ingredients together using a stand mixer or an electric hand mixer until softly whipped.

Mash the aquavit-soaked blackberries lightly with a fork and mix them into the parfait cream. Pour the cream into a loaf tin or into small ramekins and place in the freezer. Freeze the parfait for 2–3 hours before serving. You can leave it for 2–3 days in the freezer before it becomes too hard and forms large ice crystals. Remove the parfait from the freezer about 30 minutes before serving (a little less if you have used ramekins) and serve with the macaroons.

The addition of aquavit in the parfait affects both the taste and the texture – the parfait will be softer, as the alcohol prevents the mixture from freezing really hard. You can, however, also make the dessert without it.

• •

TIP This parfait doesn't require an ice-cream maker, just a bowl, a whisk and a freezer, and unlike other parfaits, you don't need to whisk the cream and egg yolks separately. It is simply an ultra-easy ice cream! I always add a little salt to my parfait mixes, as it accents the sweet and enhances the flavour of cream, eggs and vanilla. And I vary the recipe extensively – this parfait can be made with virtually any berry.

• •

Blackberries
with sugar-roasted rye bread and whipped cream

4 slices of day-old rye bread
2 tablespoons sugar
1 tablespoon melted butter
200ml whipping cream
400g fresh blackberries

Cut the bread into very small cubes. Spread the bread cubes out in an ovenproof dish, sprinkle with the sugar and drizzle with the melted butter. Bake the bread cubes in a preheated oven at 170°C/Gas Mark 3½ for 10–15 minutes until they are perfectly crispy, stirring a couple of times during baking.

Whip the cream to a light foam. Divide the blackberries between 4 individual bowls, top with the whipped cream and toasted rye bread cubes and enjoy as an effortless and lovely dessert.

We have blackberries in our garden, so we often eat them for breakfast with rye bread croutons and yogurt, but our children often ask for a scoop of whipped cream on top too!

Buttermilk dessert

3 pasteurized egg yolks
150g sugar
seeds from ½ vanilla pod
500ml buttermilk
500ml Homemade Soured Milk
  (see page 116)
finely grated zest and juice of 1 lemon
1 handful of lemon balm, chopped
Toasted Oat Flakes (see right)

Whisk the egg yolks and sugar together until pale and the sugar has dissolved.

Mix the vanilla seeds into the egg mixture, reserving the vanilla pod. Gently add the buttermilk, soured milk, vanilla pod and lemon zest and juice and stir well until thoroughly combined.

Place the buttermilk dessert in the refrigerator and leave to infuse for at least 2–3 hours before serving. When it is time for dessert, sprinkle the buttermilk with the chopped lemon balm and Toasted Oat Flakes, and serve immediately.

Toasted oat flakes

200g rolled oats
3 tablespoons honey
10g butter
10 sea salt flakes

Toast the oats lightly in a dry frying pan until golden and crisp. Add the honey, butter and salt to the pan and stir well with a wooden spoon until the oats are evenly caramelized, which usually takes just a few minutes.

Pour the oats on to a baking sheet lined with baking paper and leave them to cool. They are now ready to use.

Cream dessert
with elderflower jelly

SERVES 6

Cream dessert
3 gelatine sheets
500ml whipping cream
20g unrefined cane sugar
½ vanilla pod, spit lengthways and seeds scraped out, pod reserved
50ml elderflower concentrate or cordial

Elderflower jelly
1 gelatine sheet
100ml elderflower concentrate or cordial

For the cream dessert, soak the gelatine sheets in cold water for 5 minutes. Put the cream, sugar, vanilla seeds and pod and elderflower concentrate or cordial in a saucepan and bring to the boil. As soon as the mixture reaches boiling point, remove from the heat and add the well-drained gelatine. Leave the cream mixture to sit in the pan for 30 minutes. Pour it into a bowl

that has a spout, then pour into 6 serving glasses. Keep refrigerated for at least 6 hours before serving.

To make the elderflower jelly, soak the gelatine sheet in cold water for 5 minutes, drain it well and place in a small saucepan along with the elderflower concentrate or cordial. Heat the mixture up carefully so that the gelatine melts, then leave to cool until it begins to stiffen a little.

Spread the cooled but still liquid jelly on top of the cream dessert in the serving glasses and put them back in the refrigerator for a few hours until serving. You now have a small dessert that is sweet enough as it is but may be accompanied by a bowl of ripe strawberries. For extra flair, you can throw a few slices of strawberry or some fresh elderflowers into the jelly – my girls love it.

Tip This tastes wonderful too if you replace the elderflower jelly with pink rhubarb jelly, made in exactly the same way but instead using Rhubarb Cordial (see page 57).

Cream dessert

Gelatine-based dishes have been known for centuries and even by the late Middle Ages, more than 600 years ago, it was highly regarded to serve a clear jelly inlaid with various beautiful ingredients. Desserts using gelatine such as *risalamande*, (Danish rice pudding), mousses and cream desserts, such as the one above, grew in popularity in the second half of the 1800s. At their peak in the 20th century, every self-respecting kitchen had a ring mould in which to set cream desserts. In this recipe, I have cut down on the gelatine to achieve a more delicate consistency. You can substitute half of the cream with milk if you wish for a lighter dessert.

Autumn

Seasonal ingredients

Cultivated produce

apples
beetroot
blackberries
Brussels sprouts
cabbage
carrots
cauliflower
celeriac
chicory
cod
eel
elderberries
garfish
green beans
green tomatoes

haddock
hare
herring
horseradish
Jerusalem artichoke
kale
kohlrabi
leek
lingonberries
lobster
maize
nuts
onions
parsley
pears

plums
pumpkin
quince
salsify
sea trout
venison
weever
wild duck

In the wild

chanterelles
ceps
rowan berries
quince
apples
hazelnuts
chestnuts
cranberries
oyster mushrooms
woodcocks
horn of plenty

yellowfoot mushrooms
sea beet
sloes
sheathed woodtuft
blue stalk mushrooms

Soups and starters

Onion soup
with cheese toasts

5 large onions
2 garlic cloves
10g butter
8 thyme sprigs
sea salt flakes and freshly ground pepper
1.5 litres water or light chicken stock
2 tablespoons cider vinegar

Peel the onions and garlic cloves. Cut the onions in half and slice them finely.

Melt the butter in a large saucepan, add the onions, whole garlic cloves and thyme sprigs and sauté gently until the onions begin to caramelize and take on a little colour. Add salt and pepper to taste and sauté for a further 2–3 minutes. Add the water or stock and leave the soup to simmer over a low heat for 20 minutes.

Season the soup with the vinegar and possibly a little more salt and pepper, if necessary. Eat the soup piping hot, with warm Cheese Toasts (see below).

Cheese toasts

8 slices of day-old white bread
1 tablespoon standard rapeseed oil
100g hard cheese, such as Høost, or Grana Padano, freshly grated
sea salt flakes and freshly ground pepper

Brush the bread slices with the oil, place them on a grill rack and toast them under the grill for about 1 minute each side or until the bread is crisp and golden. Remove the bread slices from the grill, sprinkle the grated cheese over them and put them back under the grill for a further 30 seconds so that the cheese melts. Season the cheese toasts to taste with salt and pepper and serve immediately while they are warm and crisp.

Yellow split pea soup
with parsley and horseradish

250g dried yellow split peas
2 litres water
2 onions
2 garlic cloves
500g pork belly
8 sausages from Southern Jutland or any smoked pork sausage
½ handful of thyme sprigs
3 carrots
½ celeriac
5–7 large potatoes
3 leeks
300g baby onions
sea salt flakes and freshly ground pepper
2–3 tablespoons cider vinegar
½ handful of parsley
25g fresh horseradish root

Drain the split peas and put them in a pan with the measured water. Peel the onions and garlic, then cut them into fairly large chunks. Add them to the pan along with the pork belly, sausages and thyme sprigs and bring the soup to the boil. Skim off the foam and impurities, then simmer for about 45 minutes until the peas are tender.

Lift the pork belly and sausages out, then blend the split peas and onions, thyme and broth in the pan with a stick blender to a coarse purée (remove the thyme sprigs first if you like).

Peel the carrots, celeriac and potatoes, then cut the vegetables into 1cm cubes. Cut off the roots and tops of the leeks, then cut them into rings and wash them thoroughly in a bowl of cold water so that you get all the soil off. Peel the baby onions but keep them whole. Add all the vegetables to the pea soup along with the pork belly and sausages and simmer for a further 20 minutes until the vegetables are tender. Dilute the soup with a little extra water if it is too thick, and season to taste with salt, pepper and the vinegar.

Finally, rinse the parsley, leave to drain thoroughly, then roughly chop it. Peel and grate the horseradish, then mix it with the chopped parsley and stir into the soup. Serve the steaming hot yellow split pea soup in bowls with extra thyme leaves on top. Serve the pork belly and sausages as sides, and put some bread and mustard on the table as well. You may also want to consider beer and aquavit as accompaniments.

Tip Old-fashioned yellow split peas are perfect with pork, but you can just as readily make a vegetarian version of this soup – simply omit the pork belly and sausages and follow the recipe opposite.

Creamy kale soup

250g curly kale, stalks removed
sea salt flakes and freshly ground pepper
1 litre chicken stock
50ml whipping cream
2–3 tablespoons cider vinegar
2 apples

Check the kale for any bits of stalk and discard, then wash it thoroughly in cold water and leave to drain in a colander. Reserve about 50g of the kale, then blanch the rest in a pan of boiling salted water for 2–3 minutes. Drain and immediately plunge it into a bowl of cold water to stop the cooking process. Leave it to drain in a colander.

Heat the stock up in a saucepan. Chop the blanched kale roughly and put it in a blender, pour in the hot stock and blend until the soup is completely smooth. Season with the cream, salt, pepper and finally the vinegar. It is important that the vinegar is added just before serving, as otherwise the soup will lose its bright green colour.

Pour the soup back into the saucepan. Cut the apples into quarters, remove the cores and cut into small pieces. Cut the reserved raw kale into thin strips and add to the soup with the apple as a garnish. Heat the soup and serve with some good bread.

Potato soup

2 baking potatoes
800ml–1 litre water
1 shallot, peeled and finely chopped
½ garlic clove, peeled and finely chopped
250g fresh spinach, washed
1 tablespoon standard rapeseed oil
sea salt flakes and freshly ground pepper

Peel and slice the potatoes thinly. Put them in a saucepan and add the water, then cook for about 15–20 minutes until tender.

Lightly sauté the shallot and garlic in the oil in a separate saucepan without browning. Chop the spinach roughly, throw it into the pan and sauté for about 30 seconds. Pour the cooked potatoes with their cooking water into the pan and simmer the soup for a maximum of 2 minutes so that it keeps its freshness and green colour. Blend in a blender or with a stick blender until smooth, then pass it through a coarse sieve, if necessary, to make sure there are no lumps.

Season with salt and pepper to taste, then serve piping hot with a sprinkle of Crispy Croutons (see below). You can serve it as a starter, or as a main course with a nice salad, some cooked grains or cold meat.

Crispy croutons

2 slices of day-old white bread
2 tablespoons standard rapeseed oil
sea salt flakes

Cut the bread slices roughly into pieces and toss them in the oil and some salt.

Spread the bread pieces out on a baking sheet lined with baking paper and bake in a preheated oven at 170°C/Gas Mark 3½ for 5–6 minutes until crisp and golden.

• •

TIP Have some lovely pears for dessert, as they are in their prime right now. In my family we love to peel the pears at the table, and then drizzle them with a little lemon juice, which enhances their flavour.

• •

Creamy root vegetable soup
with crisp bacon and chopped parsley

700g mixed root vegetables, such as celeriac, carrots, parsley roots and parsnips
1 apple
2 garlic cloves, peeled
3 thyme sprigs
1 tablespoon standard rapeseed oil
2 litres water
50ml whipping cream
sea salt flakes and freshly ground pepper
2–3 tablespoons cider vinegar
30g streaky bacon
½ handful of parsley

Wash and peel the root vegetables, then cut them into large cubes. Core the apple, but leave the peel on and cut it into large cubes as well. Add the root vegetables, apple, whole garlic cloves and thyme sprigs to the hot rapeseed oil in a large saucepan, and sauté over a low heat for 5 minutes until the root vegetables begin to brown and caramelize. Add the measured water and leave the soup to simmer for 15 minutes, with the lid on, then add the cream and cook for a further 5 minutes.

Blend the mixture to a smooth and even consistency with a stick blender, and season to taste with salt, pepper and the cider vinegar. A note here on using vinegar: it is a basic seasoning component in line with salt, pepper and sugar, and if you haven't yet tried adjusting the taste of your food with vinegar, you will discover that the flavours unfold and come into balance. I would not dream of making a soup of heavy, sweet-tasting root vegetables without giving it a splash of acid – taste the soup before and after you add the vinegar, then you will know what I am talking about.

When the soup is cooked and seasoned to perfection, cut the bacon into small cubes and fry it in a pan until crisp.

Chop the parsley. Heat the soup up again and serve with the crisp bacon and chopped parsley on top with some good bread on the side. Toast is certainly not a bad idea!

Smoked salmon
with pearl barley, walnuts and apples

150g pearl barley (uncooked)
300ml water
sea salt flakes and freshly ground pepper
1 tablespoon standard rapeseed oil
finely grated zest and juice of ½ organic lemon
1 teaspoon acacia honey
2 celery sticks
30g fresh baby spinach
1 apple
10g walnuts
160g thinly sliced smoked salmon (or sea trout)

Rinse the pearl barley well in cold water. Put it in a saucepan, add the 300ml of water and a little salt and bring to the boil. Simmer with the lid on for about 20 minutes. Take the pan off the heat and leave the barley to stand, covered, for 5–10 minutes.

When the barley is done – it should be tender but still al dente – season to taste with salt and pepper.

Whisk the oil, lemon zest and juice, honey, salt and pepper together in a bowl to make a dressing and leave for 5–10 minutes to allow the flavours to develop.

Rinse the celery and spinach. Slice the celery very finely and mix with the spinach in a large bowl. Cut the apple into quarters, remove the core and slice it very finely. Add it to the bowl, along with the cooked pearl barley and the walnuts, coarsely chopped. Mix the dressing into the salad and serve it with thin slices of smoked salmon (or sea trout) and some good bread.

Marinated herring
with carrots and onions

2 red onions
3 carrots
100ml cold-pressed rapeseed oil
100ml cider vinegar
90g unrefined cane sugar
100ml water
4 bay leaves
1 tablespoon whole black peppercorns
1 tablespoon juniper berries
1 tablespoon coriander seeds
2 tablespoons prepared mustard
10 good-quality marinated herring fillets
1 large handful of dill

Peel the onions and carrots, then cut the onions into wedges and the carrots into slices. Place the vegetables in a saucepan along with the rest of the ingredients, except the herrings and dill, and cook until you have a syrupy consistency. Take the pan off the heat and leave to cool completely.

Put the herring fillets in a large, sterilized preserving jar, pour the cold syrup over them and finally add the dill. Seal the jar tightly, put it in the refrigerator and leave for at least 3 days before you eat the herring.

Serve the herring on rye bread, topped with raw onions and possibly some fresh dill. The marinated herring will keep fresh, unopened and refrigerated, for 2–3 months and about 20–25 days once opened.

ROWAN BERRIES
Remember to put a few bags of rowan berries in the freezer for the birds in winter.

Pan-roasted herrings
with beetroot and apple vinaigrette

10 double herring fillets
a little wasabi paste or 20–30g freshly grated horseradish
sea salt flakes and freshly ground pepper
50g rye flour
300ml cider vinegar
300ml water
270g unrefined cane sugar
2 beetroot
2 apples
1 tablespoon standard rapeseed oil
10g butter

Check that herring fillets are fresh and smell of the sea, not of the harbour. Spread a very thin layer of wasabi paste on the flesh side of the herring fillets (it is super strong, so be careful with the amount) or sprinkle the fillets with the freshly grated horseradish. Season with salt and pepper, fold the fillets together and dust the skin side with the rye flour.

Add the vinegar, 300ml of water and sugar to a saucepan and bring the mixture to the boil. Peel the beetroot and cut them into small cubes. Core the apples and cut them into thin wedges – the apple pieces should be bigger than the beetroot, since their cooking time is not the same. Add the apple and beetroot to the hot syrup and simmer for 2 minutes so that the syrup takes on both flavour and colour.

Heat up a frying pan and add the oil, and when that is hot, add the butter. When the butter has stopped bubbling, fry the herring fillets for about 3 minutes on each side until golden and crisp. It may be necessary to press down a little on the folded fillets with a fish slice just after you have put them in the pan so that they don't unfold.

Transfer the fried herrings to a dish and pour the hot syrup over them. Leave to soak in the refrigerator for a few days before you enjoy them – they will keep fresh for up to 1 week. Serve the pan-roasted herrings with the beetroot and apple vinaigrette on rye bread, preferably topped with capers and dill.

TIP Store the broth from the chicken, either in the refrigerator or in the freezer – it is always good to have at hand when making soup or risotto, or to use as a braising liquid.

Crudité of swede, pears and Savoy cabbage

½ swede
2 pears, such as Conference or Doyenne du Comice
¼ Savoy cabbage
3–4 tablespoons cider vinegar
2 tablespoons standard rapeseed oil
2 tablespoons acacia honey
sea salt flakes and freshly ground pepper
30g sunflower seeds

Peel the swede, grate it on the coarse side of the grater and place it in a bowl. Cut the pears into quarters and remove the cores, then cut them lengthways into very thin wedges and add them to the bowl. Pick off the leaves of the Savoy cabbage and wash them in cold water. Drain thoroughly and slice the leaves very finely, then add them to the bowl with the swede and pears.

Mix the vinegar, oil, honey, salt and pepper together in a separate bowl to make a dressing, then pour over the swede, cabbage and pears.

Toast the sunflower seeds in a dry pan until they are golden and begin to pop. Season the crudité with additional salt and pepper, if needed, and sprinkle the toasted sunflower seeds on top. Serve as a small everyday starter.

Rillette of pheasant

with mustard and pickled squash with dill

SERVES 8

2 cleaned pheasants
1 tablespoon rapeseed oil
2 carrots
2 onions
sea salt flakes and freshly ground pepper
2 garlic cloves
5 thyme sprigs
330ml bottle dark beer
100ml cider vinegar, plus extra to season
700ml water or chicken stock

Check the pheasants for any feather stumps and pluck them out. Pat the cavities dry with kitchen paper. Follow the instructions in the tip on page 146 to joint the birds, saving the breasts for that recipe and the carcass for making stock.

Brown the pheasant legs and any leftovers from the breast in the oil in a large, hot stewing pan. Peel the carrots and onions, cut into large chunks and throw them into the pan as well. Season with salt and pepper and leave the vegetables to brown with the pheasant for a few minutes.

Peel the garlic cloves, add to the pan whole with the thyme sprigs, beer, vinegar and stock and bring to the boil. Then simmer over a low heat, with the lid on, for 45 minutes–1 hour until the meat is very tender.

Lift the pheasant legs out of the pan and place on a chopping board. Leave the rest of the stew to reduce until a third of the broth remains.

Meanwhile, carve the meat off the legs, discarding the skin and bones. Make sure you remove the big tendons in the thighs as well and also check that there is no shot left in the meat. Add the meat to the stew again and mash around lightly with a whisk – that way, the broth, meat and vegetables integrate much better with each other to form a delicate and rustic rillette. You should probably fish the thyme sprigs out first, especially if they are coarse and hard to chew. Season with salt, pepper and a little extra vinegar, then pour the rillette into sterilized preserving jars where it will keep for 30–40 days if stored in the refrigerator.

Serve the pheasant rillette with toast and Pickled Squash with Dill (see below) as a small starter or lunch dish. If you want to make this a slightly larger dish, add a small green salad with walnuts, parsley and some good apple balsamic vinegar.

Pickled squash with dill

MAKES 2 JARS

1 winter squash, such as Hokkaido or butternut
2 tablespoons coarse sea salt

Pickling brine
500ml cider vinegar
500ml water
400g unrefined cane sugar
1 cinnamon stick
4 star anise
15 whole black peppercorns
3 dill stems

Day 1
Peel and halve the squash, then scrape out the seeds with a spoon. Cut the squash into about 1cm-thick slices, place them in a dish and sprinkle them with the coarse salt. Leave in the refrigerator for 12 hours.

Day 2
Rinse the squash slices in cold water and divide them between 2 sterilized preserving jars. Put the ingredients for the pickling brine in a saucepan and bring to the boil. Then pour the boiling mixture over the squash slices and seal the jars tightly. Place the jars in the refrigerator or in a cool cellar or other cool place and leave for about a week before eating. The pickled squash will keep fresh, refrigerated, for 6 months, and meanwhile you can enjoy it with virtually anything that simply lacks a little acidity.

Tip This pickling recipe also works really well with root vegetables like celeriac, parsley roots and parsnips, which you can prepare in exactly the same way as the squash. If using beetroot, they will need to be cooked first.

APPLES
Save a surplus of windfalls as birds' winter feed.

Marinated venison fillet
with kale purée and salad with refrigerator-pickled lingonberries

SERVES 8–10

3 whole venison fillets (filet mignon
    or tenderloin), about 300g each
    (or use lamb fillets)
125g sea salt flakes
125g unrefined brown sugar
10g coriander seeds
10g juniper berries
10 whole black peppercorns
10g fennel seeds
7–8 allspice berries
1 star anise

Trim off any tendons from the fillets and put the meat in a deep dish. Mix the salt, brown sugar and spices together, then cover the meat completely in the mixture. Cover the dish with clingfilm and leave in the refrigerator, at a temperature of about 5°C, for 2–3 days. Turn the meat every day so that it is marinated evenly – it is important that the meat is covered in liquid throughout the process.

Remove the meat from the refrigerator when it feels firm but is still red inside. Strain off the liquid and discard it, reserving the spices. Crush them roughly using a pestle and mortar. Wipe the meat lightly with kitchen paper and cover it again with the spices. Put it in a clean dish and place in the refrigerator for a further 24 hours but this time without the clingfilm so that the surface of the meat dries out a little.

Slice the meat very thinly with a very sharp knife and serve it with Kale Purée and Salad with Refrigerator-pickled Lingonberries (see right). Put some wholegrain bread on the table as well. Enjoy as a starter or lunch dish.

Tip The meat will keep fresh for 10–12 days in the refrigerator if it is tightly wrapped in clingfilm or in a container with a lid, so it does pay to marinate a few fillets in one go. If you don't have the opportunity to eat it all in that time, you can also store it in the freezer.

Kale purée and salad with refrigerator-pickled lingonberries

2 tablespoons fresh or frozen
    lingonberries (*see* tip below)
1 tablespoon unrefined cane sugar
100g curly kale, stalks removed
sea salt flakes and freshly ground pepper
finely grated zest and juice of
    ½ organic lemon
1 tablespoon olive oil

Sprinkle the lingonberries with the sugar in a bowl and leave them to marinate for 10 minutes. Meanwhile, check the kale for bits of stalk and discard, then wash it thoroughly in cold water and leave in a colander to drain.

Throw two-thirds of the kale into a pan of salted boiling water and cook for about 5 minutes until tender but still retaining its green colour. Lift the kale out into a blender with just the cooking water that is clinging to it, add salt, pepper and the lemon zest and blend to a smooth purée. Transfer the purée to a bowl.

Chop the remaining raw kale very finely, dress it with the olive oil and lemon juice and leave to marinate for 2 minutes. Season with salt and pepper. Serve with the kale purée and lingonberries to accompany the marinated venison fillet.

Tip If you can't get hold of fresh or frozen lingonberries, replace them with some good-quality and not-too-sweet lingonberry jam.

AUTUMN GAME
Autumn is game season and the hunt is now on.

Meat

Meatloaf
with lingonberries and homemade 'sauerkraut'

2 slices of day-old white bread
150ml semi-skimmed milk
100g mixed root vegetables, such as carrots, celeriac and parsley roots
1 small onion
250g minced veal, 5–7% fat
250g minced pork, 5–7% fat
sea salt flakes and freshly ground pepper
1 organic egg, lightly beaten
3 thyme sprigs, chopped
100g streaky bacon

Sauce
15g butter
1 tablespoon plain flour
600ml semi-skimmed milk
2 bay leaves
sea salt flakes and freshly ground pepper
50ml whipping cream
2 tablespoons fresh or frozen lingonberries (see tip on page 134)
5–10g blue cheese

Cut the bread slices into small cubes and leave them to soak in the milk for 10–15 minutes. Meanwhile, wash and peel the root vegetables, then grate them finely. Peel and dice the onion as finely as you can.

Put the minced meat in a bowl and add the root vegetables, onion, salt, pepper, egg, thyme and finally the soaked bread and mix well. Cut 50g of the bacon into small cubes and incorporate it into the mixture. Leave the mixture to stand in the refrigerator while you make the sauce.

Melt the butter in a saucepan and add the flour, stirring, to make a smooth roux. Turn the heat down and add the milk, a little at a time, while stirring so that the sauce cooks evenly, then add the bay leaves, salt and pepper. Simmer the sauce for 5–6 minutes.

Form the meat mixture into a loaf, place in an ovenproof dish and place the rest of the bacon rashers on top. Pour the sauce into the dish with the meatloaf and bake in a preheated oven at 170°C/Gas Mark 3½ for 50 minutes–1 hour. Check whether the meatloaf is done by inserting a metal skewer into it – if the skewer is hot when you pull it out again and the liquid that trickles out is clear, that means it is ready.

Take the meatloaf out of the oven and pour the sauce into a saucepan. Heat the sauce up, add the cream and season with the lingonberries, salt, pepper and the blue cheese. Slice the meatloaf up and serve with the sauce, potatoes and fresh Homemade 'Sauerkraut' (see right).

A history of meatloaf

When Denmark was a major producer of bacon for the UK market around 1900, Danish housewives were duty bound to use more pork when cooking, with the industry lobbying for using half minced pork to the traditional veal and beef in the minced meat dishes that had already become fashionable in the first decades of the 20th century. This trend was aided by the meat mincer, with which most kitchens in Denmark had been equipped during this period. The combination of pork and veal or beef appeared not least in the many substitutes for a roast that were created at the time. One of them was the meatloaf, first mentioned in the last edition of A. M. Mangor's cookbook from 1910 under the name 'Chinese hare', but later renamed as 'meatloaf' by Miss Jensen, who also supplemented the dish with brown gravy, browned potatoes and currant or lingonberry jelly. I have made a lighter version by adding root vegetables and also some crunchy cabbage, as the loaf itself doesn't have a lot of bite to it.

Homemade 'sauerkraut'

1 small white cabbage
10 caraway seeds
10 dill seeds
8 juniper berries
200ml dry cider
200ml cider vinegar
1 tablespoon sea salt flakes
2 tablespoons honey, plus extra to season
freshly ground pepper
4 shallots

Cut the white cabbage into quarters, shred it very finely using a knife and put it in a large bowl.

Crush the spices using a pestle and mortar and add them to a saucepan along with the cider, vinegar, salt and honey. Bring to the boil and then pour over the cabbage. Mix well so that all the cabbage is marinated and season with pepper.

Peel the shallots, slice them very finely and add them to the bowl as well, tossing everything around thoroughly. Now season with more honey, salt and pepper to taste. Leave the cabbage to marinate for 1 hour at room temperature before serving.

The cabbage will keep fresh for 10–12 days in the refrigerator, and the flavour is actually enhanced after a few days.

TIP If you don't have any cider, use some good apple juice instead. I often make this same fresh sauerkraut with red cabbage instead, using a cherry or plum vinegar and a little cherry juice instead of cider vinegar and cider.

Braised beef ribs
with potato and squash purée

2kg forerib of beef
sea salt flakes and freshly ground pepper
3 garlic cloves
2 onions
2 carrots
3 large parsley stems
2 thyme sprigs
5 bay leaves
3 rosemary sprigs
400ml strong red wine
200ml water
2 tablespoons cider vinegar
a little sugar
10–15g cold butter

Score the ribs by making small cuts through the meat and fat and season with salt and pepper. In an ovenproof dish, make a bed using the whole garlic cloves, onions and carrots, peeled and cut into chunks, parsley stems, thyme sprigs, bay leaves and rosemary sprigs. Place the forerib on top and pour the red wine and the measured water into the dish. Roast the forerib in a preheated oven at 170°C/Gas Mark 3½ for 1½ hours, regularly basting the meat with the sauce. Add a little extra water, if necessary, to prevent too much of the sauce from evaporating.

Take the dish out of the oven and strain the sauce into a saucepan. Skim off the fat and adjust the flavour with the vinegar, salt, pepper and sugar. Pour the sauce into a blender, add the parsley stems and rosemary sprigs (discarding the thyme and bay leaves) and blend it with the cold butter into a smooth, creamy sauce. Remove the bones from the meat (they should come away easily), then cut the meat into thick slices and pour the sauce over it. Serve immediately with the Potato and Squash Purée (see right) and some wholegrain bread.

Potato and squash purée

1kg baking potatoes
400g winter squash, such Hokkaido
    or butternut
200ml semi-skimmed milk
50g butter
sea salt and freshly ground pepper

Peel the potatoes and squash. Halve the squash and scrape out the seeds with a spoon. Cut the potatoes and squash into 3–4cm chunks and place them in a saucepan with enough water to cover them. Bring to the boil and cook for 25–30 minutes until they are tender. Drain and leave to sit in the pan for 2–3 minutes to cool slightly.

Heat up the milk in a small saucepan. Cut the butter into small cubes. Mash the vegetables with a potato masher or whisk, add the hot milk and butter and beat until completely smooth and soft. Then season with salt and pepper. The purée is now ready to be served.

HAZELNUTS
If you are lucky enough to find crisp, fresh hazelnuts, they are a real delicacy at this time of year.

Roasted veal rump
with potato and root vegetable rösti and beetroot sauce

SERVES 4–6

1kg veal rump
sea salt flakes and freshly ground pepper
5 thyme sprigs, leaves picked
2 garlic cloves, peeled

Trim the rump, removing the tendons and some of the fat. Score a criss-cross pattern into the fat side and sprinkle with salt, pepper the thyme leaves and whole garlic cloves.

Put the rump in an ovenproof dish and roast it in a preheated oven at 250°C/Gas Mark 10 (or your highest Gas Mark setting) to brown for 5 minutes. Then lower the temperature to 170°C/Gas Mark 3½ and roast the rump for a further 20–25 minutes. If you have a meat thermometer, you can check the core temperature of the meat, which should be about 58–60°C when you remove it from the oven. At that temperature it will be beautifully pink and juicy inside.

Leave the roast to rest for 7–8 minutes before you cut it into thin slices and serve with Potato and Root Vegetable Rösti (*see* below) and Beetroot Sauce (*see* right).

Tip Save 200g of the veal rump for the Beetroot Tartare with Horseradish and Cold Veal Rump (*see* page 199).

Potato and root vegetable rösti

400g baking potatoes
500g mixed root vegetables, such as celeriac, parsley roots and carrots
sea salt flakes and freshly ground pepper
3 thyme sprigs, chopped
1 garlic clove, chopped
100ml olive oil

Wash and peel the potatoes and other root vegetables, then grate them on the coarse side of the grater and squeeze out as much moisture as possible. Put the grated vegetables in a bowl and season with salt, pepper and the chopped thyme and garlic.

Heat up a medium-sized frying pan with the olive oil (if you have a nonstick pan, this is the time to use it). Add the grated vegetables to the pan and press to form a firm pancake. Fry the rösti over a medium heat for about 10 minutes on each side until it becomes golden and crisp. If you find it too hard to control the cooking process on the hob, you can finish the rösti in the oven – transfer it to a baking sheet (if your pan isn't ovenproof) and bake in a preheated oven at 180°C/Gas Mark 4 for 10–15 minutes. Slide the finished rösti on to a plate and cut it into wedges, like a cake, before serving.

Beetroot sauce

2 large shallots
2 garlic cloves
a little standard rapeseed oil
5–6 thyme sprigs
2 bay leaves
500ml beetroot juice (*see* tip)
200ml cherry vinegar or other fruit vinegar, plus extra if needed
500ml chicken or beef stock
50g cold unsalted butter, cut into cubes, plus extra if needed
sea salt flakes and freshly ground pepper

Peel the shallots and garlic, then roughly chop them. Sauté them in a hot pan lightly greased with oil for a few minutes, taking care not to burn them. Add the thyme sprigs and bay leaves and then the beetroot juice and vinegar, and cook the mixture until reduced to a third of its original volume.

Add the stock and leave the sauce to boil until it has a dense, shiny texture and the taste is intense, maybe still with a slight rawness to it.

Strain the reduced sauce through a fine sieve into a small saucepan. Add the cubes of cold butter while whisking vigorously. Season to taste with salt and pepper and add a little more butter if needed and perhaps a little vinegar.

Tip Beetroot juice can be purchased at a health food store – or make it yourself by putting 600–700g beetroot through a juicer.

Braised pork knuckle
with spicy sugar-browned cabbage

2 onions
3 carrots
20g butter
1 teaspoon sea salt flakes
1 teaspoon whole black peppercorns
1 teaspoon cumin seeds
1 teaspoon juniper berries
3 rosemary sprigs
1 garlic clove, peeled
50ml plum vinegar or other fruit vinegar
1 tablespoon brown sugar
1 tablespoon tomato purée
50ml standard rapeseed oil
500ml chicken stock
330ml bottle dark beer
2 pork knuckles (hocks or shanks), about 1.5–2kg in total

Peel the onions and carrots, then cut them into chunks. Sauté them in the butter in a pan until they just start to soften, then transfer them to a large ovenproof dish or roasting tin. Add the rest of the ingredients, except the pork, to a food processor and blend into a smooth braising liquid.

Rub the pork knuckles with the braising liquid, sit them on top of the vegetables and pour the excess liquid over the meat. Cover the dish or tin with foil so that the knuckles are well covered and place in a preheated oven at 150°C/Gas Mark 2 to braise for 3–3½ hours until they are very, very tender. Remove the foil when 30 minutes of cooking time remain, scoop the braising liquid from the base of the dish or tin and pour it over the pork about every 5 minutes to create a beautiful caramelized crust.

Serve the knuckles and braised vegetables with Spicy Sugar-browned Cabbage (see below). Make sure you put a jar of good-quality strong mustard on the table as well as some rye bread. Add some nice cold beer, and everyone should be more than satisfied.

Spicy sugar-browned cabbage

100g sugar
1 white cabbage
2 tablespoons sea salt flakes
freshly ground pepper
2 bay leaves
2 crushed allspice berries
2 thyme sprigs
100ml dark beer
300ml chicken stock
a little cider vinegar

Melt the sugar to a lightly golden caramel in a saucepan. Shred the cabbage finely and add it to the pan along with the salt, pepper, spices and thyme, then sauté for 5 minutes.

Add the beer and chicken stock and simmer, with the lid on, over a low heat for about 45 minutes–1 hour until the cabbage is very soft and all the liquid has evaporated. Season to taste with salt, pepper and a few drops of cider vinegar until your cabbage has just the right flavour.

Burning love

1kg baking potatoes
400g smoked bacon in one piece
6 onions
sea salt flakes and freshly ground pepper
200ml full-fat milk
100g butter

Peel and halve the potatoes, then put them in a pan with water to just cover them. Bring to the boil and cook for 25–30 minutes until tender. Meanwhile, prepare the

bacon. Cut the whole piece of bacon into 1cm cubes and put them in a sizzling-hot sauteuse so that they begin to fry immediately they hit the pan. Fry over a medium heat until golden and crisp.

Peel and halve the onions, then slice them very finely. Lift the fried bacon out of the pan with a slotted spoon so that the rendered fat remains in the sauteuse and place in a bowl on the side. Add the sliced onions to the sauteuse and fry over a low heat until they are golden and tender – be careful not to burn them. Return the cubes of smoked bacon to the pan and let it all heat up and mingle, then season with salt and pepper.

Drain the potatoes when they are tender and leave for 2–3 minutes in the pan to cool slightly. Meanwhile, heat the milk up in a small saucepan and cut the butter into small cubes. Mash the potatoes (see tip) and add the hot milk and butter cubes until the mash is heavenly smooth and soft. Season with salt and pepper.

Prepare portions of the mashed potatoes with a good scoop of onion and fried bacon on top, and serve the Burning Love sizzling hot, possibly with a palliative spoonful of plum chutney or lingonberry jam.

Tip When making mashed potatoes, it is important not to mash it for too long. If you use an electric mixer or whisk, you risk ending up with a wallpaper glue-like consistency, which happens as a result of overworking the naturally occurring starch in the potatoes. The best way is actually to fold the butter and milk into the mashed potatoes with a spoon or spatula.

The story of burning love

This beautiful name appeared for the first time in the early 1900s, referring to a dish made from leftovers: mashed potatoes with roasted, possibly salted and smoked pork belly and roasted onions. But a similar dish, a kind of thick potato soup served with fried pork belly, had previously been served in Southern Jutland in the 1800s, and on the island of Lolland it was common to have 'picked pork' – the delicious meat left on the bones when the pork belly had been cut off. Even before the potato secured a foothold in the Danish South Sea Islands, this meat was fried, served with roasted onions and perhaps supplemented with 'extenuating circumstances', which was *stikkelsbær* or rhubarb compote. So the story of burning love is actually an old tale.

Apart from bacon, any kind of rich pork leftovers can be used in your burning love. Some leftover roast pork or the last bits of meat carved from the bones of a roast fried in some fat with onions – that is true love!

Pork tenderloin medallions
with caramelized onions

6 onions
20g cold butter
2 thyme sprigs, leaves picked
sea salt flakes and freshly ground pepper
2 tablespoons cider vinegar
1 trimmed pork tenderloin, about 600g

Peel the onions, cut them in half and slice them finely. Add the onions to a sauté pan along with 10g of the cold butter, the thyme leaves, salt and pepper and sauté over a medium heat for 15–20 minutes until they start to soften. Season to taste with salt, pepper and the vinegar once the onions begin to caramelize, then sauté for a further few minutes until they have lightly browned.

Cut the tenderloin into 8 small medallions and press them slightly so that they flatten out a bit.

Throw the rest of the butter into a very hot frying pan and let it bubble away. Fry the medallions for 2–3 minutes on each side until they have a gorgeously golden surface, then season with salt and pepper. Put them in an ovenproof dish, cover with the onions and cook in a preheated oven at 170°C/Gas Mark 3½ for 6–7 minutes. Serve the tenderloin medallions with Pickled Squash with Dill (see page 132) and boiled potatoes.

> ### The making of a Danish classic
>
> Historically, tenderloin was one of the cuts from the pig that wasn't suitable for salting and therefore ended up as sausage meat with the knuckle, among others. However, when fresh meat was more readily available in the latter half of the 1800s, dishes featuring fresh tenderloin started appearing. For many years, this pork muscle was used only as a substitute for other more expensive meats, for example, by stuffing it with lard and served with a cream sauce in the same way as game meat, stuffed with apples and prunes to mimic roast goose. Pork tenderloin can also be stuffed with parsley and served in a cream sauce, as a pork version of roast chicken. In this recipe, pork is a substitute for beef, which is traditionally served as medallions with caramelized onions. This pork dish is now a Danish classic that appears among the hot dishes on a smorgasbord. The vinegar added to the onions takes them to a whole new level.

Braised pork knuckle
with cabbage and apples

8 pork knuckles (hocks or shanks), about 200g per person (see tip)
2 tablespoons standard rapeseed oil
sea salt flakes and freshly ground pepper
8 shallots
3 apples
½ Savoy cabbage
5 thyme sprigs
3 garlic cloves, peeled
½ x 330ml bottle of lager or wheat beer
50ml cider vinegar, plus extra to season
500ml water, poultry or light veal stock
a little sugar
½ handful of parsley

Cook the pork knuckles in the oil in a large ovenproof sauté pan or flameproof casserole dish until well browned on all sides. Season with salt and pepper. Meanwhile, peel and halve the shallots, cut the apples into quarters and remove the cores and cut the cabbage into large chunks.

When the knuckles are browned, add the thyme sprigs, whole garlic cloves, shallots, apple and cabbage to the pan and sauté for another minute. Add the beer, vinegar and measured water or stock, bring to the boil and skim off any foam and impurities. Cover the pan with a lid, place it in a preheated oven at 150°C/Gas Mark 2 and braise for about 1½–2 hours. Stir the knuckles around a few times during the braising so that they are beautifully glazed on all sides.

Remove the pan from the oven and season the sauce with salt, pepper, a splash of vinegar and a little sugar. You don't need to reduce the sauce any further, as it should be fine the way it is – not too thick but intense in flavour. Serve the knuckles with the parsley on top. They are lovely with mashed potatoes, or you can serve them with the Jerusalem Artichoke and Apple Purée (see page 142).

Tip The knuckle (also called the hock or shank) is part of the pig's leg, and is cheap and absolutely delightful to stew for hours until the meat is so tender that it falls off the bone. Remember to pre-order the knuckles at the butcher's, as it may not be something they keep in stock.

Karbonader (Veal and pork patties)

2 slices of day-old white bread, crusts removed
50ml semi-skimmed milk
500g mixed minced veal and pork, 5–7% fat
sea salt flakes and freshly ground pepper
50g boiled potato, mashed
1 organic egg, beaten
75g fresh breadcrumbs
1 tablespoon standard rapeseed oil
10g butter

Soak the bread in the milk for 10 minutes. Mix the minced meat with salt, pepper, the mashed potato and soaked bread in a bowl. Knead the mixture thoroughly and then form into 4 equally sized patties.

Press the patties out to a thickness of approximately 2cm. Dip them in the beaten egg and then in the breadcrumbs. Heat up a frying pan and add the fat – first the oil, and when that is hot, then the butter. When the butter has finished bubbling, add the patties and fry over a medium heat for 3–4 minutes on each side until they become golden and crisp on the outside and cooked through but still juicy on the inside.

Serve the patties with Glazed Carrots and Shallots (see below) and boiled potatoes, if you like, or just a fresh salad, maybe of grated raw carrots, apples and oranges.

Glazed carrots and shallots

300g carrots
200g shallots
10g butter
50ml water
1 rosemary sprig
sea salt flakes and freshly ground pepper
100ml cider vinegar, plus extra to taste
1 tablespoon honey, plus extra to taste

Peel the carrots and shallots, then cut the carrots into chunks and the shallots in half lengthways. Put the carrots and shallots in a pan with the butter, measured water and rosemary, and season with salt and pepper. Leave the vegetables to steam, with the lid on, for 3–4 minutes, then remove the lid and add the vinegar and honey. Cook for a further 5–6 minutes until the liquid is absorbed by the onions and carrots, which should start to look quite glossy and beautifully glazed.

Season the vegetables with salt, pepper, honey and vinegar to achieve just the right balance of flavour. Serve with the patties, or with any dish that could use a sweet and sour garnish. Other dishes it goes well with are Pan-fried Garfish (see page 36) or braised meat or game dishes.

Braised shoulder of venison
with Jerusalem artichoke and apple purée

1 shoulder of venison, about 1.5kg
100ml cider vinegar
½ handful of thyme
sea salt flakes and freshly ground pepper
5 onions
3 red onions
5 shallots
2 garlic bulbs
2 cooking apples
300ml ale or other dark beer
500ml apple juice
½ handful of parsley, chopped

Score the shoulder a few times so that it absorbs the seasoning better, and rub it with some of the vinegar and thyme and salt and pepper.

Peel the onions and shallots, then cut them into chunks. Peel all the garlic cloves but leave them whole. Put the onions, shallots and garlic in a roasting tin. Core the apples, cut into wedges and add to the roasting tin, then toss all the ingredients in the beer, the rest of the vinegar, the apple juice, the remaining thyme, salt and pepper. Place the shoulder on top of the vegetables, cover with foil and braise in a preheated oven at 160°C/Gas Mark 3 for 2½–3 hours until it is so tender that it is almost falling off the bone. Remember to glaze the meat by scooping some of the liquid in the roasting tin up and basting the shoulder with the delicious broth a few times during the cooking process.

When it is cooked, leave the meat to rest for 10 minutes before you carve into it (in fact, the meat should be so tender that you can just lift it from the bone!). Serve the braised shoulder of venison with the baked onions in the glorious braising liquid, together with the Jerusalem Artichoke and Apple Purée (see below). Finish off by sprinkling the freshly chopped parsley on top.

Jerusalem artichoke and apple purée

1kg Jerusalem artichokes
1 apple, such as Belle de Boskoop or Cox
20g skinned hazelnuts (see method on page 171)
20g butter
1–2 tablespoons cider vinegar
sea salt flakes and freshly ground pepper

Wash and scrub the Jerusalem artichokes thoroughly with a sponge so that all the dirt is removed, then cut them into large cubes. Cut the apple into quarters, remove the core and cut it into large cubes. Add both the artichokes and apple to a saucepan of boiling water and cook for about 15 minutes until tender. Drain and leave the apples and artichokes to sit in the pan until slightly cooled.

Transfer the artichokes and apple to a food processor, add the hazelnuts, butter and 1 tablespoon of the vinegar and blend to a coarse purée. Season the purée with salt, pepper and a little extra vinegar to taste, and serve immediately.

Roast chicken and carrot purée
with dill seeds and vinegar

SERVES 4–6

1 large organic chicken, about 1.5kg
5 thyme sprigs
5 rosemary sprigs
2 tablespoons cold-pressed rapeseed oil
2 tablespoons cider vinegar
sea salt flakes and freshly ground pepper
1 handful of parsley, chopped

Check the chicken for any feather stumps and pluck them out. Remove any blood or intestine residues from the cavity and wipe with kitchen paper. Stuff the chicken with the whole thyme and rosemary sprigs. Rub the skin with the oil, vinegar, salt and pepper.

Place the chicken in an ovenproof dish and roast in a preheated oven at 180°C/Gas Mark 4 for 50 minutes. Then turn the oven off but leave the chicken in the oven for 10–15 minutes.

Take the chicken out and cut it into 8 pieces – breasts, wings, thighs and drumsticks. Serve with the Carrot Purée with Dill Seeds and Vinegar (see below) and the chopped parsley, together with some good bread and cooked grains or roast potatoes.

Carrot purée with dill seeds and vinegar

7–8 large carrots
10 dill seeds
4 tablespoons standard rapeseed oil
3–4 tablespoons cider vinegar
1 tablespoon acacia honey, plus extra if needed
sea salt flakes and freshly ground pepper

Peel the carrots, cut them into smaller pieces and cook in a pan of water with the dill seeds for about 20 minutes until tender.

Drain the carrots and place with the dill seeds in a food processor or blender. Add the oil, vinegar, honey, salt and pepper and blend to a smooth purée. As the sweetness of carrots varies with the season, it is important to taste the purée when it is finished – but that is the case for pretty much all the food you make! There is a good chance that the purée could do with a bit more vinegar or honey before there is perfect harmony between acidity and sweetness. Serve the purée while it is warm.

· ·

Tip Any leftovers can be used as a spread in a sandwich or similar. Should you also happen to have some leftover cold chicken, you can make yourself quite a luxurious sandwich. Add some crunchy walnuts or crispy bacon on top and a sprinkle of chopped parsley to finish the snack off.

· ·

Griddled pheasant breast
with squash, mushrooms and mushroom velouté

4 pheasant breasts (see tip)
1 tablespoon standard rapeseed oil
sea salt flakes and freshly ground pepper
100g mixed wild mushrooms, such as penny bun, chanterelle, boletus, horn of plenty and funnel chanterelle
1 Hokkaido squash
10g butter
1 rosemary sprig, chopped
finely grated zest and juice of ½ organic lemon

Marinate the pheasant breasts in the oil, salt and pepper for 10 minutes.

Clean the mushrooms with a brush or a small vegetable knife. If they are very dirty, you can wash them gently. Cut them into smaller pieces. Peel and halve the squash, then scrape out the seeds with a spoon.

Cut the squash into 2cm cubes. Sauté the mushrooms and squash in the butter in a hot sauté pan for a few minutes – the mushrooms should shrink quite a bit and the squash cubes should become tender. Add the chopped rosemary and lemon zest and juice and season to taste with salt and pepper.

Cook the pheasant breasts on a very hot griddle pan for 3–4 minutes on each side. Remove the breasts from the pan and leave them to rest for 3–4 minutes. Slice them and serve with the squash and mushrooms, along with the Mushroom Velouté (see right) and, if you desire, some boiled or fried potatoes or boiled wheat grains.

· ·

Tip Buy two whole pheasants and joint them yourself so that you have the breasts to griddle in this recipe, the legs for the Rillette of Pheasant (see page 132) and a pair of carcasses to make stock. To joint the pheasants, first, cut the legs off by cutting between the thigh and the body all the way down to the thigh joint. Break the leg off at the joint and then finally cut through the skin so that the thigh is completely released from the body. Carve off the pheasant breasts by cutting down either side of the breastbone and loosening the fillets from the body, then divide the carcass into smaller pieces with a big, heavy knife.

· ·

Mushroom velouté

**400g mixed wild mushrooms, such as
   penny bun, chanterelle, boletus, horn
   of plenty and funnel chanterelle**
25g butter
40g plain flour
600–700ml chicken stock
sea salt flakes and freshly ground pepper
2 tablespoons cider vinegar

Clean the mushrooms with a brush or a
small vegetable knife. If they are very dirty,
you can wash them gently. Cut them into
smaller pieces if you want to. Sauté the
mushrooms in half the butter in a sauté pan
until lightly golden. Pour the mushrooms
and any juice they may have given off into
a bowl (the juice is perfect flavouring for
the sauce later).

Melt the remaining butter in a pan over a
low heat, add the flour and cook, stirring,
until the mixture turns golden brown and
smooth. Stir the chicken stock into the
roux little by little, then bring the sauce to
the boil and simmer for about 15 minutes,
giving it the occasional stir to make sure it
is completely smooth and all the flour taste
has cooked away.

Add the mushrooms and their juice and
let the sauce simmer for another couple
of minutes. Season with salt, pepper and
the vinegar before serving your velvety
mushroom velouté.

Tip Velouté is one of French cuisine's
'mother sauces'; it forms the base of other
sauces and thus can be flavoured with
virtually anything. The options include
herbs, mushrooms, mustard or a nice
bouillon that goes with the dish you want
to serve the sauce with. Velouté means
'velvety' or 'mellow', and that is just what
this dish is.

Game stew
with white barley
risotto

**600g boneless shoulder of venison with
   fat removed**
1 tablespoon olive oil
2 onions
4 carrots
5 thyme sprigs
1 garlic clove, peeled
4 juniper berries, lightly crushed
sea salt flakes and freshly ground pepper
200ml red wine, plus extra if needed
1 litre venison or beef stock
15g cold butter, cut into cubes
15g dark chocolate, grated

Check the meat for tendons and remove,
then cut it into 2cm cubes (or get your
butcher or supplier to do the work for you).
Cook the meat over a high heat in the olive
oil in a large pan so that it is beautifully
browned on all sides.

Peel the onions and carrots, then cut them
into pieces the same size as the meat.
Throw the vegetables into the pan along
with the thyme sprigs, whole garlic clove
and lightly crushed juniper berries, and
brown them as well until they are lightly
golden. Season with salt and pepper.
Add the red wine and cook until reduced
to half its original volume. Add the stock
and bring the stew to the boil. Skim off any
foam and impurities and then simmer for
about 1½ hours over a low heat until the
meat is tender.

Just before serving, add the cubes of cold
butter and grated chocolate – this will
round off the taste of the stew and give it
a delicious thick and 'sticky' texture. Don't
allow the stew to boil after the chocolate
has been added, as it may give it a slightly
grainy texture. Season with salt and pepper
and if necessary a dash of fresh red wine.
Serve with the White Barley Risotto (*see*
right) and a good-quality lingonberry jam.

White barley risotto

1 shallot
30g butter
200g pearl barley (uncooked)
100ml white wine
1 litre boiling chicken stock or water
sea salt flakes
2 tablespoons soured cream, 18% fat
**50g hard cheese, such as Høost
   or Grana Padano, freshly grated**
freshly ground pepper
2 tablespoons cider vinegar
½ handful of flat leaf parsley, chopped

Peel and chop the shallot, then sauté it
in half the butter in a saucepan until it is
translucent but has not taken on any colour.
Rinse the pearl barley well in cold water,
then add it to the pan and sauté for a few
minutes. Add the white wine and cook
until the grains have absorbed it. Then
add the boiling stock or water little by
little so that the grains are covered at all
times, and stirring occasionally to prevent
them sticking to the base of the pan. It is
important to season with salt during the
cooking so that it is absorbed by the pearl
barley. Cook the grains for 25–30 minutes
until they are tender but still al dente.

Remove the pan from the heat and add the
soured cream, the remaining butter, cut into
cubes, and the grated cheese so that the
barley risotto has a more liquid and creamy
consistency. Season with salt, pepper and
the vinegar. Sprinkle with the chopped
parsley and serve immediately.

In this recipe, where the creamy barley is
matched with a potent game stew, I have
chosen not to garnish it with wild mushrooms
and a little squash or celeriac purée, which
could otherwise be a nice accompaniment
to the dish.

Chanterelles

The chanterelle is a firm-fleshed fungus with a 2–10cm-diameter cap and a characteristic apricot fragrance. The stem is 6–8cm in length and usually slightly pointed at the base. Chanterelles don't have gills on the underside like button or flat mushrooms, but ridges that run down to the stem. The chanterelle is easy to recognize, with its colour varying from pale yellow to bright orange. It can only be confused with the false chanterelle, which often has a stronger orange colour, no smell and a more velvety surface. The chanterelle grows in acidic soil in deciduous as well as coniferous forests. There are many different species to be found in uplands and lowlands, along trail edges or country dirt roads with mixed woodland and lots of shade, and they can be picked from midsummer to mid-November.

How to pick chanterelles

Pick the mushrooms gently, cut off the root and roughly clean them on the spot. Finish cleaning them at home without the use of water, as that will wash away some of the flavouring substances. Gently tear the bigger chanterelles into smaller pieces and fry them in a pan until they begin to sizzle. Chanterelles are good in sauces but have enough flavour to give a distinguished character to a homemade stock, and they are fantastic stewed in cream and served on a piece of bread.

Dried chanterelles

If you find a lot of chanterelles or other wild mushrooms during the summer and autumn, more than you can eat, drying them is a great idea. Clean the mushrooms, again not using water to avoid washing away some of the flavour. Cut them into small pieces or thin slices, place them on a baking sheet lined with baking paper and dry them in a preheated fan-assisted oven at 60°C/ lowest Gas Mark setting (you can leave the oven door slightly ajar) for about 1–1½ hours or until they are completely dry – this is important, otherwise they will quickly rot once you store them. Leave the mushrooms to cool, then pack into sterilized glass jars, seal tightly and store in a cool, dry place. You can dry most mushrooms in this way and thus enjoy them well beyond their normal season. Use your dried mushrooms in risottos, sauces and soups or as a tasty sprinkle on top of a good stew.

Fish

Boiled lobster
with lemon mayonnaise

1 tablespoon salt
1 teaspoon sugar
2 live lobsters, about 700–800g each

Bring a large pan of water with the salt and sugar added to the boil. Kill the lobsters by inserting a large kitchen knife into the neck of the lobster and then quickly cutting down straight through the head so that the lobster dies instantly. Then plunge the lobster into the boiling water and boil for 5 minutes. Take the pan off the heat and put the pan and its contents in the refrigerator for the lobster to cool in the cooking brine. When the lobster has cooled, you should aim to remove the flesh from the shell in whole pieces as far as possible. The easiest way to do this is to cut the lobster in half with a large knife, then crush the claws with the side of the knife or use a pair of seafood scissors. A hammer could also be used, but just be careful that you don't smash the claws altogether. Once all the lobster meat has been removed, check the meat for any remnants of shell, and remove the dark vein (intestinal tract) running all the way down the tail.

Serve the lobster meat with Lemon Mayonnaise (see right) and good bread, and remember to put the pepper mill on the table too – freshly ground pepper is mandatory when there is seafood on the menu.

Lemon mayonnaise

2 pasteurized egg yolks
½ tablespoon French mustard
finely grated zest of ½ organic lemon, and juice of 1
sea salt flakes and freshly ground pepper
150ml cold-pressed rapeseed oil

Using an electric whisk or a balloon whisk, whisk the egg yolks, mustard, half the lemon juice, salt and pepper together in a bowl until thick and white. Slowly add the oil in a thin stream while whisking vigorously. It is of the utmost importance to add the oil gently and slowly so that the mayo doesn't curdle. Should it begin to curdle, you can try and save it by adding a few drops of cold water while still whisking vigorously. Season the finished mayonnaise with the lemon zest and extra juice and, if needed, additional salt and pepper.

Orange and fennel-marinated cod

400g cod fillets
1 teaspoon sea salt flakes
1 tablespoon sugar
1 red onion
1 fennel with feathery tops
50ml cider vinegar
finely grated zest and juice of 1 organic orange
6 fennel seeds, coarsely crushed
5 juniper berries
2 tablespoons standard rapeseed oil
freshly ground pepper

First, check that the cod fillets are nice and fresh and smell of the sea, not of the harbour. Remove the skin and any bones from the fillets, put them in a dish and sprinkle with salt and the sugar. Cover the dish with clingfilm and leave in the refrigerator for 2 hours.

Cut the fillets into very thin slices and place them on a platter.

Peel the onion. Cut the fennel in half, rinse it thoroughly in cold water and drain. Chop both the onion and fennel very finely (save the feathery leaves from the fennel for the garnish). Put the vegetables in a saucepan, add the vinegar, orange zest and juice, coarsely crushed fennel seeds, juniper berries and oil and bring it to a rapid boil. Turn off the heat and leave the marinade to cool slightly, then pour it evenly over the thin slices of cod while it is still warm. Leave the cod to soak for about 10 minutes before serving.

Finish the cod off with a sprinkle of the chopped fennel fronds and some freshly ground pepper. The marinated cod is a delightful starter or lunch served with good bread, but it could also be part of a main dish together with a few other small dishes, such as the Mushroom and Savoy Cabbage Pie (see page 155) or the Brussels Sprout Salad with Orange, Walnuts and Pearl Barley (see page 238).

BLUE STALK MUSHROOMS
In autumn, these mushrooms light up the forest floor.

Fish and chips

8 large baking potatoes
600g skinless haddock or cod fillet
sea salt flakes
100g plain flour, plus extra for sprinkling
1 teaspoon fine salt
600ml dark beer
3 litres rapeseed oil, for deep-frying

Peel the potatoes, cut into chips about 1cm thick and 10cm long and put them in a bowl of cold water. Leave to soak for about 30 minutes, then leave to drain thoroughly.

Check that the fish is fresh and smells of the sea, not of the harbour. Remove any bones or stray scales and cut the fish into 8 evenly sized pieces. Sprinkle with salt and a little flour, then leave to rest in the refrigerator for 10 minutes.

Meanwhile, mix the 100g flour, fine salt and beer together in a bowl to make a sticky batter and put that in the refrigerator as well for 10 minutes.

Pour the oil into a large pan and heat it up to about 170–180°C, or until the wooden end of a match sizzles when you drop it in the oil. Dip the pieces of fish in the batter to coat, then put them straight into the hot oil – 3–4 pieces at a time so that the oil doesn't lose too much heat. Fry the fish for about 3–4 minutes until golden and crisp. Remove with a slotted spoon, place them on a piece of kitchen paper and sprinkle with sea salt flakes.

Double-cook the chips in the sizzling oil so that they become deliciously crisp and golden. First cook them at a lower temperature, around 130–140°C, for about 4–5 minutes until they become tender but without taking on any colour, then remove from the oil. Fry a second time at a higher temperature, around 180°C, for about 3–4 minutes until crisp and golden. Lift the chips out, drain on kitchen paper and season with sea salt. Eat both fish and chips while they are hot. Serve with Homemade Mayonnaise (see page 68) for dipping and beer to wash it down.

Fish cakes
with quick tartare sauce

600g skinless cod or haddock fillet
1 teaspoon sea salt flakes
2 organic eggs
2 tablespoons plain flour
150ml whipping cream
1 carrot
1 baking potato
½ handful of dill, chopped
freshly ground white pepper
10g butter
1 tablespoon rapeseed oil, for frying

Check that the fish is fresh and smells of the sea, not of the harbour. Put the fish in a food processor and mince coarsely. Add the salt and pulse the minced fish until it is sticky – this way, it will bind with the liquid much better and the cakes will be less likely to fall apart. Place the fish in a mixing bowl.

Add the eggs, flour and then the cream, a little at a time, and stir well until the minced mixture has a good, firm consistency.

Peel the carrot and potato, then grate them finely. Squeeze the moisture out of the vegetables with your hands, then stir them into the fish cake mixture. Finally, add the chopped dill and white pepper. Refrigerate the mixture for 30 minutes before frying.

Fry large spoonfuls of the mixture in the butter and oil over a medium heat – it is important to be patient so that they form a beautiful crust on the underside before you turn them, and that way they will also keep their shape and become firmer, producing a better end result. Serve the golden fish cakes with a bowl of boiled potatoes or good rye bread, as well as a green or more rustic salad and a generous dollop of Quick Tartare Sauce (see right).

••••••••••••••••••••••••••••••••

TIP It is important that all the ingredients are at the same temperature, as they will combine a lot more easily.

••••••••••••••••••••••••••••••••

Quick tartare sauce

1 fennel bulb
2 carrots
½ cauliflower
2 tablespoons standard rapeseed oil
sea salt flakes and freshly ground pepper
20g unrefined cane sugar
3 tablespoons cider vinegar
2 pasteurized egg yolks
1 tablespoon prepared mustard
1 tablespoon cider vinegar, plus extra to season
300ml cold-pressed rapeseed oil
50g gherkins, chopped
½ handful of chervil, chopped

Prepare and wash all the vegetables. Grate the outer parts of the cauliflower on the coarse side of the grater and place in a bowl. Then cut the rest of the cauliflower (discarding any tough stalk) and the other vegetables into 5mm cubes.

Put the vegetables in a saucepan along with the standard rapeseed oil, salt, pepper, sugar and vinegar, and steam them, with the lid on, for 3–4 minutes until slightly soft but still with a bite – stir a few times during the steaming so that the vegetables are evenly cooked. Take the pan off the heat and leave the contents to cool.

While the vegetables are cooling, it is time to make the mayonnaise. Using an electric whisk or a balloon whisk, whisk the egg yolks, mustard, vinegar, salt and pepper together in a bowl until thick and white. Slowly add the cold-pressed rapeseed oil in a thin stream while whisking vigorously – be careful not to make the mayo curdle. When all the oil has been added, adjust the flavour with a little additional salt, pepper and vinegar. Finally, fold the steamed vegetables, grated cauliflower and chopped gherkins into the mayonnaise, and finish with the freshly chopped chervil.

••

Baked potatoes
with salmon tartare and dill yogurt

4 large baking potatoes
coarse sea salt
200ml Greek yogurt, 10% fat
finely grated zest and juice
  of 1 organic lemon
½ handful of dill, chopped
sea salt flakes and freshly ground pepper
2 anchovy fillets
1 tablespoon capers
1 small shallot
200g very fresh skinless salmon fillets

Wash the potatoes and put them in an ovenproof dish on a little bed of coarse salt. Bake the potatoes in a preheated oven at 180°C/Gas Mark 4 for 45 minutes–1 hour until tender.

Meanwhile, combine the yogurt with the lemon zest and juice, chopped dill, salt and pepper in a bowl. Finely chop the anchovies and capers, and peel and finely chop the shallot. Cut the salmon into very small cubes with a sharp knife – when making tartare, it is important to cut the fish, not chop it. Put the salmon in another bowl and season with the anchovies, capers and shallot. Mix well so that the ingredients are evenly distributed, and season with salt and pepper.

Take the potatoes out of the oven and cut a cross in the top of each potato. Squeeze them a little so that they open up and serve with the salmon tartare and dill yogurt so that the diners can garnish their own potato. Remember to set the table with teaspoons for scraping out the delicious potatoes!

. . . .

Tip If you want to serve baked potatoes as a main course, allow 1½–2 potatoes per person, and preferably make an additional filling: maybe one of my herb butters on page 102 or perhaps some stewed mushrooms. Earlier in the year, in the transition between late winter and early spring, baked potatoes with lumpfish roe and crème fraîche are a real treat.

. . . .

Pan-fried herrings
marinated in cider vinegar

10 double herring fillets
100g prepared wholegrain mustard
sea salt flakes and freshly ground pepper
100g rye flour
1 tablespoon standard rapeseed oil
10g butter
300ml cider vinegar
300ml water
270g unrefined cane sugar
5 bay leaves
10 whole black peppercorns

Check that the herring fillets are fresh and smell of the sea, not of the harbour. Place the herring fillets in a dish, skin side down, rub the flesh side with the mustard and season with salt and pepper. Fold the fillets together and dip them in the rye flour to coat.

Heat a frying pan and add the fat – first the oil, and when that is hot, then the butter. When the butter has stopped bubbling, fry the herring fillets for about 3 minutes on each side until golden and crisp. It may be necessary to press down a little on the folded fillets with a fish slice just after you have put them in the pan so that they don't unfold.

Combine the rest of the ingredients in a saucepan and bring to the boil. Pour the hot syrup over the fried herrings so that they are covered and leave to cool slightly

before you put the dish in the refrigerator to marinate for a couple of days.

Eat the pan-fried marinated herrings on good rye bread with thin slices of raw onion on top.

. . . .

Tip You can heat up the herring and marinade a little by briefly placing it in a preheated oven at 150°C/Gas Mark 2, then serve warm with some boiled potatoes and fried onions – another great way to enjoy the dish.

. . . .

OYSTER MUSHROOMS
The autumn forest is full of these delicate translucent stemmed caps – look for them cascading from the surface of dead hardwood trees.

Light dishes

Salted cod sandwich
with mustard cream and pickled Jerusalem artichokes

Salted cod
200g skinless cod fillet (or use other cod-like fish such as pollock, hake, ling or tusk)
1 teaspoon sugar
2 tablespoons sea salt flakes

Mustard cream
200ml Greek yogurt, 2% fat
2 tablespoons prepared mustard
1 teaspoon acacia honey
sea salt flakes and freshly ground pepper

To serve
8 slices of good wheat bread
1 tablespoon olive oil
8 small cocktail tomatoes
100g Pickled Jerusalem Artichokes (see page 167)
2 handfuls of mixed herbs, such as flat leaf parsley, chervil and chives

Check that the cod fillet is nice and fresh and smells of the sea, not of the harbour. Check the fish for bones and use a knife to scrape off any stray scales. Put the cod fillet in a dish and sprinkle with the sugar and salt. Cover the dish with clingfilm and leave in the refrigerator for at least 2–3 hours, preferably longer. Alternatively, the cod can be left to salt over a few days, if that fits better with your schedule.

When ready to serve, brush the sugar and salt mix from the cod and cut it into thin slices.

For the mustard cream, mix all the ingredients together in a bowl until smooth and a good consistency for spreading on to the toasted bread.

Oil the bread slices with the olive oil and toast them in a preheated oven at 220°C/Gas Mark 7 for 5–6 minutes until crisp and golden. Leave the toasted

bread to cool slightly, then spread 4 slices with the mustard cream and top with the thin slices of salted cod, the tomatoes, halved, and the pickled artichokes. Finish off with a good sprinkling of herbs and then place the remaining toasted bread slices on top. Serve the warm sandwiches with a green salad.

Mushroom and Savoy cabbage pie

Pastry
150g plain flour, plus extra for dusting
50g spelt flour
a little salt
90g softened butter, plus extra for greasing
1 organic egg

Filling
300g mixed mushrooms, such as button, oyster or chanterelle
300g Savoy cabbage
10g butter
3 thyme sprigs, freshly chopped
sea salt flakes and freshly ground pepper
3 organic eggs
150g cottage cheese
100ml semi-skimmed milk
a little grated nutmeg
30g hard cheese, such as Høost, or ripe Gouda or Grana Padano, freshly grated

First, make the pastry. Put the flours and salt in a bowl, add the softened butter, cut into small pieces, and rub in with your fingertips until the mixture resembles breadcrumbs. Stir in the egg and knead into a smooth dough. Place the dough in a floured bowl, cover it with clingfilm and leave to rest in the refrigerator for 30 minutes.

Roll the dough out on a lightly floured surface to a thickness of about 5mm and place in a greased 24cm diameter pie dish. I usually carry the dough from the table to the pie dish by rolling the dough around the rolling pin and then rolling it out into the dish. Press the dough into the dish

and trim the excess dough from the edge. Place a piece of baking paper on top of the pastry and add coarse salt, rice, dried beans or other heavy ingredients that will keep pressure on the pastry while it is pre-baking.

Pre-bake the pie crust in a preheated oven at 180°C/Gas Mark 4 for 10–15 minutes until it is firm and slightly golden.

While the pie crust is in the oven, clean the mushrooms with a brush or a small vegetable knife, then cut them into small pieces. Rinse the cabbage, drain thoroughly and then slice finely. Sauté the mushrooms in the butter in a frying pan until softened slightly, then add the cabbage. Season with the freshly chopped thyme, salt and pepper, and remove the pan from the heat.

Remove the pie crust from the oven and remove the baking paper and weights. Tip the mushroom and cabbage mixture into the pie crust. Mix the eggs, cottage cheese and milk together in a bowl, and season with salt, pepper and nutmeg, then pour over the vegetables. Sprinkle the grated cheese on top. Bake the pie in the oven at 170°C/Gas Mark 3½ for 30–35 minutes until the filling has set and the pie is golden on top. Take the pie out of the oven and leave to rest for 5 minutes before you cut it.

Serve the pie on its own or with the Orange and Fennel-marinated Cod (see page 150). If you want to serve it as a more substantial meal, supplement it with some boiled wheat grains flavoured with a little cider vinegar and rapeseed oil.

• •
Tip The pie can be made the day before and served cold.
• •

Fynbo
with pear mostarda and homemade crispbread

200g firm yellow cheese, such as
   Danish Fynbo or Vesterhavsost,
   or ripe Gouda
Pear Mostarda (*see* below)
Homemade Crispbread (*see* right)

Cut the cheese into blocks or batons and serve it with the Pear Mostarda (*see* below) and Homemade Crispbread (*see* right) after a nice dinner.

Pear mostarda
MAKES 1 SMALL JAR

3 ripe pears, such as Clara Frijs
   or Grise Bonne, or Williams
50ml water
2 tablespoons wholegrain mustard
1 tablespoon honey
a little cider vinegar
1 tablespoon standard rapeseed oil
sea salt flakes and freshly ground pepper

Peel the pears, cut them into quarters and remove the cores. Cut them into large cubes. Put the cubes in a saucepan with the measured water, cover with a lid and steam over a low heat for about 15–20 minutes until tender. Then remove the lid and let the water evaporate.

Put the pears in a blender with the mustard and honey and blend to a purée. Season with a little vinegar, the oil, salt and pepper. Pour the mostarda into a small sterilized preserving jar and store it in the refrigerator, where it will keep for 30–40 days unopened and 15–20 days once you have opened it.

· ·

Tip Although the name is Italian, the spicy-sweet fruit condiment mostarda is not unknown in ancient Nordic cuisine, and pear mostarda is also fabulous with Nordic cheeses, cold meats and most smoked products.

· ·

Homemade crispbread
MAKES ABOUT 35–40 CRISPBREADS

50g wholemeal flour
200ml semi-skimmed milk
15g fennel seeds, plus extra for
   sprinkling, coarsely crushed
220g plain flour
coarse sea salt, for sprinkling

Mix the wholemeal flour and milk together in a bowl.

Toast the fennel seeds in a dry frying pan until they begin to pop, then crush them using a pestle and mortar and add them to the bowl of flour and milk mixture. Leave to stand for 10 minutes in the kitchen.

Mix the plain flour into the milk mixture, a little at a time, until you have a smooth dough (save a little of the flour for rolling out the dough). Leave the dough to rest in the refrigerator for 15 minutes.

Roll the dough out thinly on a lightly floured surface, cut into long strips about 3 x 20cm and place on baking sheets lined with baking paper. Brush the crispbreads with water and sprinkle with coarse sea salt and some extra fennel seeds. Bake in a preheated oven at 170°C/Gas Mark 3½ for about 6–8 minutes until golden and crisp. Leave the crispbreads to cool, then store in an airtight container for up to 2–3 months.

Apple, Jerusalem artichoke and bacon compote

500g Jerusalem artichokes
500g apples, such as Ingrid Marie or Cox
1 tablespoon cider vinegar, plus extra
   to season
8 slices of thick bacon, preferably
   dry-salted
sea salt flakes and freshly ground pepper
50ml water
2–3 thyme sprigs, leaves picked
1 teaspoon sugar

Wash and peel the Jerusalem artichokes, then cut them into smaller pieces. Core the apples, dice them into small cubes and toss them with the vinegar.

Cook the bacon either on a baking tray in a preheated oven at 150°C/Gas Mark 2 or in a frying pan on the hob over a very low heat for 40–50 minutes or so that the bacon is crisp and releases most of its fat – you will need the fat later. Remove the bacon from the pan and keep it warm.

Sauté half the Jerusalem artichokes and apples in a little of the bacon fat in a sauté pan until slightly softened. Then add salt, pepper and the measured water and steam, with the lid on, over a medium heat for about 10–15 minutes until the apples and artichokes are tender but still retain some structure.

You can now choose to either fry the remaining apples and artichokes over a high heat in a little bacon fat for a beautiful, golden exterior, then sprinkle with the thyme, or you can add the rest of the Jerusalem artichokes to the compote along with the thyme leaves. In the latter case, steam the compote for a further 3–4 minutes until the Jerusalem artichokes are tender, and finish by mixing the raw apple pieces into the hot compote so that there is a crispy element to the dish and the compote is not too soft. Add salt, pepper, the sugar and extra vinegar to taste.

Serve the compote in the pan, with the bacon on top and, if you like, the roasted apples and artichokes on the side. Serve with plenty of great rye bread. This is also a very nice dinner for the apple season.

Homemade crispbread »

Warm pheasant salad
with scorzonera and carrots

1 cleaned pheasant
2 tablespoons standard rapeseed oil
sea salt flakes and freshly ground pepper
300g mixed root vegetables, such as
carrots, celeriac, parsley roots, parsnips
3 thyme sprigs
2 bay leaves
5 whole black peppercorns
500–600ml water
2–3 scorzonera (black salsify),
or regular salsify
2 carrots
100ml fruity vinegar, such as raspberry,
sherry or red wine
¼ handful of flat leaf parsley, leaves only
1 tablespoon cold-pressed rapeseed oil

Brown the pheasant thoroughly on all sides in 1 tablespoon of the standard rapeseed oil in a frying pan. Season with salt and pepper. Transfer the pheasant to a roasting tin and roast in a preheated oven at 170°C/ Gas Mark 3½ for 35–40 minutes until it is well done but still juicy. Remove from the oven and leave to rest for 10–12 minutes.

Remove the pheasant meat from the bones and put it in a bowl (save the bones to make the stock you need for the dressing).

Wash and peel the mixed root vegetables, then cut them into large cubes and brown them in the remaining 1 tablespoon standard rapeseed oil in a sauteuse along with the pheasant carcass, chopped into smaller pieces. When the vegetables are golden, add the thyme, bay leaves, peppercorns and enough of the measured water to cover, then bring to the boil and skim off any foam and impurities. Lower the heat and simmer the broth for 1–1½ hours.

Strain the broth through a fine sieve, then reduce to an intense stock of only about 50ml.

Wash and peel the scorzonera and carrots, then cut them into long, thin strips with a

vegetable peeler. Pour the vinegar into a small saucepan and boil it until it has a syrupy consistency, then mix with the hot, reduced broth. Toss the vegetable strips, pheasant meat and parsley leaves in the broth, and season with salt, pepper and the cold-pressed rapeseed oil. Serve immediately while it is warm.

• •

Tip You can make this salad with quail instead – two small quail will yield the equivalent amount of meat to one pheasant.

• •

Open rye bread sandwich
with smoked haunch of venison and compote of swede, apples and horseradish

½ swede, about 200g
sea salt flakes
1 tablespoon cold-pressed rapeseed oil
1 tablespoon cider vinegar
1 tablespoon acacia honey
freshly ground pepper
2 apples
30g freshly grated horseradish
1 handful of chives, chopped
200g thinly sliced smoked haunch of
venison (order at the butcher's)
4 slices of rye bread

Peel the swede and cut it into 1cm cubes, then rinse them in cold water. Bring a saucepan of salted water to the boil and cook the swede for about 2 minutes until tender but still with a bite.

Drain the swede and put the warm cubes in a bowl, then marinate them in the oil, vinegar, honey, salt and pepper.

Cut the apples into quarters, remove the cores and dice into cubes the same size as the swede. Add to the swede along with the horseradish, mix well and leave to cool slightly. Finish by adding the chives.

Put the smoked venison slices on the rye bread, pile a generous portion of the warm swede compote on top and serve immediately.

Omelette
with crispy Jerusalem artichokes

400g Jerusalem artichokes
40g bacon
1 tablespoon cold-pressed rapeseed oil
1 courgette
2 thyme sprigs, leaves picked
sea salt flakes and freshly ground pepper
6 organic eggs
150ml semi-skimmed milk

Wash and peel the Jerusalem artichokes, then dice them into large cubes. Cut the bacon into cubes as well, and put both the artichokes and bacon in a hot ovenproof frying pan with the oil. Fry for 4–5 minutes over a medium heat until the artichokes are tender and lightly golden and the bacon is crisp.

Cut the courgette into cubes and add them to the pan along with the thyme leaves, salt and pepper.

Crack the eggs into a bowl – one at a time so that you can check that they are fresh. Add the milk and whisk together, season with salt and pepper and pour the egg mixture into the pan. Stir lightly around so that the artichokes, courgette and bacon are evenly distributed, then leave the egg mixture to firm for a few minutes.

Transfer the pan to a preheated oven at 250°C/Gas Mark 10 (or your highest Gas Mark setting) and bake the omelette for about 5–6 minutes. You may want to use the grill function in the oven at the end so that the omelette is nice and golden on top. Remove the omelette from the oven, turn out on to a platter and serve as part of a Sunday brunch.

Vegetable accompaniments

Pearl barley salad

160g pearl barley (uncooked)
300ml water
sea salt flakes and freshly ground pepper
2 tablespoons cider vinegar, plus extra
　if needed
2 tablespoons olive oil
1 tablespoon acacia honey, plus extra
　if needed
1 swede
2 apples
½ handful of chervil

Rinse the pearl barley well in cold water. Put it in a saucepan, add the measured water and bring to the boil. Simmer with the lid on for about 20 minutes. Take the pan off the heat and leave the barley to stand for 5–10 minutes, still with the lid on.

Put the barley in a bowl and season with salt, pepper, vinegar, oil and honey so that the hot grains absorb all the nice flavours. Place the bowl in the refrigerator.

Peel the swede and cut it into very thin slices, using a mandoline or a sharp knife, then put the slices in a bowl. Cut the apples into quarters and remove the cores. Cut the wedges into very thin slices and mix with the swede. Add the cooked pearl barley and season, if necessary, with a little extra vinegar, salt and pepper.

Chop the chervil roughly and mix it into the salad. Taste again and add salt, pepper, vinegar or honey to your taste. Mix well once more and serve.

Serve this salad as an alternative to potatoes, rice, cooked grains or other filling side dishes. It has the crispness, acidity and sweetness to accompany heavier meat dishes, and I am particularly fond of it as a side to pork; the combination of swede, apple and the aniseed-flavoured chervil is absolutely brilliant with, for instance, roast pork.

Baked beetroot
with yogurt and dill

1kg beetroot
4 tablespoons coarse sea salt
200ml Greek yogurt, 2% fat
1 tablespoon cider vinegar
2 tablespoons acacia honey
10 dill seeds, crushed
1 handful of dill, chopped
sea salt flakes and freshly ground pepper

Wash the beetroot clean of soil, place them in an ovenproof dish and sprinkle with the coarse salt. Bake the whole beetroot in a preheated oven at 170°C/Gas Mark 3½ for 1 hour 10 minutes–1 hour 20 minutes until tender and wrinkled (the baking time can vary, of course, if the beetroot are very large or very small).

Remove the beetroot from the oven and scrape the skin off with a small, sharp knife as soon as they are cool enough to handle. Cut them into chunks and put them in a bowl.

Mix the yogurt with the vinegar, honey, crushed dill seeds, chopped dill, salt and pepper in a bowl. Pour the dressing over the beetroot when they have cooled but are still slightly warmer than room temperature and mix well. Leave the beets to absorb the flavours of the dressing for 10 minutes before serving. It is a good idea to give them one last round of seasoning – the balance often changes once the flavours of the beetroot and dressing have blended.

The beetroot pairs well with fish, light meats and poultry. And if you fancy a meat-free day, serve them with cooked grains and a salad of raw, grated vegetables or fruits like carrots, apples, cabbage and so on.

Baked carrots

12 carrots
30g smoked bacon
2 tablespoons standard rapeseed oil
100ml apple juice
50ml cider vinegar
1 basil sprig, leaves picked
1 tablespoon dark brown sugar
sea salt flakes and freshly ground pepper

Peel the carrots and cut them into rough batons, then place in an ovenproof dish. Cut the bacon into cubes and put in a bowl with the rest of the ingredients. Stir everything together and pour over the carrots. Toss around a few times so that the batons are well coated.

Bake in a preheated oven at 220°C/Gas Mark 7 for 6–8 minutes. The temperature is quite high in order for the carrots to get a nice caramelized exterior.

Remove the carrots from the oven and leave to cool slightly, then serve as a side dish to grilled pork, meatloaf, meatballs or poultry.

Salad of squash, lingonberries, bacon and chestnuts

1 large butternut or Hokkaido squash
2 tablespoons cider vinegar
2 tablespoons cold-pressed rapeseed oil
sea salt flakes and freshly ground pepper
1 tablespoon acacia honey
75g fresh or frozen lingonberries, defrosted if frozen
1 tablespoon unrefined cane sugar
30g whole blanched almonds
1 handful of chervil, chopped
8 baked chestnuts
50g bacon

Peel the squash – I think it is easiest to use a knife – halve it, then scrape out the seeds with a spoon. Cut it into chunks or wedges, place them in a large roasting tin lined with baking paper and toss them well in the vinegar, oil, salt, pepper and honey. Bake in a preheated oven at 180°C/Gas Mark 4 for 7–8 minutes until tender but still al dente.

The squash will give off a little liquid during cooking. Pour this liquid into a small saucepan and reduce it to half its original volume. Blend it with a stick blender so that it becomes thick and smooth, then pour it over the baked squash. Put the dish in the refrigerator.

Mix the lingonberries with the sugar and leave them to stand for 10 minutes in the kitchen.

Roast the almonds in a dry pan until golden, then tip them out on a chopping board and chop them roughly. Mix the almonds with the baked squash, then add the lingonberries and chopped chervil, and maybe a little extra salt and pepper to taste.

Peel the baked chestnuts, then cut them into slices – as thin as possible without them crumbling apart. Sprinkle the chestnuts over the salad. Dice the bacon and fry in a hot frying pan until crisp. Sprinkle the crispy bacon over the salad and serve.

The squash salad can be served with fish or seafood or as an independent starter or a main course accompanied by some good-quality bread.

Baked mushrooms
with cider and garlic

500g button or Portobello mushrooms
3 garlic cloves, lightly crushed
3 rosemary sprigs, plus extra, finely chopped, to serve
2 tablespoons olive oil, plus extra to serve
sea salt flakes and freshly ground pepper
100ml cider

Clean the mushrooms with a brush or a small vegetable knife, then place them in an ovenproof dish with the lightly crushed garlic, rosemary sprigs, olive oil, salt and pepper. Pour over the cider.

Bake in a preheated oven at 150°C/Gas Mark 2 for 12 minutes. Eat the mushrooms warm with a little finely chopped rosemary, giving them a light drizzle of olive oil just before serving.

The mushrooms can be served as a small dish on its own or as an accompaniment to most meats and fish.

CHESTNUTS
Take a walk in the forest and you may be lucky enough to find genuine sweet chestnuts.

Baked parsley roots
with salsa of Savoy cabbage and almonds

1kg parsley roots
2–3 tablespoons cider vinegar
5 thyme sprigs, chopped
1 tablespoon standard rapeseed oil
sea salt flakes and freshly ground pepper

Salsa
50g Savoy cabbage, cut into chunks
1 shallot, peeled
½ handful of parsley
30g whole blanched almonds
100ml standard rapeseed oil
50ml cider vinegar, plus extra if needed
sea salt flakes and freshly ground pepper
a little unrefined cane sugar or honey

Peel the parsley roots and cut them into chunks. Put the roots in an ovenproof dish and toss them with the vinegar, chopped thyme, oil, salt and pepper. Bake the parsley roots in a preheated oven at 180°C/Gas Mark 4 for 7–8 minutes until the roots are tender but still have a bite to them. Take the roots out of the oven and leave them to cool.

Now make the salsa. Add the cabbage, shallot, parsley, almonds, oil and vinegar to a food processor and blend to a coarse dip. Season with salt, pepper and the sugar or honey, then toss the salsa with the parsley roots. Add extra salt, pepper, sugar or vinegar to taste.

The baked parsley roots are a great side to a variety of dishes, especially classic pork dishes such as sausages, meatballs, fillet steaks and pork collar, but they are also quite delicious with a piece of steamed fish or as a (lunch) side dish with charcuterie.

Brussels sprouts salad

with chickpeas, apple and capers

100g dried chickpeas, soaked in cold
    water for 12 hours
1 garlic clove, peeled
½ handful of flat leaf parsley
2 tablespoons olive oil
finely grated zest and juice of 1 organic
    lemon, plus extra juice if needed
sea salt flakes and freshly ground pepper
10 Brussels sprouts
2 apples
2 tablespoons capers

Drain the soaked chickpeas and rinse them
thoroughly in clean water. Put the chickpeas
in a pan, cover with water and add the whole
garlic clove and the stems from the parsley.
Bring to the boil, then simmer the chickpeas
gently for 35–45 minutes until tender.

Drain the chickpeas, pour them into a bowl
and, while they are still hot, season with
the olive oil, lemon zest and juice, salt and
pepper so that they absorb the flavours.

Wash the Brussels sprouts, drain and
chop them very finely. Cut the apples into
quarters, remove the cores and slice into
thin wedges. Wash the parsley thoroughly
and chop it roughly. Add the sprouts, apples,
parsley and capers to the bowl of chickpeas
and toss well. If necessary, season with more
pepper, salt or lemon juice to taste – now the
salad is ready to serve.

'Burnt' leeks and lemon in oil

with dill flowers, coriander and fennel seeds

MAKES 1 JAR

4 winter leeks
1 organic lemon
4 dill flower heads
1 tablespoon coarse sea salt
1 tablespoon coriander seeds
1 tablespoon fennel seeds
1 bay leaf
about 2 litres good olive oil

Cut off the roots and tops of the leeks, then
rinse them thoroughly in cold water. Drain
them well and cut them into pieces about
10cm in length (or any length that will suit
the preserving jar you want to use). Heat
a griddle pan until it is sizzling hot, place
the leeks on it and cook them for about
3–4 minutes on each of their four 'sides'
so that they have beautiful grill marks all
around. Cut the lemon into quarters and
griddle the lemon wedges on the flesh
sides until they have a golden colour.

Put the leeks, lemon, dill flower heads, salt
and spices in a sterilized preserving jar
and pour over the olive oil to cover. Seal
tightly, place the jar in the refrigerator and
leave to pickle for about 14 days before you
serve the leeks. If the jar is kept chilled and
the leeks and lemons are covered by the
oil, the shelf life is 2–3 months. Both leeks
and lemons (thinly sliced) can be used as
a garnish for almost any dish, but I would
suggest in particular grilled chicken and
Fried Flounder with Braised Chicory (*see*
page 218) or the Seared Hanger Steak with
Frisée lettuce (*see* page 75), where you can
cut the leeks into thin slices and mix them
into the salad.

Tip When you have eaten all the leeks
and lemons, you can reuse the oil for
frying or use it as a dressing for salads
as well as cooked and steamed vegetables
so that nothing is wasted.

SHEATHED WOODTUFT
This mushroom can be commonly
foraged as late as November.

Pickled squash
with onions and bay leaves

MAKES 4 LARGE JARS

2 winter squashes, such as butternut
   or Hokkaido
100g coarse sea salt
125g shallots
20g fresh horseradish root
5 bay leaves
2 teaspoons whole black peppercorns
2 teaspoons mustard seeds (any type)
2 litres cider vinegar
1kg sugar
1 litre water

Day 1
Peel and halve the squash, then scrape out the seeds with a spoon. Cut the squash into slices, place them in a bowl and sprinkle with the coarse salt. Leave the squash to sit for 12 hours in the refrigerator.

Day 2
Wipe the squash slices free of salt and put them in sterilized preserving jars. Peel and roughly chop the shallots, and peel and slice the horseradish. Add them along with the spices between the slices of squash.

Bring the vinegar, sugar and the measured water to the boil in a saucepan, then pour the boiling syrup over the squash in the jars. Seal the jars and leave the squash to pickle in the refrigerator or in a cool cellar or other cool place for about a week, before enjoying them with boiled, fried or braised meats and poultry or as pickles in sandwiches.
The pickled squash will keep fresh, stored in the refrigerator, for up to 6 months.

Pickled cabbage
with juniper, chervil and pears

½ white cabbage, about 500–750g
sea salt flakes
1 teaspoon cumin seeds
10 juniper berries, chopped
100ml cider vinegar
freshly ground pepper
2 pears, such as Conference or
   Doyenne du Comice
1 handful of chervil, chopped

Remove the outer leaves of the cabbage and chop the rest of the cabbage very finely. Bring a large pan of lightly salted water to the boil and throw the cumin seeds and chopped juniper berries into the water. Cook the cabbage for 2–3 minutes until it is tender but still has some bite. Drain the cabbage and flavour with the vinegar, salt and pepper, then leave to cool.

Cut the pears into quarters, remove the cores and cut them into long, thin strips. Mix the cooled cabbage with the pears and chopped chervil just before serving.

Serve the pickled cabbage as an accompaniment to the Braised Shoulder of Venison with Jerusalem Artichoke and Apple Purée (see page 142) and other dishes with game, or with the Braised Pork Knuckle with Spicy Sugar-browned Cabbage (see page 139) as an alternative to the browned cabbage.

Pickled Jerusalem artichokes

3 tablespoons cold-pressed rapeseed oil
3 tablespoons cider vinegar
1 tablespoon clear honey
sea salt flakes and freshly ground pepper
200g Jerusalem artichokes
½ bunch flat-leaf parsley

Put the oil, vinegar, honey, salt and pepper a small saucepan and bring to the boil.

Wash the Jerusalem artichokes thoroughly and slice them into very fine slices using a mandolin or a sharp knife. Spread the slices in the base of a shallow dish and pour over the hot dressing, then leave to marinate for 10–15 minutes.

Finely chop the parsley and stir into the Jerusalem artichokes just before serving.

Baking and sweet things

Apple muffins
with rosemary

MAKES ABOUT 25–30 MUFFINS

200g softened butter
400g unrefined cane sugar, plus extra
    for sprinkling over the vanilla seeds
5 organic eggs
100g whole blanched almonds
200g plain flour
4 apples, such as Cox or Ingrid Marie
1 rosemary sprig, leaves picked and
    finely chopped
½ vanilla pod, split lengthways and
    seeds scraped out

Beat the softened butter and sugar together thoroughly, then beat in the eggs, one at a time – incorporate each egg well before you add the next to avoid the mixture splitting.

Chop the almonds finely in a food processor and stir them into the muffin mixture along with the flour. Mix well until the mixture is smooth and supple.

Cut the apples into quarters, remove the cores and dice them into small cubes. Put the apples in a bowl and mix them with the finely chopped rosemary and the seeds from the vanilla pod – if you scrape the vanilla seeds out on to a chopping board and sprinkle a little sugar on them, you can separate the grains from each other by crushing the sugar and vanilla seeds with the flat side of a chef's knife. That way, the vanilla is easy to mix well with the apple filling. Add the apple filling to the batter and pour the batter into the cups of a muffin tin lined with paper cases or a silicone muffin tray.

Bake the muffins in a preheated oven at 200°C/Gas Mark 6 for about 15 minutes until they are baked through and golden on top. Remove the muffins from the oven and leave them to cool slightly on a wire rack.

This muffin recipe is something between a traditional very light and airy muffin and a more dense sponge cake. I am aware that rosemary is a flavour that doesn't agree with everyone when it comes to using it in the sweet kitchen, and if you really don't connect with the slightly soapy pine-needle taste, you should not feel obliged to include it. But I promise you, rosemary and apples is an extraordinary combination.

Tip Using this batter as a foundation, you can add whatever filling the season prescribes – hazelnuts, pear and ginger, for example, or plums, almonds and cinnamon. Obviously, you can also just fill it with chocolate, orange zest and dried fruit – in fact, you can pretty much tailor-make the filling with your own favourite additions.

Apple pie with hazelnuts and vanilla

SERVES 10

Filling
1kg apples, such as Filippa, Gråsten
    (Gravenstein) or Cox
100ml apple juice (preferably unfiltered)
50ml dry cider
½ vanilla pod, split lengthways and
    seeds scraped out
1 tablespoon honey

Batter
375g skinned hazelnuts (*see* method
    on page 171)
200g softened butter, plus extra for
    greasing
375g sugar
2 organic eggs
2 organic egg whites
100g plain flour

Peel and core the apples, then cut them into smaller pieces. Put them in a bowl and toss them in the apple juice, cider, the seeds from the vanilla pod and the honey, then leave them to soak for 10–15 minutes in the kitchen.

Chop the hazelnuts finely and beat them with the butter and sugar until completely smooth and creamy. Add the whole eggs and egg whites – one at a time, so that each egg is incorporated well into the batter before adding the next – then add the flour.

Pour the batter into a buttered 26–28cm springform tin. Drain the apples (save the juice for later) and arrange them on top of the batter, giving them a light press with the flat of your hand so that they sink in a bit. Bake the apple pie in a preheated oven at 170°C/Gas Mark 3½ for 1 hour– 1 hour 10 minutes. If the pie browns too fast, you can cover it with foil for the remaining baking time. Remove from the oven and leave it to cool slightly.

Reduce the liquid from the apples to a thick syrup and pour it over the slightly cooled apple pie. The pie will benefit from having 3–4 hours to absorb the syrup – it is almost better the day after, when it has 'set'. Enjoy the pie with lightly whipped cream, Yogurt Ice Cream (*see* page 246) or crème fraîche.

Crispy puff pastry apple pie

150g frozen puff pastry (2 sheets),
    defrosted
plain flour, for dusting
4–5 apples, such as Cox or Ingrid Marie
150g icing sugar
30g butter, melted
4 tablespoons Calvados

Roll the puff pastry out thinly on a lightly floured surface, creating long rectangular sheets. Cut each sheet in half to make 4 pie crusts. Alternatively, cut out 4 circles 12–14cm in diameter. Place the pie crusts on a baking sheet lined with baking paper and leave to rest in the refrigerator for 10 minutes.

Core the apples and cut them into very thin slices (or leave the cores in the apples – it looks beautiful). Place the apple slices in a thin layer on the puff pastry, each slightly overlapping the last, sprinkle with the icing sugar and drizzle with the melted butter. Bake the pies in a preheated oven at 220°C/Gas Mark 7 for 15 minutes until the pastry has puffed up and the apples are beautifully golden and lightly caramelized.

Remove the pies from the oven and sprinkle with the Calvados while they are still hot. Serve warm with crème fraîche, Greek yogurt or vanilla ice cream.

Apple sauce and apple sorbet
with roasted hazelnuts, dried apples and sugar beet syrup

SERVES 6

Apple sorbet
500g apples, such as Ingrid Marie, Belle de Boskoop or Cox
300ml water
180g unrefined cane sugar
40g glucose syrup
150ml apple juice
lemon juice
cider

Apple sauce
500g apples, such as Ingrid Marie, Belle de Boskoop or Cox
50–75g sugar
½ vanilla pod, split lengthways and seeds scraped out
1 handful of lemon verbena leaves (can be left out or replaced by lemon zest)

To serve
35g hazelnuts
2 tablespoons sugar beet syrup (see tip)
Dried Apples (see right)

First, make the sorbet. Wash the apples and remove the cores, but leave the peel on. (Reserve the cores – they contain lots of

pectin, which helps to stabilize the finished sorbet.) Cut the apples into small pieces, put them in a saucepan with the measured water, sugar, glucose, apple cores and apple juice and boil for about 3–4 minutes until the apples are tender.

Remove the cores, put the apples and the syrup in a blender and blend until creamy. Pass the pulp through a fine sieve so that the blended apple mixture is completely smooth. Add the lemon juice and cider to taste. Now follow the recipe for Rhubarb Sorbet on page 60 from the third step to finish making the sorbet, including alternative methods if you don't have an ice-cream maker.

While the sorbet is freezing, make the apple sauce. Wash the apples, remove the cores and cut them into large cubes. Put the apples in a saucepan with the sugar and the split, scraped vanilla pod and vanilla seeds. Cover with a lid and slowly bring the apples to the boil so that they release some juice, then simmer for about 10–15 minutes to create a dense and chunky apple sauce. Pass the sauce through a coarse sieve for a beautifully smooth consistency and season, if necessary, with a little extra sugar along with the chopped verbena. Leave the sauce to cool in a bowl.

Meanwhile, skin the hazelnuts. Place the nuts in a small ovenproof dish and toast them in a preheated oven at 180°C/Gas Mark 4 for 7–10 minutes. Remove the nuts from the oven, turn them directly on to a clean tea towel and rub off the skins inside the towel.

Put them in a dry frying pan, add 1 tablespoon of the sugar beet syrup and bring to the boil, then simmer the nuts in the syrup for about 30 seconds until they are glazed and sticky (be careful, as they easily burn). Remove the nuts from the pan and leave them to cool.

Arrange the apple sauce in deep dessert plates with the Dried Apples, roasted hazelnuts, a scoop of apple sorbet and the last of the sugar beet syrup on top, then serve.

True dessert fanatics would probably like to pour something like cream, crème Anglaise, ice cream or another creamy substance on top – and I guarantee that to be a winner as well. But sometimes I really like the pure and fresh juiciness of a fruit dessert such as this, so serve it to suit your taste.

Tip Sugar beet syrup is concentrated, unrefined sugar beet juice, as opposed to Swedish dark syrup, which is a mixture of white refined sugar and molasses derived from sugar cane. Sugar beet syrup has considerably more character and nuances than plain dark syrup. You will find it in most Meyers Deli shops and from online suppliers, or you can of course replace it with a good dark syrup.

Dried apples

100ml water
25g sugar
2 apples, such as Ingrid Marie or Cox

Put the measured water and sugar in a saucepan and heat to dissolve the sugar, then leave the syrup to cool.

Wash the apples, then cut into very thin slices about 1mm thick – this is unquestionably easiest if you have a mandoline. I usually leave the cores in the apples because it looks so beautiful in the dried apples, but if you don't like the extra crunch, remove them with an apple corer.

Dip the apple slices in the cooled syrup and place them on a baking sheet lined with baking paper. Place the apples in a preheated oven at 60°C/lowest Gas Mark setting, preferably with the fan on, and with the oven door ajar. Dry the apple slices for about 2½–3 hours until they are absolutely crisp but have not browned.

Remove the apples from the oven and leave them to cool before storing them in a tightly sealed, sterilized glass jar for up to 3 days.

Stewed apples
with vanilla yogurt

750g apples, such as Ingrid Marie or Cox
2 tablespoons water
2–4 tablespoons unrefined cane sugar
(depending on sweetness of apples)
½ vanilla pod, split lengthways and
seeds scraped out

Wash the apples but leave the skin on, since there is plenty of nice apple flavour and lots of vitamins in it. (If you use apples with very thick skin, pass the apple sauce through a coarse sieve after cooking.) Cut the apples into quarters, remove the cores and dice.

Put the apples in a saucepan with the measured water, sugar and the split and scraped vanilla pod and vanilla seeds. Simmer, with the lid on, over a low heat for about 8–10 minutes until tender and a bit mashed. If necessary, add a little extra sugar to taste, then leave the apple sauce to cool and serve cold or at room temperature topped with Vanilla Yogurt (see below).

Vanilla yogurt

300ml Greek yogurt, 2% fat
½ vanilla pod, split lengthways and
seeds scraped out
2 tablespoons icing sugar
10 lemon verbena leaves (see tip), very
finely chopped

Stir the yogurt with the seeds from the vanilla pod, the icing sugar and the very finely chopped lemon verbena in a bowl.

Leave the creamy mixture to stand for 15 minutes before it is served so that the taste of verbena and vanilla is fully infused into the yogurt.

Tip Lemon verbena is an overlooked herb with a very fine lemon flavour. Verbena is great in September, but if you can't find it, lemon balm can be substituted. The dessert will also still be great without any herbs.

The staple apple

In the parts of Denmark where apples grow well, that is East Jutland, Funen, Zealand and the Danish South Sea Islands, apples have for centuries played an important role as a year-round food staple. That is especially true in Lolland-Falster, where both fresh and dried apples and pears are included in many of the local dishes. The oldest recipe for apple pie dates back to the 1600s, but it was only when sugar beet made the Danish production of inexpensive white sugar possible in the last decades of the 1800s that sweet dishes such as apple pie become an everyday dish for the Danes.

Baked apples
with beer ice cream

SERVES 6

2 star anise
100ml porter
2 tablespoons dark brown sugar
finely grated zest and juice of
1 organic lemon
2 tablespoons cold-pressed rapeseed oil
seeds from 1 vanilla pod
6 Cox apples

Crush the star anise a little using a pestle and mortar or with the flat side of a chef's knife. Combine with the porter, brown sugar, lemon zest and juice, oil and split, scraped vanilla pod and vanilla seeds in a bowl to make a pickling brine.

Wash the apples, place them in an ovenproof dish and pour the liquid on top. Bake in a preheated oven at 150°C/ Gas Mark 2 for 50 minutes–1 hour – stir the apples around a few times during baking, and scoop up and pour the pickling liquid over them so that they are baked evenly, while becoming beautifully glazed and shiny. Serve the apples warm with Beer Ice Cream (see right) and a little syrup from the dish.

Beer ice cream

500ml half cream
150g sugar
100ml porter
½ vanilla pod, split lengthways and
seeds scraped out
5 organic egg yolks

Combine the cream, sugar, porter and split, scraped vanilla pod and vanilla seeds in a pan. Gently warm the mixture so that the sugar dissolves.

Put the egg yolks in a bowl that is large enough to accommodate all the ingredients. Pour the hot cream mixture into the egg yolks slowly and carefully while whisking vigorously. Pour it all back into the pan and cook over a low heat to thicken the cream until it reaches a temperature of 84–85°C and, although still runny, easily sticks to a wooden spoon.

When the texture is right, pour the cream through a sieve into a bowl. Leave the cream to cool for a while before pouring it into an ice-cream maker and churning it until it has the consistency of soft ice cream. You can now choose to serve the ice cream immediately, or you can transfer it to a plastic box with a lid and store it in the freezer for 1–2 hours for a firmer texture.

In contrast to other ice creams, it is not necessary to let this one sit at room temperature before serving – it is soft and delicious from the moment you take it out of the freezer.

Tip The beer ice cream is not well suited to alternative freezing methods. But if you don't have access to an ice-cream maker, you can freeze it in a container, chop it into small pieces and blend in a food processor into a kind of soft-serve ice cream.

Elderberries

Elderberries begin to mature in September, and the birds are always the first to discover them. They also know which trees have the best berries. You will find elder trees in woods, thickets, managed hedges and abandoned gardens. They can grow up to 8 metres tall, but often form shorter shrubs, especially if regularly cut back. The young branches are filled with soft, white marrow, and the leaves are divided into five to seven elliptical, jagged leaflets. The plant itself has a characteristic slightly sickly smell.

Using elderberries

Pick the ripe berries off the trees in bunches and rinse them. If are using them for juice, cut off the coarser stems. If you want to make a preserve, you will need to pick the berries off the stems with your fingers or using a fork. Be careful not to get the juice on your clothes, as it is a very intense colourant and virtually impossible to get out of your clothes. Try making some *grevskabets* preserve to have with your *æbleskiver* (Doughnut Holes, see page 243)

using equal parts elderberries and tart apples cooked with sugar and seasoned with lemon juice. You can pickle the ripe red berries with cider vinegar and sugar just like beetroots, while the unripe green berries can be pickled.

Dried elderberries

You can also try drying elderberries. Carefully pick the berries off the stems, preferably using a fork so that they remain nice and whole, as you may accidentally squash the berries if you use your fingers. Spread the berries on a sheet of baking paper, sprinkle with icing sugar and bake in a preheated fan-assisted oven at 60°C/lowest Gas Mark setting for about 1½ hours, preferably with the oven door ajar. They should shrivel up a little and look a bit like raisins. Leave the elderberries to cool, then store in a sterilized glass jar or other airtight container in a cool, dry place. Eat them with yogurt or use them in a salad, on a cake or in ice cream or cream – delicious.

Cinnamon swirls

MAKES 16 SWIRLS

Dough
500ml cold full-fat milk
50g fresh yeast
1 large organic egg, plus 1 extra,
  beaten, to glaze
1kg plain flour, plus extra for dusting
150g sugar
15g fine sea salt
12g ground cardamom
150g butter

Filling
125g softened butter
125g sugar, plus extra for sprinkling over
  the swirls
2 tablespoons ground cinnamon

Pour the cold milk into a bowl and stir in the yeast. Add the egg, flour, sugar, salt and cardamom, and knead the dough until it is supple and glossy and has stopped sticking to the bowl. This will take about 20 minutes, so use a stand mixer fitted with a dough hook and set it on a medium speed.

Now cut the butter into small cubes and add them to the dough, then let the machine continue kneading for a further 20 minutes until the dough is smooth and shiny. (The long kneading times are absolutely crucial for the final result!)

Cover the bowl with a clean tea towel and leave the dough to rest for 1½ hours in the kitchen.

Place the dough on a floured surface and roll it out into a rectangle 40cm wide and 50cm long. Spread the softened butter over the dough, then sprinkle the sugar and cinnamon evenly on top and rub them into the butter with your fingertips. Fold one-third of the dough towards the centre and fold the other third over the first so that you have 3 layers of dough. Roll out the dough again until it is 30cm wide and 50–60cm long, then cut it into 16 strips.

Hold each strip at either end and give it 4–5 twists – don't twist it so hard that you squeeze out the filling. Take the end of a twisted strip in one hand and wrap it twice around the index and middle finger of your other hand. Place the remaining snippet of dough over the 2 rings, put it between your index and middle finger and pull it down with your fingers to secure the snippet inside the bun.

Put the cinnamon swirls on a couple of baking sheets lined with baking paper, twists facing up. Cover with a clean tea towel and leave to rise in a warm room until doubled in size – about 2 hours.

Brush the cinnamon swirls with beaten egg, sprinkle them with a little sugar and bake in a preheated oven at 200°C/Gas Mark 6 for about 12–14 minutes. Leave them to cool on a wire rack.

• •

Tip These cinnamon swirls are of Norwegian origin. When I wrote my baking book *Meyers Bakery*, we went on a field trip to visit Bakeriet in Lom where I had previously sampled these wonderful, twisted little pastries that surpassed anything I had experienced before in the way of cinnamon buns. You can of course just shape the dough into ordinary cinnamon buns and still have some tasty baked goods, but you will not get quite as much caramelized cinnamon filling as when you form it into swirls.

• •

Pears poached in elderberry juice
served with skyr and elderberry syrup

4 pears, such as Conference or Doyenne
  du Comice
400ml water
200g unrefined cane sugar, plus extra
  if needed
300ml unsweetened elderberry juice
2 tablespoons cider vinegar
200ml skyr

Peel the pears beautifully from the stalk to the base, leaving the stalks on. Place the pears in a pan with the measured water, sugar and elderberry juice. Bring the pears to the boil and then cook gently over a low heat for 20–25 minutes until tender but still with some bite. Stir a few times during the cooking so that they are evenly cooked.

Lift the pears out and place them on a plate. Reduce the pear juice until two-thirds remain and it has reached a syrupy consistency. Add the vinegar and possibly a little extra sugar to taste so that the balance between sweet and sour is perfect.

Place the pears back in the syrup and leave them to cool in the refrigerator, where they will keep for 25–30 days as long as they are covered by the syrup (and if you can leave them alone for that long!).

Flavour the skyr with some of the elderberry syrup and eat it with the beautiful, elderberry-coloured pears. I highly recommend munching an Almond Macaroon (see page 114) or a toasted crumpet with your free hand.

Pear sorbet

with fennel seeds and aquavit

300ml water
180g unrefined cane sugar
40g glucose syrup (*see* tip)
3g fennel seeds
500g ripe pears
juice of 2 limes
25ml aquavit (pear brandy is also
    a great option)

Combine the measured water, sugar, glucose and fennel seeds in a pan and bring to the boil.

Wash the pears, cut them into quarters and remove the cores, then cut them into small pieces – just leave the peel on. Put the pear pieces and the hot syrup in a blender and blend for 1 minute until the pear pieces are blended completely.

Strain the fruit syrup through a fine sieve to make it perfectly smooth, and season with the lime juice and aquavit. Now follow the recipe for Rhubarb Sorbet on page 60 from the third step to finish making the sorbet, including alternative methods if you don't have an ice-cream maker.

Serve the pear sorbet as a refresher for your palate after a heavy autumn dinner. I like to eat it as it is, with its crystal clear pear and aquavit taste, but you can serve it with a little crunchy cookie or a sprinkle of Crispy Crumbles (*see* page 60).

• •

Tip Glucose syrup is extracted from corn and is less sweet than ordinary sugar or sugar beet syrup, but it gives elasticity and creaminess when you use it in caramels, dessert creams or, as here, in ice cream and sorbet. Glucose syrup is available in well-stocked supermarkets and online shops for confectionery making.

• •

Rye bread crumble,

apple sauce and blackcurrant preserve with whipped cream

250g dark rye bread (choose one that
    doesn't have too many whole grains)
80g sugar
30g butter
4–6 large apples, such as Cox
    or Belle de Boskoop
50ml water
seeds from ½ vanilla pod (optional)
4 tablespoons blackcurrant preserve
250ml whipping cream, freshly whipped

Grate the bread on the coarse side of the grater and mix it with 40g of the sugar.

Melt the butter in a saucepan and add the bread and sugar mixture. Toast the bread over a medium heat for 2–3 minutes until it starts to smell caramelized, then remove it from the pan and leave to cool. When it cools, the sugar will harden and the rye bread mixture will become nice and crisp.

Peel the apples (or leave the peel on if you like them more rustic), cut them into wedges and remove the cores. Cook the apples to a sauce with the remaining 40g sugar, measured water and possibly the split, scraped vanilla pod and vanilla seeds. The combination of vanilla and apple is a great marriage, but once in a while it can also be nice to let the apple flavour shine on its own, especially if you are dealing with an interesting old apple variety or a variety with a very short season, which should be enjoyed to the full.

When the apple sauce is ready, after 15–20 minutes (maybe more or less depending on the apple variety), take the pan off the heat and leave to cool completely.

Add the rye bread crumble, apple sauce and blackcurrant preserve in layers to a bowl – the first and last layer should be the rye bread crumble. Decorate with the freshly whipped cream before serving.

Princess pudding

SERVES 6–8

65g butter, plus extra for greasing
65g sugar
65g plain flour
finely grated zest and juice of
    ½ organic lemon
¼ vanilla pod, split lengthways and
    seeds scraped out
250ml semi-skimmed milk
8 organic egg yolks
4 organic egg whites

Melt the butter in a heavy-based pan, add the sugar, flour, lemon zest and juice and vanilla seeds from the pod and cook, while whisking, until the mixture becomes smooth and comes away from the side of the pan.

Heat the milk in separate pan, and when it reaches the boil, add it to the roux. Stir the batter well with a large spoon and let it cook lightly so that it firms and almost lifts from the pan. Leave the batter to cool slightly, then stir in the egg yolks, one at a time.

Whisk the egg whites until stiff and then fold them into the batter. I always briskly stir in a spoonful of the egg whites first, making it easier to gently fold in the rest of the whites and keep their airy texture.

Pour the batter into 12–16 small buttered ramekins or ovenproof dishes. Make a bain-marie by standing the dishes in a shallow baking tin and pouring boiling water from a kettle into the tin to come halfway up the sides of the dishes. Bake the princess puddings in a preheated oven at 180°C/Gas Mark 4 for around 30–35 minutes until the batter has souffléd.

Turn the puddings out on a serving platter and serve them while they are still warm with Apple Sauce (*see* left) or fresh fruit.

Winter

Seasonal ingredients

Cultivated produce

apples
beans and lentils
beetroot
Brussels sprouts
cabbage
carrots
celeriac
chicory
Chinese artichokes
cod
cod roe
grains
haddock
hare
horseradish

Jerusalem artichokes
kale
kohlrabi
leeks
lumpfish roe
nuts
onions
oysters
parsley
parsnips
partridge
pears
pumpkin
red cabbage
redfish

salsify
Savoy cabbage
whiting

In the wild

oyster mushrooms
mussels
chickweed
velvet shank mushrooms
water mint
watercress
venison
Scots pine bark
perch
ramsons
scurvy grass

lumpfish
mussels
nettles
daisies
ground elder
wood sorrel
birch sap
coltsfoot
violets
dandelion leaves

Soups and starters

Mushroom soup
with wheat berries and chicken meatballs

500g field mushrooms
2 shallots
1 garlic clove
5 thyme sprigs
2 tablespoons olive oil
sea salt flakes and freshly ground pepper
100ml dry sherry, plus extra if needed
1 litre chicken stock or water
200g cooked wheat grains
Chicken Meatballs (see below)

Clean the mushrooms using a brush or a small vegetable knife, then cut them into thin slices. Peel and chop the shallots and garlic.

Sauté the mushrooms, shallots, garlic and thyme in the olive oil until they are tender and the shallot turns translucent, then season with salt and pepper. Add the sherry and reduce to half its original volume, then add the chicken stock or water. Simmer for 10–15 minutes so that the mushrooms are still al dente but have imparted their flavour to the broth.

Add the cooked wheat grains to the broth and season to taste with salt and pepper and, if necessary, a little extra sherry.

Finally, add the Chicken Meatballs to the soup and let them heat up. Serve the soup with good bread.

Chicken meatballs

1 boneless chicken breast
sea salt flakes
1 organic egg, lightly beaten
100ml whipping cream
freshly ground pepper
1 thyme sprig, chopped

Remove any skin or tendons from the chicken breast and cut it into large cubes. Season the chicken with salt, chop it in a food processor and then mix it with the egg and cream. Season with pepper and the chopped thyme. The mixture should be worked until soft and smooth, but not for too long otherwise it might split.

Take a small lump of the meatball mixture, then poach it and taste it to check the seasoning. When you're happy with the flavour, form the mixture into balls with a small spoon, aiming for 1.5cm in diameter.

Poach the meatballs in a pan of salted water for 2–3 minutes. These meatballs are suitable for both clear soups and asparagus or pea soups (see pages 19 and 66).

Fish soup
with root vegetables and broad bean mash

Soup
1 large apple
1 leek
1 parsnip or parsley root
1 onion
3 garlic cloves
1kg bones of flatfish, such as flounder, halibut or turbot
a few parsley stems
12 whole black peppercorns
½ x 75cl bottle white wine
50ml whipping cream
50ml wheat beer
1 tablespoon cider vinegar
sugar, to taste
sea salt flakes and freshly ground pepper

Filling
1 carrot
100g celeriac
50ml water
sea salt flakes
100g cooked dried broad beans (or use canned beans)
2 tablespoons olive oil
grated zest and juice of ½ organic lemon
freshly ground pepper
¼ handful of parsley, chopped

First, make the soup. Wash the apple (keep the peel on) and vegetables, then cut them all into small pieces and put in a pan along with the fish bones, parsley stems and peppercorns. Pour over the white wine and add enough water to cover the vegetables. Bring the soup to the boil and skim off any foam and impurities, then lower the heat and simmer for 25 minutes.

Turn the heat off and leave the soup to stand for 20 minutes, then strain through a sieve and return to the pan. Add the cream and then reduce to the desired intensity and consistency. Season with the wheat beer and vinegar, and sugar, salt and pepper to taste.

Now make the filling. Peel and cut the vegetables into large cubes. Put the vegetables in a small pan with the measured water and some salt. Steam the vegetables, with the lid on, for about a minute until tender but still al dente.

Mash the beans coarsely, adding the oil, lemon zest and juice and salt and pepper to taste.

Pour any excess water from the steamed vegetables into the soup, then add the mashed beans to the pan along with the vegetables and let it all warm through. Serve a large spoonful of vegetables and mashed beans in shallow soup dishes. Whisk the soup quite vigorously with a whisk so that it is lightly foaming, then pour the hot soup over the vegetables and finish with a sprinkle of chopped parsley on top. Serve with good bread.

Potato soup
with lumpfish roe and dill

400g baking potatoes
1 leek
15g butter
3 thyme sprigs, leaves picked
1 garlic clove, very finely chopped
sea salt flakes and freshly ground pepper
700ml water
50ml whipping cream
200g fresh lumpfish roe with all
    membranes removed (see right)
1 handful of dill

Peel and slice the potatoes thinly, place them in a bowl of cold water and leave them to soak for 10 minutes. Cut off the root and top of the leek, then slice into thin rings and rinse them thoroughly in cold water to remove all the soil.

Drain the potato slices and leek thoroughly. Melt the butter in a pan and sauté the vegetables for 3–4 minutes until they have softened a little. Season with the thyme leaves, garlic, salt and pepper, and sauté for about a minute.

Add the measured water and simmer the soup over a low heat for 15–20 minutes until the potato slices are tender. Add the whipping cream and cook for another 5 minutes.

Pour the soup into a blender and blend until smooth, but not for long otherwise it will become sticky in consistency.

Pour the soup back into the pan, warm it through and season to taste with salt and pepper. Serve in soup plates with a good spoonful of lumpfish roe and the dill on top. Eat with some nice wholegrain bread.

Cleaning lumpfish roe

Lumpfish roes are held together by big membranes, and for the best dining experience they should be removed completely. It is pretty easy to remove the membranes yourself and much cheaper than buying the precious roe in a purified form. Just do the following. Remove the outer coarse membrane by hand. Put the roe in a bowl with a little cold water and salt. Whisk for a while so that the rest of the membranes cling to the whisk instead of the roe. Remove the membranes from the whisk a few times while whisking and continue until the roe is totally free of membranes. At this point, I usually leave the roe in the bowl and put it under the cold tap for a few minutes. When there are no more bits of membranes rising to the surface and into the sink, that means your roe is clean. Pour the roe in a sieve and leave it to drain for a while. Season with salt and your lumpfish roe is ready to be served. The roe can be stored in the refrigerator for a few days, or you can even freeze it.

Split pea soup
with parsley and rapeseed oil

150g dried green split peas
1 onion
1 rosemary sprig
1 garlic clove, peeled and finely chopped
2 tablespoons standard rapeseed oil
sea salt flakes and freshly ground pepper
2 tablespoons cider vinegar
½ handful of flat leaf parsley
a little cold-pressed rapeseed oil

Pour the split peas into a colander, rinse them with cold fresh water and leave them to drain thoroughly. Peel and chop the onion.

Sauté the onion, split peas, rosemary and garlic in the standard rapeseed oil in a saucepan for 1–2 minutes without colouring. Add enough water to cover the ingredients by a depth of about 5cm and bring to the boil, then simmer gently, with the lid on, for 45 minutes until the split peas are tender.

Take the pan off the heat, save a few tablespoons of the split peas for the garnish and scoop the rest of the soup into a blender. Remember to discard the rosemary sprig – it should definitely not go in the blender, as it could ruin both your soup and your blender. Blend the soup until smooth, and season to taste with salt, pepper and the vinegar. If necessary, dilute the soup with a little water so that it has the consistency of yogurt.

Wash the parsley thoroughly, leave it to drain well and then chop it. Serve the soup topped with the chopped parsley and the reserved cooked split peas, and finish off with a drizzle of cold-pressed rapeseed oil.

This soup makes a really nice starter, especially with a good sprinkle of Crispy Croutons (see page 128).

Gravad salmon
with sweet and spicy mustard sauce

SERVES 8–10

1 handful of dill (*see* tip)
20g fennel seeds
10g allspice berries
10g coriander seeds
10g juniper berries
1 star anise
150g unrefined cane sugar
150g sea salt flakes
½ side of very fresh salmon, skin on, scaled and pin-boned, about 2–2.5kg

Day 1
Wash the dill very, very carefully and leave it to drain, then chop finely. Crush all the spices thoroughly using a pestle and mortar and mix with the sugar, salt and chopped dill. Place the side of salmon in a dish, skin side down, sprinkle the spice mixture over it and cover the dish tightly with clingfilm. Leave the salmon to marinate in the refrigerator for at least 24 hours and preferably 48 hours, turning it a few times during the process.

Day 2 or 3
Take the salmon out of the dish, slice thinly and serve with good wholewheat bread and the Spicy and Sweet Mustard Sauce (*see* right).

Gravad salmon is a classic on the breakfast table, but it is also nice as a starter for a big dinner. I like to pair it with a beetroot salad, such as the Beetroot Tartare with Horseradish (*see* page 199), whose sweetness goes really well with the gravad fish. If you don't finish all the gravad salmon in one go, it can keep for about 8 days in a tightly sealed container in the refrigerator.

• •

TIP I have used fresh dill when making gravad salmon throughout my life and have had no problems, but the fact is that soil bacteria can sometimes lurk in fresh dill,

and therefore in the professional kitchen we are forced to use dried dill. At home, however, I still always use the fresh herb, washing it thoroughly of course. Well, now you know the reality, and should you wish to use dried dill instead, you will need about 50g for this recipe.

• •

Spicy and sweet mustard sauce

100g prepared Dijon mustard
100g prepared sweet French mustard
100g brown sugar
3 tablespoons cider vinegar
50ml cold-pressed rapeseed oil
10g fennel seeds
½ handful of dill, chopped
sea salt flakes and freshly ground pepper

Combine the 2 kinds of mustard in a bowl along with the brown sugar and vinegar, and stir until most of the sugar has dissolved. Then add the oil, a little at a time, whisking vigorously until the sauce thickens and becomes smooth.

Season the sauce with the fennel seeds, first giving them a quick crush using a pestle and mortar or with the flat side of a chef's knife, the chopped dill and salt and pepper to taste. Now the sauce is ready to be served.

Oysters
with apple and horseradish vinaigrette

2 apples
2 tablespoons rapeseed oil
3 tablespoons cider vinegar
sea salt flakes and freshly ground pepper
1 teaspoon honey
2 tablespoons freshly grated horseradish, or to taste
16 Limfjord (native European) oysters (Brittany oysters can also be used)

Peel the apples, cut them into quarters and remove the cores.

Mix the oil, vinegar, salt, pepper and honey together in a bowl. Cut the apples into small cubes and add them to the vinaigrette. Season to taste with the horseradish. Leave the vinaigrette to stand for 5 minutes so that the flavour of the horseradish really develops.

To shuck the oysters, hold an oyster cupped side down firmly in one hand with a tea towel. Insert the tip of an oyster knife close to the hinge between the 'lid' and bottom shell and then twist the knife to prise the shells open, keeping the oyster level to prevent the juices from spilling out. Check them for stray pieces of shell and make sure they are nice and fresh (an oyster should smell fresh from the sea and have lots of lovely juice in the shell; if there is any doubt about the freshness, the oyster must be discarded).

Pour a little vinaigrette over each oyster and serve immediately.

Lumpfish roe
with blinis, red onion and soured cream

Blinis
400ml semi-skimmed milk
15g fresh yeast
½ organic egg
½ teaspoon fine salt
180g buckwheat flour
180g plain flour
1–2 tablespoons butter, for frying

Accompaniments
300g fresh lumpfish roe
   (uncleaned weight)
sea salt flakes and freshly ground pepper
1 red onion
1 organic lemon
200ml soured cream, 18% fat

Warm the milk to around 37°C – there is no need for a thermometer, just bring it to the warmest point your little finger can bear – and pour some of it into a bowl, then dissolve the yeast in it. Add the egg, salt and both kinds of flour, then mix in the rest of the milk and whisk into a smooth batter. Leave the batter in the kitchen to rise for about 1 hour.

Fry the batter in a little butter in a special blini pan for 1–2 minutes on each side until golden, to make small, thick pancakes. If you don't own a blini pan, use an ordinary small frying pan. Keep the cooked blinis warm in a dish covered with foil while you cook the rest.

Clean the lumpfish roe (see page 188) and season with a little salt and pepper. Peel the onion and chop finely, and cut the lemon into wedges. Serve the warm blinis straight away with the lumpfish roe, chopped red onion, soured cream and lemon wedges.

Fried tartare of cod
with beetroot, smoked bacon and horseradish cream

150g beetroot, about 2
50ml plum vinegar
1 tablespoon unrefined cane sugar
1 tablespoon olive oil
200g very fresh skinless cod fillet
sea salt flakes and freshly ground pepper
8 thin slices of smoked bacon
a few beetroot leaves or other bitter
   salad leaves

Wash the beetroot, put them in a saucepan of water and bring them to the boil, then simmer for about 20–30 minutes until tender but still al dente. Drain the cooked beetroot, submerge in cold water to cool a little and then slip the skins off to expose the silky interior – you can wear plastic gloves if you don't want your hands to be stained red.

Cut the beetroot into large cubes and place them in a saucepan with the vinegar, sugar and oil. Boil until the beets have absorbed the vinegar, and they are glazed and the marinade has the consistency of syrup.

Check that there are no stray bones left in the cod fillet and that the fish is really nice and fresh, smelling of the sea, not of the harbour. Cut the fillet into very small cubes – use a sharp knife so that the flesh is cut cleanly and not mashed. Put the cod in a bowl, season with salt and pepper and mix well. Form into 4 small patties and place them in the refrigerator for 10 minutes so that they firm up before frying.

Heat up a frying pan and fry the thin slices of bacon until they are crispy and starting to curl a little. Take the bacon out of the pan and place on kitchen paper.

Pour off the excess fat from the pan and then fry the tartare patties for about 30 seconds on one side only – that way, they get a beautiful crust while still remaining

raw. Serve the patties with the warm, glazed beetroot, the crispy bacon, a small salad and freshly grated Horseradish Cream (see below).

I love the classic Danish dish of boiled cod with the works – pickled beets, bacon, grated horseradish, fish mustard and butter sauce – and this starter is my modern take on that ever-good combination.

Horseradish cream

100ml semi-skimmed milk
sugar, to taste
sea salt flakes and freshly ground pepper
finely grated zest and juice of
   ½ organic lemon
freshly grated horseradish, to taste

Heat the milk up in a saucepan and season to taste with sugar, salt, pepper and the lemon zest and juice.

Remove the pan from the heat and season with as much freshly grated horseradish as you would like. Personally, I like it so that it tingles a little up the nose.

Pour the horseradish milk into a bowl and place it in the freezer for a few hours until completely frozen. Scrape the ice with a spoon to form a fine horseradish powder and use immediately as a garnish.

Salted halibut
with squash purée and chervil dressing

200g very fresh skinless halibut fillet
1 tablespoon sea salt flakes
1 teaspoon sugar
freshly ground pepper

Squash purée
1 butternut squash
25g butter
50ml cider vinegar, plus extra if needed
sea salt flakes and freshly ground pepper
1 tablespoon acacia honey

Chervil dressing

1 shallot
3 tablespoons cider vinegar
3 tablespoons cold-pressed rapeseed oil
1 teaspoon acacia honey
sea salt flakes and freshly ground pepper
1 handful of chervil

Day 1

Check the halibut for any remaining bones and mucus. Put it in a dish and sprinkle with the salt, sugar and some pepper. Cover the dish with clingfilm and leave to marinate in the refrigerator for 12 hours before serving.

Day 2

For the squash purée, peel and halve the squash, then scrape out the seeds with a spoon. Cut it into large cubes, saving a small piece for the chervil dressing. Put the rest of the squash cubes in a pan, cover with water and bring to the boil, then simmer for about 20 minutes until tender. Drain and place in a blender along with the remaining ingredients for the purée, then blend until you have a completely smooth purée.

For the chervil dressing, peel the shallot and chop it very finely. Dice the reserved piece of squash. Put both vegetables in a bowl and toss in the vinegar, oil, honey, salt and pepper. Chop the chervil roughly and add it to the dressing.

Pour the squash purée into a pan, heat it up and, if necessary, season with a little extra vinegar, salt and pepper.

Take the halibut out of the refrigerator, cut it into very thin slices and serve with the warm squash purée and the chervil dressing on top as a nice starter.

• •

TIP Make some extra squash purée (about half the quantity or so), put it in the refrigerator and save it for the Bruschetta with Squash Purée and Goats' Cheese (see page 224).

• •

Terrine of wild boar
with squash chutney

SERVES 6–8

1kg shoulder of wild boar, boned and skinned (you can also use pork shoulder)
1 tablespoon olive oil
2 carrots
2 onions
sea salt flakes and freshly ground pepper
2 garlic cloves, peeled
5 thyme sprigs
600ml dark Danish beer
100ml cider vinegar, plus extra if needed
1.5 litres chicken stock

Cut the shoulder into small pieces and brown in the olive oil in a large cast-iron pan. Peel and cut the carrots and onions into chunks, add them to the pan and season with salt and pepper. Sauté until they start to brown as well.

Add the garlic, thyme, beer, vinegar and stock, and bring the stew to the boil, then simmer with a lid on either on the hob over a low heat or in a preheated oven at 150°C/Gas Mark 2 for 1–1½ hours until the meat is very tender.

Fish the meat out of the pan and cook the broth with the vegetables on the hob to reduce to a third of its volume. Put the meat back into the broth and mash the stew lightly using a whisk so that the broth, meat and vegetables combine to a soft and rustic consistency. Season with salt, pepper and, if necessary, a little extra vinegar.

Transfer the stew to a terrine mould, cover with a piece of baking paper and add a little weight on top, such as an unopened milk carton and maybe a chopping board on top of that. Put the terrine in the refrigerator for 4–6 hours to set before slicing it. Serve the terrine with Squash Chutney (see right), some bitter salad leaves (frisée, chicory or radicchio) and bread.

Squash chutney

MAKES 2 MEDIUM JARS

1.5kg winter squash, such as Hokkaido or butternut
500g red onions
500g apples
650g unrefined cane sugar
500ml cider vinegar
2 tablespoons coarse sea salt
2 tablespoons coriander seeds
2 tablespoons fennel seeds
5 cardamom pods
2 whole red chillies
50g fresh root ginger, peeled and sliced
2 garlic cloves, peeled and finely chopped
200g raisins

Peel and halve the squash, then scrape out the seeds with a spoon. Peel the red onions. Wash and core the apples, leaving the peel on. Then cut the squash, onions and apples into large cubes.

Put the vegetable and apple cubes in a saucepan with all the remaining ingredients, except the raisins. Simmer over a low heat, with the lid on, for 30–40 minutes until you have a dense compote, but don't cook the vegetables to the point of collapse. Remember to stir the chutney a few times while it cooks so that it doesn't burn.

Finally, stir in the raisins and then pour the chutney into sterilized preserving jars.

In my family, we often serve the squash chutney with meatballs or cold meat from the day before, and we also frequently use it in sandwiches. The chutney will keep fresh in the refrigerator for 4–5 months unopened, and 3–4 weeks after you have opened it.

Christmas terrine
with pickled beetroot

SERVES 12–14

500g pigs' liver
200g duck liver
300g duck meat, such as duck breast
400g fresh or frozen hard pork back fat
2 apples, cored and cut into wedges
10 pitted prunes
1 onion, peeled
3 teaspoons ground allspice
2 teaspoons ground cloves
2 tablespoons Christmas aquavit
4 organic eggs
200ml semi-skimmed milk
5 tablespoons plain flour
sea salt flakes and freshly ground pepper
butter, for greasing

Run the livers, duck meat, pork back fat, apples, prunes and onion through a meat mincer into a bowl. The sweetness of the fruits goes really well with the liver.

Add the spices, aquavit, eggs and milk to the minced mixture and mix to a soft consistency. Add the flour towards the end of mixing, and mix it in gently. Season with salt and pepper. I always taste the raw pâté mixture at this stage to check it for seasoning, but if that's a bit too challenging for your stomach, bake a small sample in the oven.

Divide the mixture between 12–14 small buttered ramekins or individual foil trays. Bake the terrines in a bain-marie – stand the dishes in a shallow baking tin and pour boiling water from a kettle into the tin to come halfway up the sides of the dishes – in a preheated oven at 160°C/Gas Mark 3 for 35–40 minutes until they have set and are golden on top.

Serve on good rye bread with pickled beetroot as an accompaniment (*see* right). The baked terrines will stay fresh for 4–5 days in the refrigerator.

Tip When making quite a large quantity of pâté, as in this recipe, you can freeze some of the uncooked mixture directly in the dishes and then bake fresh terrines for any occasion. Take the dishes out of the freezer a few hours before you need to bake them so that the mixture can defrost, then bake as described in the recipe.

Two kinds of pickled beetroot

Here are my recipes for two ways of pickling beetroot – the first one is slightly spicy, and the other fruity, fresh and slightly less sweet. Whichever you choose, you will end up with some very lovely pickled beets, excellent as an accompaniment to liver pâtés, cold cooked and cured meats, ham and sausages, among others.

Pickled beets with orange, chilli and cinnamon
MAKES 3 MEDIUM JARS

2kg beetroot
sea salt flakes

Pickling brine
1 litre water
1 litre cider vinegar
650g unrefined cane sugar
1 red chilli
pared strips of zest and juice
    of 1 organic orange
1 cinnamon stick
3 star anise
10 whole black peppercorns
15 fennel seeds
1 small handful of coarse sea salt

Wash the beetroot free of soil and place them in a saucepan of salted water. Bring to the boil and skim off any foam and impurities, then simmer for 20–30 minutes, depending on their size, until just tender when pierced with a small knife – be careful not to overcook them. It is therefore important that the beetroot are all are about the same size so that their cooking time is the same. If they are not evenly sized, you will need to adjust their cooking time to ensure that even the smallest still have some bite to them.

Drain the cooked beetroots and rinse them under the cold tap, then slip their skins off – you can wear plastic gloves if you want to avoid staining your hands red. When the beetroot have cooled, put them in sterilized preserving jars.

Put all the ingredients for the pickling brine in a saucepan and bring to the boil. Take the brine off the heat and leave it to stand for 10 minutes in the kitchen. Then pour the still-hot pickling brine over the beetroot, seal the jars tightly and leave them to pickle in the refrigerator for a minimum of 3 days before you eat them. The beets can be kept, unopened, for 6 months in the refrigerator and almost get better with time. Use within 3 months of opening

Pickled beetroot with blackcurrant and anise
MAKES 2 MEDIUM JARS

2kg beetroot
sea salt flakes

Pickling brine
900ml cider vinegar
500ml water
15g coarse sea salt
400g sugar
4 star anise
50ml blackcurrant concentrate or cordial
6 lightly crushed black peppercorns
6cm piece of fresh horseradish root,
    peeled and sliced

Follow the first 3 steps of the previous recipe to prepare, cook and skin the beetroot, then put in sterilized preserving jars.

Put all the ingredients for the pickling brine, except for the horseradish, in a saucepan and bring to the boil. Take the brine off the heat and then add the horseradish slices – if the horseradish is boiled, it becomes bitter and can give the brine an unpleasant aftertaste. Pour the still-hot pickling brine over the beetroot, seal and store as above.

Meat

My mother-in-law's glazed ham
with stewed kale

SERVES 12–14

3kg lightly salt-cured smoked boneless gammon joint in netting (order from your butcher's)
4 tablespoons Homemade Christmas Mustard (*see* right, or buy some good-quality mustard)
4 tablespoons brown sugar
finely grated zest and juice of 1 organic orange
1 teaspoon crushed star anise

Wrap the gammon in foil nice and tightly – you will need a few layers so that the ham is completely covered. Place the gammon on an oven or roasting rack with a roasting tin filled with water underneath. Roast the gammon in a preheated oven at 160°C/ Gas Mark 3 for 2–2½ hours until it is quite firm and cooked through while juicy on the inside. If you own a meat thermometer, you can check the core temperature of the meat, which should be about 65°C.

Take the ham out of the oven and leave it to rest for 30 minutes in the foil. Meanwhile, combine the mustard, sugar, orange zest and juice and crushed star anise.

Unwrap the ham, remove the netting and score a criss-cross pattern in the fat with a sharp knife. Spread the glaze on to the scored side of the ham – the pattern will help it stick to the meat. Then put the ham back in the oven at 190°C/Gas Mark 5 for 8–10 minutes until the glaze is completely crisp and golden on top.

Remove the ham from the oven and serve it immediately with Stewed Kale (*see* right) and boiled potatoes. Homemade Christmas Mustard should also be on the table (*see* right).

TIP You can cook the ham the day before you need it and then glaze it just before serving. There is a lot of meat in a ham and it may be too much for certain occasions. If that is the case, you can just use a *kassler* (lightly salt-cured smoked loin of pork) or a saddle of pork instead of a whole ham and follow the instructions left.

Homemade Christmas mustard
MAKES 1 SMALL JAR

3 tablespoons yellow mustard seeds
3 tablespoons black mustard seeds
6 tablespoons water
6 tablespoons cider vinegar
4–5 tablespoons brown sugar
1 teaspoon sea salt flakes

Roast the mustard seeds lightly in a dry pan until they begin to pop. Pour them into a mortar and grind them to a fine powder with a pestle (you can also use an electric coffee grinder, which you should only use for grinding spices so that they don't taste of coffee).

Pour the ground mustard into a bowl and add the measured water, little by little, while stirring constantly. Add the vinegar and season to taste with the brown sugar and salt.

Pour the mustard into a small sterilized glass jar and leave it in the refrigerator for 1–2 days for the flavours to combine well before using it. The mustard will keep fresh for several months in the refrigerator and will only taste better with time. Use within 6 months of opening.

TIP You can vary the flavour of the mustard by adding Christmas spices like star anise, cinnamon and cloves.

Stewed kale

250g curly kale, stalks removed
sea salt flakes
30g butter
30g plain flour
750ml semi-skimmed milk
2–3 gratings of fresh nutmeg
1 teaspoon sugar
2–3 tablespoons cider vinegar

Check the kale for any bits of stalk and discard, wash it thoroughly in cold water and leave in a colander to drain.

Blanch the kale in a large pan of salted boiling water for 3–4 minutes and then immediately plunge it into a bowl of cold water. Now press all the liquid out of the kale and chop it roughly.

Melt the butter in a saucepan, whisk in the flour and cook to make a smooth roux. Add the milk, a little at a time, while stirring vigorously until you have added it all and the sauce is smooth and lump free. Simmer the sauce until all the flour taste is cooked out and the sauce is completely smooth and supple.

Add the chopped, blanched kale to the sauce and let it stew for a while. Season with 1 teaspoon salt, the nutmeg, sugar and vinegar to taste, and serve immediately.

Pigs' cheeks

1kg pigs' cheeks
2 tablespoons standard rapeseed oil
1 carrot
1 onion
1 garlic clove
5 thyme sprigs
200ml dark beer (ale or porter)
400ml apple juice
100ml cider vinegar, plus 2 tablespoons
sea salt flakes and freshly ground pepper
500ml chicken or beef stock
800g potatoes
300g Brussels sprouts
50g cold butter, cut into cubes
1 handful of flat leaf parsley or chervil
20g whole almonds
¼ preserved lemon from the 'Burnt'
    Leeks and Lemon in Oil (*see* page 166)

Start by removing the tendons from the pigs' cheeks. Put the cheeks on your chopping board with the tendon facing down so that it lies flat against the board. Take a long, sharp knife and cut a small incision in the jaw just where the tendon is. Grip the tendon and then let the knife slide down the tendon so that it comes off in one long, clean cut. It is not easy the first few times, but let it take the time it takes. The key is not to carve off too much meat while cutting off the tendon. You may want to get your butcher to do the work for you (and the butcher may already have removed the tendons as a matter of course).

Brown the cheeks in the oil in a large cast-iron pan so that they are golden on all sides.

Peel the carrot, onion and garlic clove, then chop everything into large chunks, throw them into the pan and let them brown with the meat. Lastly, add the thyme sprigs, beer, apple juice, the 100ml vinegar, salt and pepper, bring to the boil and cook until reduced by half. Then add the stock, bring to the boil and skim off any foam and impurities. Cover the pan with a lid and place in a preheated oven at 150°C/Gas Mark 2 to braise for 1½–2 hours.

While the cheeks are braising, peel the potatoes, cut them into large cubes and bring them to the boil in a saucepan of lightly salted water. Rinse the Brussels sprouts and remove the outer leaves, reserving the nicest ones for the garnish. Cut the rest into quarters and add them to the pan with the potatoes after they have cooked for 10 minutes. Cook the sprouts and potatoes together for a further 5 minutes until both are tender. Drain and add 40g of the cold butter along with salt and pepper until the compote is seasoned to perfection.

When the cheeks are done, remove the pan from the oven and strain the broth into another pan, discarding the vegetables, as they have done their job, and leaving the cheeks in the cast-iron pan. Reduce the broth by half so that it is a beautiful, slightly sticky consistency with a shiny surface. Season to taste with the remaining butter, salt and the remaining 2 tablespoons vinegar. When the sauce is flavoured as desired, add the cheeks and heat them up.

Finally, make a quick salad of the reserved sprout leaves and parsley or chervil. Roast the almonds in a dry pan until they take on some colour, then chop them roughly and mix them into the sprout salad. Cut the preserved lemon into small pieces and add it to the delicious salad, then dress this fresh bowl of goodness with a little oil from the preserved lemon. Serve the compote accompanied by a few pieces of cheek with a little sauce on top. Finish off with a handful of the salad and serve immediately.

Beetroot tartare
with horseradish and cold veal rump

500g beetroot
2 tablespoons cherry vinegar
sea salt flakes and freshly ground pepper
1 red onion
1 apple
1½ tablespoons prepared coarsely
    ground mustard
1 tablespoon olive oil
2 tablespoons freshly grated
    horseradish
1 tablespoon honey
½ handful of chervil, chopped
200g cold Roasted Veal Rump
    (*see* page 138), thinly sliced

Peel 100g of the beetroot and cut it into very small cubes. Put the beetroot cubes in a bowl and marinate them in the vinegar seasoned with salt and pepper.

Cook the rest of the beetroot in a pan of boiling water for 40–45 minutes until soft. Drain the cooked beetroot, submerge in cold water and slip them out of their skins – you can wear plastic gloves if you don't want your hands to be stained red, but then you will miss the lovely feeling of the silky beetroot slipping between your hands.

Peel the red onion and chop it very finely. Core the apple and cut it into tiny cubes. Then cut the cooked beetroots into very small cubes as well and toss them with red onion, apple, mustard and olive oil in a bowl. Add the raw marinated beetroot to taste along with the freshly grated horseradish, salt, pepper, honey and chopped chervil.

The beetroot tartare should be fresh, sweet, spicy and also have a hot element thanks to the horseradish and mustard. Serve the thin slices of roasted veal rump with the beetroot tartare. The tartare also goes well with smoked or Gravad Salmon (*see* page 190) or with hot-smoked salmon, meatballs (*see* pages 26, 137, 186 and 200) or meat patties (*see* pages 76 and 142). It is one of the few salads I know that goes with almost anything.

. . . .

Tip The beetroot tartare is great for practising your seasoning skills. If you season it just a little, it is almost like a salad, but if you season it quite a bit, the tartare almost tastes like a pickle – both of which can be really nice with the meat.

. . . .

Lamb rump

with celeriac and apple compote and 'stamped' potatoes

2 lamb rumps, about 350–400g each
sea salt flakes and freshly ground pepper
5 thyme sprigs
2 garlic cloves, crushed

Cut the largest sinews and most of the fat away from the lamb rumps. Score the remaining fat with a sharp knife.

Heat a dry frying pan and fry the rumps on all sides until brown, starting with the fatty side so that enough of it renders to fry the other sides in. Transfer the rumps to an ovenproof dish and season with salt, pepper, the thyme and crushed garlic. Cook the rumps in a preheated oven at 180°C/Gas Mark 4 for 10–12 minutes so that they are slightly pink in the middle.

Leave the rumps to rest uncovered for 3–4 minutes before cutting them into slices. Serve with the Celeriac and Apple Compote and 'Stamped' Potatoes (see below) or cooked grains or rice.

Celeriac and apple compote

1 celeriac, peeled and cut into 1cm cubes
sea salt flakes and freshly ground pepper
4 tablespoons cider vinegar, plus extra to taste
4 tablespoons olive oil
2 apples
2 onions
1 garlic clove
2 tablespoons curry powder
1cm piece of fresh root ginger, peeled and thinly sliced
100ml apple juice
100ml whipping cream
4 celery sticks

Put the celeriac cubes into an ovenproof dish and season with salt, pepper, 2 tablespoons of the vinegar and 2 tablespoons of the olive oil. Bake in a preheated oven at 180°C/Gas Mark 4 for 5–7 minutes or until softened but al dente.

Peel and core the apples, and peel the onions and garlic, then roughly chop them all and put in a pan with the remaining 2 tablespoons of olive oil. Sauté for a couple of minutes, then add the curry powder and ginger and sauté for a further 2 minutes. Add the apple juice and the remaining 2 tablespoons vinegar and bring to the boil, then add the cream. Let the delicious mixture simmer for 10 minutes over a low heat.

Use a stick blender to blend the mixture into a chunky compote. Add the baked celeriac cubes as well as salt, pepper and vinegar to taste – it might need an extra touch of acidity.

Rinse and finely chop the celery, then add it to the compote shortly before serving with the lamb so that it stays crisp. This compote is also good with chicken or pork chops.

'Stamped' potatoes

1kg small potatoes
sea salt flakes
20g butter
1 tablespoon prepared coarsely ground mustard
finely grated zest of ½ organic lemon
freshly ground pepper

Rinse the potatoes thoroughly, add them to a pan of salted water and bring to the boil, then simmer for 12–14 minutes. Turn off the heat and leave the potatoes to sit in the hot water for a further 5–7 minutes. Drain the potatoes and leave in the pan for a minute or so for the steam to rise. Roughly mash with a whisk and add the butter, mustard, lemon zest and salt and pepper to taste.

Firmly press the mashed potatoes into 4 small bowls, then turn them out on to a baking tray lined with baking paper. Place the tray in a preheated oven at 220°C/Gas Mark 7 for 10–15 minutes or until they are crisp and golden. Serve the 'stamped' potatoes with the lamb, or whatever you like – they go well with almost anything.

Meatballs in celeriac sauce

SERVES 6

2 slices of wheat bread, crusts removed
300ml semi-skimmed milk
500g mixed minced veal and pork, 5–7% fat
sea salt flakes and freshly ground pepper
2 organic eggs

Sauce
1 litre water or light stock (chicken or veal)
1 tablespoon sea salt flakes
3 bay leaves
1 celeriac
1 tablespoon cornflour mixed with a little cold water
50ml whipping cream
freshly ground pepper
juice of ½ lemon
a little sugar, if needed
1 handful of flat leaf parsley, chopped

Soak the bread in the milk for about 10–15 minutes.

Put the minced meat in a bowl with salt, pepper, the eggs and soaked bread and mix together to make a smooth meat mixture. It is a good idea to mix it for quite a while, as that will make it extra juicy when cooked. Leave the mixture in the refrigerator for 15–20 minutes before making the meatballs.

To make the sauce, bring the measured water or stock to the boil in a saucepan and add the salt and bay leaves. When the water reaches boiling point, start forming the meat mixture into meatballs using a spoon. Submerge the balls in the broth, a few at a time, and poach them over a very low heat for 4–5 minutes until they become firm and start floating to the surface. Lift the cooked meatballs out and put them in a bowl. Continue until you have used up all the meat mixture.

Peel the celeriac and cut it into 1cm cubes, then cook in the broth for about 3–4 minutes until tender. Strain the broth into another saucepan and simmer for 5 minutes, then add the cornflour paste and simmer for another few minutes. Add the cream and cook the sauce for a further 4–5 minutes. Season with salt, pepper, the lemon juice and possibly a little sugar to taste.

Add the meatballs and celeriac to the sauce and let everything cook together to thoroughly combine all the flavours. Finally, sprinkle the chopped parsley on top and serve with rice, boiled potatoes or grains.

Roast pork
with crispy skin and gravy

800g loin of pork on the bone, skin on
coarse sea salt
10–15 bay leaves
600–700ml water
2 tablespoons plain flour
1–2 tablespoons Apple Gastrique
   (see page 10)
sea salt flakes and freshly ground pepper

Check that the skin is scored all the way down into the meat – if not, you will just have to do it yourself by taking a sharp kitchen or utility knife and scoring the skin at 5mm intervals. Wet your hand and rub the skin side of the loin with plenty of coarse salt. This makes the salt stick better, and the salt starts 'cooking' the skin before the meat even reaches the oven so that it ends up nice and crisp. Insert the bay leaves into the cuts. Place the loin, skin side up, on an oven or roasting rack with a roasting tin containing the measured water underneath.

Roast the pork in a preheated oven at 180°C/Gas Mark 4 for 1 hour 5 minutes– 1 hour 10 minutes.

Halfway through the cooking time, pour the liquid from the roasting tin into a saucepan for making the gravy; if you wait until the very end, there will be too much steam in the oven and the skin will end up not being properly crispy. Leave the liquid to stand

for a while and then skim off most of the fat from the surface. Bring it to the boil and reduce it to about 400–500ml.

Turn off the heat and again leave the liquid to stand until the fat settles on top. Sprinkle with the flour and let the fat absorb it. Then whisk vigorously and bring the gravy back to the boil. This way the gravy will come together nicely and the fat will also give it a little extra body (beware not to leave too much fat in the gravy).

Simmer the gravy for 6–7 minutes and then season to taste with Apple Gastrique, salt and pepper. Strain the gravy if necessary.

Check the core temperature of the roast with a meat thermometer, which should be around 65°C when it is time to take the roast out of the oven – this will give you a pale pink and juicy pork loin (if the core temperature is higher than 65°C, the meat may well be dry). Leave the meat to rest for at least 15 minutes before slicing it up. Serve with boiled potatoes, Warm Red Cabbage (see page 201) and the delicious gravy.

Tip Roast an extra 800g of meat and save until the following day to make a delightful roast pork sandwich – see page 222 for the recipe for the sandwich we sell in Meyers Deli. Also make sure that you have some extra cabbage for the sandwich.

Warm red cabbage
SERVES 10–12

1 red cabbage
juice of 2 organic oranges
1 cinnamon stick
3 star anise
4 bay leaves
120g caster sugar
300ml concentrated cherry juice
200ml cherry vinegar
400ml red wine
1 tablespoon sea salt flakes

Cut the red cabbage into quarters and cut out and discard the stalk. Slice the cabbage finely and place in a large saucepan with the remaining ingredients and stir over a high heat. Bring to the boil, then reduce the heat and let the cabbage simmer, covered, for 1–1½ hours, stirring occasionally. The liquid should all be absorbed, to result in a blank and clear appearance.

Crispy pork skin

There have been several techniques through the years for getting your pork skin crispy. Some pour water into the roasting tin and then put the rind face down in the water for the first 15 minutes so that it is cooked first, before turning the roast back rind side up for the rest of the cooking, so that it ends up nice and crispy. I have found that you need to drain the liquid from the roasting tin halfway through the cooking, otherwise too much steam is formed for the skin to become properly crisp. When I roast pork, I keep the meat on the bone because it gives extra flavour and intensity to both the meat and gravy.

I rub the pork skin with a damp hand and plenty of coarse sea salt, then pour a small amount of water into the roasting tin to collect the juices, which I later use as the base for the gravy. I then pour off the juices into a pan halfway through the roasting time so there is not too much moisture in the oven and the skin can get nice and crisp. I roast the pork joint for 1 hour 5 minutes–1 hour 10 minutes in a preheated oven at 180°C/Gas Mark 4, and this way my roast turns out perfectly each time. And no cooking with the oven door open at the end, i.e. using the grill function – you will just end up burning the skin.

Pork braised in milk, garlic and rosemary

SERVES 6

1kg boneless pork neck joint
1 tablespoon olive oil
sea salt flakes and freshly ground pepper
1 whole garlic bulb
½–1 organic lemon, plus extra lemon
    juice to season
3 rosemary sprigs
5 bay leaves
10 whole black peppercorns
1.5 litres full-fat milk

Brown the pork neck well on all sides in the oil in a frying pan, then season with salt and pepper and add the garlic bulb (leave intact with the skin on, but cut it in half), the lemon, cut into quarters, rosemary sprigs, bay leaves and peppercorns. Leave it all to sauté lightly before adding the milk. Once the milk reaches the boil, lower the heat and simmer for 1½–2 hours with the lid halfway on so that the milk can evaporate and the sauce is lightly browned. Turn the meat around a few times during braising.

When the pork is done, lift it out of the sauce, cut it into slices and serve with White Barley Risotto (see page 147) or mashed potatoes and the lovely sauce seasoned with a little extra lemon juice, salt and pepper.

• •

TIP You can also milk braise veal rump or neck – just make sure that the meat is marbled with fat so that it doesn't become too dry.

• •

Pork ribs
with apple mostarda

800g lightly salt-cured pork ribs (see tip)
1.5 litres water
1 bouquet garni, consisting of thyme
    sprigs, bay leaves and parsley stems
sea salt flakes and freshly ground pepper
Apple Mostarda (see right)

Put the pork ribs in a large pan along with the measured water, bouquet garni and some salt. Bring to the boil and skim off the foam and any impurities, then simmer for about 40 minutes.

Take the pan off the heat and leave to cool slightly before placing in the refrigerator and leaving the meat to cool completely in the broth. For practical reasons, I usually do this part of the preparation the day before.

Lift the cold pork ribs out and season the broth with salt and pepper. Leave the ribs to marinate in half the quantity of Apple Mostarda for 30 minutes in the kitchen.

Cook the ribs under the grill of the oven preheated to 220°C/Gas Mark 7 for 15–20 minutes so that they are beautifully caramelized and crispy.

Serve the grilled pork ribs straight from the grill with the Crudité of Swede with Wild Garlic and Apple (see right), the remaining fresh Apple Mostarda and good bread.

Apple Mostarda

6 red apples
2–3 tablespoons water
3–4 tablespoons cider vinegar
2 tablespoons brown sugar
2 tablespoons prepared mustard
sea salt flakes

Wash the apples and cut them into quarters, then put them straight into a pan with the measured water, without removing the skin or cores. Steam them, with the lid, on for about 7–8 minutes until they start to form a compote but some whole pieces still remain.

Pour the tender apples into a blender or food processor and blend well, then pour them through a sieve to remove the cores and seeds. Season with the vinegar, brown sugar and mustard so that there is a good balance between sour, sweet and 'hot'. Then season ever so slightly with salt.

The first time I came by mustard pickled fruit was many years ago in Italy, but

since then I have found out that we also used to pickle with mustard in medieval Scandinavia. This apple mostarda is my version of a medieval apple sauce. In addition to using it for barbecues and for dishes with white meat, it is a lovely accompaniment to cheese and smoked meats, as well as in a sandwich or in place of butter on a slice of rye bread with cold cuts, like Danish rolled sausage.

• •

TIP You can order lightly salt-cured pork ribs from the butcher, or you can do the salting yourself. If so, sprinkle the ribs with 2 tablespoons coarse sea salt in a dish, cover the dish with clingfilm and place in the refrigerator for 12 hours so that they are ready to be cooked the next day. Remember to brush the excess salt off first if necessary.

• •

Crudité of swede

½ swede
2 red apples
2 wild garlic leaves (or equivalent
    quantity of lovage), chopped
1 small garlic clove, peeled
1 tablespoon cold-pressed rapeseed oil,
    plus extra to season
2 tablespoons cider vinegar, plus extra
    to season
sea salt flakes and freshly ground pepper

Peel the swede and cut or grate it into matchstick-thin strips about 4cm long. Wash in cold water and leave to drain in a colander.

Peel the apples, cut them into quarters and remove the cores. Cut into small cubes and then mash them into a creamy dressing with the chopped wild garlic, garlic and oil using a pestle and mortar. Adjust the consistency and flavour with the vinegar, and season to taste with salt and pepper.

Toss the swede in the dressing and season with some more vinegar, oil, salt and pepper.

Pork braised in milk, garlic and rosemary »

Hotpot
with veal, liquorice root and beer

SERVES 6

1kg veal blade or brisket
sea salt flakes and freshly ground pepper
2 onions
2 carrots
2 garlic cloves
2 celery sticks
25g plain flour
1 tablespoon standard rapeseed oil
¼ red chilli, deseeded
5 bay leaves
4 rosemary sprigs
1 liquorice root
100ml cider vinegar, plus extra to taste
100g prunes, pitted
100g dried apricots
500ml dark ale (I use Gl. Carlsberg Porter)
1 litre thin veal stock or water

Inspect the veal and cut away the sinews and fat, then cut it into 4–6 big pieces. Season with salt and pepper and leave to rest at room temperature for an hour. I don't always have enough time to let the meat rest that long, but it is absolutely fine just to leave it while preparing the vegetables.

Peel the onions, carrots and garlic, and rinse the celery, then dice them all roughly. Dust the meat with the flour. Heat the oil in a deep ovenproof pan or casserole and fry the meat until browned on all sides. Then add the vegetables and sauté them with the meat for a couple of minutes. Add the chilli, herbs, liquorice root and vinegar and leave to soak into the meat for a few minutes before adding the dried fruit. Now add the beer and stock or water, bring to the boil and skim off any foam (impurities) that rises to the surface.

Cover the pan with a lid and put in a preheated oven at 150°C/Gas Mark 2. Leave the meat to braise for 2–3 hours until it is so tender that it just about falls apart.

Take the pan out of the oven, strain the liquid into a pan and reduce to a sauce consistency. Season with additional vinegar, salt and pepper if needed. Pour the sauce back into the meat pan and mix well but carefully so that the tender meat and vegetables don't fall apart completely. Serve the hotpot with cooked grains, mashed potatoes or some good bread and a green salad.

....

TIP I often make this hotpot with boneless leg of goat or beef cheek – both are surprisingly delicious given this beer, liquorice and dried fruit treatment.
....

Pan-fried veal liver
with compote of apples and onions

Compote
3 onions
15g butter
3 thyme sprigs
sea salt flakes and freshly ground pepper
2 apples
a little cider vinegar

Liver
600g veal liver
plain flour, for dusting
sea salt flakes and freshly ground pepper
10g butter, for frying
2 teaspoons standard rapeseed oil

For the compote, peel and chop the onions finely, then put them in a cold pan with the butter and thyme sprigs. Sauté the onions lightly and season with salt and pepper as they begin to brown. Wash the apples, cut them into quarters and remove the cores, then cut them into large cubes. Add the apples to the pan, mix well and sauté until they have softened slightly but are still al dente. Season the compote with vinegar, salt and pepper until there is a good balance between acidity and sweetness.

Remove any outer membrane or tendons from the liver and cut into slices about 2cm thick. Dust the liver slices with flour, season with salt and pepper and fry in the butter and oil in a large frying pan for about 1 minute on each side. Don't fry the liver until just before serving so that it is piping hot and delicious (liver should not be reheated, as it will become very dry). Serve the liver on rye bread with the warm compote on top and a nice cold pilsner in your other hand.

WATERCRESS
These crisp, dark, peppery leaves can often be found in winter growing in warm streams and channels.

Veal chops and pearled spelt salad
with apples and parsley

**4 bone-in veal chops with fat,
250–300g each
1 tablespoon standard rapeseed oil
sea salt flakes and freshly ground pepper**

Scrape the chops with a knife to remove any bone fragments, and score the fat a few times so that it doesn't contract too much when fried. Rub the chops with the rapeseed oil and season with salt and pepper.

Brown the chops in a hot frying pan for about 1 minute on each side so that they get a beautiful golden crust.

Transfer the chops to an oven or roasting rack with a roasting tin underneath to collect any fat and juices and cook in a preheated oven at 180°C/Gas Mark 4 for 7–8 minutes. By then they will be done but still pink and juicy around the bone.

Take the chops out of the oven and serve them with the Pearled Spelt Salad with Apples and Parsley (see below) and, if you wish, some herb butter and a green salad.

Pearled spelt salad with apples and parsley

**80g pearl barley or pearled spelt
sea salt flakes
600ml boiling water
2 tablespoons cider vinegar, plus extra
    if needed
2 tablespoons cold-pressed rapeseed oil
freshly ground pepper
1 tablespoon honey
1 parsley root
1 red onion
2 apples
1 handful of flat leaf parsley**

Rinse the pearled spelt in cold water. Put it into a pan with the lightly salted measured boiling water and boil, with the lid on, for

20 minutes – it should be soft but still have some bite.

Take the pan off the heat and leave to stand, still with the lid on, for 5–10 minutes. Drain off any excess water and season the grains with the vinegar, oil, salt and pepper to taste and the honey while still warm, as they will absorb the flavours better.

Peel the parsley root and onion, and wash and core the apples. Cut the vegetables into very small cubes and mix them with the pearled spelt. Chop the parsley roughly and mix it into the salad. Mix well and if necessary season with additional salt, pepper and vinegar.

Eat the salad with the fried veal chops. It is also a great accessory to meatballs, good sausages or other fried food that could use a little edge and acidity.

Roasted duck
with prunes, baked apples and gravy

SERVES 6

**1 duck, about 3–3.5kg
sea salt flakes
1kg apples, such as Cox or Belle de Boskoop
500g whole pitted prunes
4 thyme sprigs, chopped
freshly ground pepper
40g plain flour
1.5 litres water
a little cider vinegar or other
    light fruit vinegar
a little sugar or Apple Gastrique
    (see page 10)**

Wipe both the cavity and outside of the duck with kitchen paper and then rub both with salt. Wash the apples, cut them into quarters and remove the cores, then cut them into large cubes. Mix with the prunes, chopped thyme, salt and pepper. Stuff the duck with the fruit mixture – it is important that you stuff it as full as possible, as the

filling helps to retain the juices and thereby prevent the meat from becoming dry. Tie the thighs tightly up against the breast with kitchen string, which will help to keep the breast fillets nice and juicy as well.

Place the bird, breast side up, on an oven or roasting rack with a roasting tin containing the duck's neck, wing tips and giblets underneath. Brown in a preheated oven at 250°C/Gas Mark 10 (or your highest Gas Mark setting) for 15 minutes. Remove the roasting tin from the oven, add the flour to the tin and turn all the duck pieces around a few times so that all the fat is absorbed by the flour. Pour the measured water into the roasting tin and put back underneath the duck. Turn the oven down to 150°C/ Gas Mark 2 and roast for another 2–2½ hours. The duck is ready when the skin is beautifully golden and crisp and the thigh meat is creeping up the bone, which, by the way, should be about to fall off by itself.

Take the duck out of the oven and leave to rest for 20–25 minutes before you start carving it. Meanwhile, strain the gravy from the roasting tin into a saucepan – the flour you added earlier will have thickened the juices into a sauce. If there is excess fat on top, skim it off (you can save it and use it another time). Adjust the consistency of the sauce, if necessary, and season with a little vinegar and sugar or Apple Gastrique, along with some salt and pepper, until it is just as good as your mother's gravy.

Cut the bird into 8 pieces (4 breasts, 2 thighs and 2 drumsticks) and serve it with the fruit stuffing, gravy and boiled, browned or butter-fried potatoes or whatever you usually eat with roast duck. Red cabbage is probably just about mandatory, and as far as I am concerned, the warm vinegary version on page 201 is a good accompaniment.

Gravad beef topside
with celeriac pickles

1 tablespoon coriander seeds
1 tablespoon fennel seeds
1 tablespoon cumin seeds
1 tablespoon juniper berries
200g coarse sea salt
200g unrefined cane sugar
    or brown sugar
800g beef topside

Roast the spices in a dry pan until they begin to give off some aroma, and then mix them with the salt and sugar. Put the beef in a dish and spread the mixture out over it. Cover the dish with clingfilm and place in the refrigerator overnight.

The following day the spices and salt will have transformed into a brine. Turn the meat to coat it in the brine.

Repeat the turning and coating procedure every day for the next 5 days. The meat is then ready to be served. Scrape some of the spice mixture off the beef and cut it into thin slices. Serve with Celeriac Pickles (see below) and a little bread.

Celeriac pickles

1 small celeriac
sea salt flakes and freshly ground pepper
2 tablespoons cold-pressed rapeseed oil
2 tablespoons cider vinegar, plus extra
    to taste
4 celery sticks
100ml Homemade Mayonnaise
    (see page 68)
300ml Greek yogurt, 2% fat
2 tablespoons prepared mustard
4 tablespoons capers, chopped
grated zest and juice of ½ organic lemon

Peel the celeriac and cut it into thin sticks. Place the celeriac sticks in an ovenproof dish, toss them with some salt and pepper, the oil and vinegar and bake them in a preheated oven at 180°C/Gas Mark 4 for 20–25 minutes. Toss them around a few times during the cooking time so that they are evenly baked. Take the celeriac out of the oven and leave to cool.

Wash the celery, cut it into very fine strips and then mix with the baked celeriac. Combine the mayonnaise, yogurt, mustard, chopped capers, lemon zest and juice, salt and pepper in a bowl to make a dressing. Pour the dressing over the celery and celeriac and toss to coat thoroughly. Finish by adding more salt, pepper and vinegar to taste.

Leg of wild boar
SERVES 6

1 leg of wild boar, 1.5–2kg
1 organic lemon
3–4 garlic cloves
3 rosemary sprigs
sea salt flakes and freshly ground pepper

Lightly score the top of the leg with a sharp knife. Place the leg on an oven or roasting rack with a roasting tin filled with water underneath to collect the fat and juices while the meat is roasting. Cut the lemon into small pieces, and peel and crush the garlic cloves with the flat blade of a knife. Distribute the pieces of lemon, rosemary sprigs and garlic evenly across the leg, and season with salt and pepper.

Roast in a preheated oven at 160°C/Gas Mark 3 for 2–2½ hours. Scoop up and baste the leg with the juices that are collected in the roasting tin about every 30 minutes, and add a little more water to the tin if the liquid is about to evaporate completely. Check the core temperature of the leg with a meat thermometer before you take it out of the oven – at 65–70°C the meat will be nice and juicy and slightly pink.

Leave the meat to rest for 15–20 minutes before carving it into thin slices. Serve with Baked Squash and Potato Mash and Warm Vinaigrette with Orange, Red Onion and Rosemary (see right).

Baked squash and potato mash

1.5kg baking potatoes
500g squash, such as Hokkaido or butternut
200ml semi-skimmed milk
100g butter, plus extra for greasing
sea salt flakes and freshly ground pepper

Peel the potatoes and squash, then halve the squash and scrape out the seeds with a spoon. Cut the potatoes and squash into small pieces and place them in a saucepan with water to cover. Bring to the boil, then simmer for 25–30 minutes until the vegetables are tender. Drain and leave to cool in the pan for 2–3 minutes.

Heat the milk in a saucepan. Cut the butter into small cubes. Mash the potatoes and squash using a masher or a whisk, add the hot milk and butter and mash until completely smooth and soft. Season to taste with salt and pepper.

Fill a large buttered ovenproof dish with the mash, place on a baking sheet and bake in a preheated oven at 200°C/Gas Mark 6 for 15–20 minutes until golden and crispy on top. Take the dish out of the oven and serve immediately.

Warm vinaigrette with orange, red onion and rosemary

2 oranges
1 red onion, peeled and finely chopped
1 rosemary sprig, leaves chopped
50ml olive oil
50ml cider vinegar
sea salt flakes and freshly ground pepper
1 teaspoon honey

Peel the oranges, making sure that all the white pith is removed. Cut the oranges into small cubes and put in a pan with the onion, rosemary, oil, vinegar, some salt and pepper and the honey, and gently bring to the boil. Stir with a spoon until the dressing is smooth. Take the pan off the heat and leave to stand for 10 minutes before serving it warm with the wild boar and to balance the sweet Baked Squash and Potato Mash.

Fish

Pan-fried salmon
with warm salad of pearl barley, broccoli, pea shoots and hazelnuts

1 head of broccoli
sea salt flakes and freshly ground pepper
freshly grated nutmeg, to taste
500g low-fat natural yogurt
800g salmon fillet, skin on
2 tablespoons cold-pressed rapeseed oil, plus extra to season
200g cooked pearl barley
100g fresh pea shoots
25g hazelnuts, roughly chopped
2–3 tablespoons cider vinegar
1 pack or tray growing salad cress, chopped

Break the broccoli into small florets and rinse them in cold water. Bring a pan of salted water to the boil and blanch the broccoli for 30 seconds, then immediately transfer to cold water so that they keep their crispness and colour.

Stir grated nutmeg, salt and pepper to taste into the yogurt in a bowl and leave to stand for 20–25 minutes before serving.

Use a knife to scrape the scales off the skin of the salmon. Divide the salmon into 4 pieces approximately 200g each.

Heat a frying pan and fry the salmon pieces in 1 tablespoon of the rapeseed oil on the skin side for about 2–3 minutes, then turn over and fry for a further 2–3 minutes so that the salmon has a beautiful crust on both sides.

Transfer the salmon fillets to an ovenproof dish and roast them in a preheated oven at 170°C/Gas Mark 3½ for 4–6 minutes.

Meanwhile, drizzle the remaining tablespoon of rapeseed oil into the frying pan and fry the cooked barley over a high heat for 1–2 minutes, tossing it around a few times. Add the broccoli florets, pea shoots and hazelnuts, and toss around so that all the ingredients are evenly mixed. Season the grain salad with the cider vinegar, extra rapeseed oil, lots of chopped cress, salt and pepper. Give the salad another stir and add some more salt and pepper if needed.

Serve the salmon pieces with the warm grain salad, the yogurt dressing and some good bread.

. . . .

TIP The grain salad is also good served cold, so if you have leftovers from dinner, they will make a nice lunch box for the following day.

. . . .

Spicy fish cakes
with white cabbage salad

1 onion
1 garlic clove
15g fresh root ginger
500g skinless cod fillet (or pollock or coley)
200g crabmeat
100g boiled potato, mashed
finely grated zest of 1 organic lime
1 organic egg, plus extra if you wish
½ handful of fresh coriander, chopped
1 tablespoon prepared mustard
sea salt flakes
1 tablespoon groundnut oil, for frying

Peel and grate the onion, garlic and ginger into a bowl. Roughly chop the fish and add to the bowl with the crabmeat, mashed potato, lime zest, egg, chopped coriander, mustard and salt. Work the fish mixture until you have a good, firm texture, adding an extra egg or so if you want a softer consistency.

Using a spoon, form the mixture into little crab cake-sized patties. Fry the patties in hot oil in a frying pan for 3–4 minutes on each side until golden and crisp.

Eat the fish cakes with some good-quality sweet and sour chilli sauce or Homemade Apple Ketchup (see page 235) for dipping. Pack in your lunch box or serve for lunch or dinner with the White Cabbage Salad (see below), rice and vegetables.

White cabbage salad

¼ white cabbage, 300g
2 shallots
1 apple
2 tablespoons cider vinegar
1 teaspoon caster sugar
2 tablespoons cold-pressed rapeseed oil
sea salt flakes and freshly ground pepper

Using a sharp knife, cut the cabbage into fine strips and put into a bowl. Peel the shallots and cut the apple into quarters, discarding the core. Slice the shallots and apple thinly and add them to the bowl as well.

Toss the cabbage, shallots and apple with the vinegar, sugar, rapeseed oil, salt and pepper, and leave to marinate for 2–3 minutes. The cabbage will absorb the marinade and become soft.

. . . .

TIP Cabbage is a spectacular vegetable and it very often ends up in the salad bowl at my house. I vary the recipe depending on what I have in the refrigerator – for example, this salad could be made with kale, red cabbage or finely shredded Brussels sprouts. The latter, because of their size, might be a bit of a struggle to shred, but trust me, they make a delicious salad! A nice cabbage salad such as this makes a great accompaniment to almost any dish.

. . . .

Spicy fish cakes »

Steamed razor clams
with jerusalem artichokes, onions and white beans

1.5kg razor clams (or mussels or cockles)
1 onion
1 garlic clove
4 Jerusalem artichokes
2 tablespoons olive oil
100g cooked white beans, such as haricot or cannellini
10 thyme sprigs
300ml white wine
sea salt flakes and freshly ground pepper

Sit the razor clams in some fresh cold water for 5–10 minutes or until they have rinsed themselves through and discharged as much sand as possible, as unfortunately they usually store up quite a bit. If you are using mussels, check that they are fresh – they should smell of the sea. Clean the mussels by scrubbing them thoroughly under cold water and removing the beards. Discard any mussels that don't close after lightly tapping on the work surface, and those with damaged shells.

Peel the onion, garlic and Jerusalem artichokes, and chop them finely. Heat the olive oil in a large pan and throw in the vegetables, beans and thyme. Sauté for 1 minute, then add the razor clams or mussels and sauté for another minute. Add the white wine, cover the pan with a lid and steam for 2–4 minutes. All the razor clams or mussels should open during steaming, but if there are any that remain closed, discard immediately as they are bad.

Serve the razor clams or mussels straight from the pan or in a large bowl. Season beforehand with a little salt and pepper. Eat with some good bread to soak up all the delicious broth.

Octopus salad
with beans, leeks and tarragon

1 octopus, 1.5–2kg
1 onion
1 garlic clove
1 carrot
sea salt flakes
10 whole black peppercorns
100g dried broad beans (or green split peas), soaked in cold water overnight
finely grated zest and juice of 1 organic lemon
2 tablespoons olive oil
freshly ground pepper
2 winter leeks
5 tarragon sprigs, leaves picked

Wash the octopus in cold water and remove the beak and any ink (or have the fishmonger do the work for you). Peel the onion, garlic and carrot, then cut them into chunks.

Put the octopus in a pan along with the vegetables, some salt, the peppercorns and enough water to cover. Bring to the boil, then simmer for about 45 minutes– 1 hour. Turn the heat off and leave the octopus to soak in the broth for about 30–40 minutes until done – it should be tender but still al dente.

Drain the soaked beans (or split peas), place in a pan of fresh cold water and bring to the boil, then simmer for about 25–30 minutes until tender. Drain in a colander.

Lift the octopus out of its broth and cut it into small pieces. Put it into a bowl and add the beans. Toss thoroughly with the lemon zest and juice, olive oil, salt and pepper.

Cut off the roots and tops of the leeks, then cut into rings about 1cm thick and rinse them thoroughly in cold water so that all the soil is washed away. Bring a pan of salted water to the boil and blanch the leeks for about 1 minute, then immediately plunge them into cold water so that they retain their colour and crispness.

Toss the blanched leeks and tarragon leaves into the octopus and bean salad, and season with additional salt and pepper if necessary. Serve the salad as a starter or a small lunch dish.

....
TIP Soak and then cook 100g extra dried beans, then put them in a tightly sealed container in the refrigerator and save them for the Fish Soup with Root Vegetables and Broad Bean Mash (see page 186).
....

SCURVY GRASS
When the winter frosts retreat, scurvy grass can be found on the beach or in meadows.

Pan-fried herrings
with dill, mustard and melted butter

8 double herring fillets
2 tablespoons prepared mustard
1 handful of dill, chopped, plus extra
   to garnish
sea salt flakes and freshly ground pepper
50g plain flour
40g butter
2 tablespoons cider vinegar

Check that the herring fillets are fresh and smell of the sea, not of the harbour. Put them in a dish, skin side down, then spread the mustard on to the flesh side, sprinkle with the chopped dill and season with salt and pepper. Fold the fillets together and toss them in the flour to coat.

Fry the fillets in a little of the butter (about 10g) in a medium-hot frying pan for about 3 minutes on each side so that the skin is beautifully golden and crisp. It may be necessary to press down slightly on the folded fillets with a fish slice when you first add them to the pan to make sure they don't unfold.

Lift the herrings out of the pan and place them on a plate. Add the rest of the butter to the hot pan and let it bubble into a golden brown butter sauce. Season the sauce with the vinegar and salt and pepper to taste.

Serve the fried herrings with the butter sauce and boiled potatoes, sprinkled with some chopped dill.

Pan-fried cod
with leeks, dill and carrot and egg sauce

600g skinless cod fillet (or use other
   cod-like fish such as haddock, ling,
   tusk, coley or hake)
sea salt flakes
4 winter leeks
1 shallot
1 tablespoon cold-pressed rapeseed oil
1 tablespoon cider vinegar
freshly ground pepper
1 tablespoon capers
½ handful of dill, chopped
1 tablespoon standard rapeseed oil

Check that the cod is fresh and smells of the sea, not of the harbour, and remove any remaining bones. Cut the cod into 4 evenly sized pieces, place in a dish and season with a little salt, then leave to lightly salt cure in the refrigerator for 10 minutes.

Cut off the roots and tops of the leeks, then cut into slices about 5cm thick and rinse them thoroughly in cold water so that all the soil is washed away. Bring a pan of lightly salted water to the boil and boil the leeks for 3–4 minutes until tender but still al dente.

Drain the leeks in a colander and swiftly shake all the water out of them, then put them in a bowl. Peel the shallot and slice it finely. Fold it into the hot leeks and add the cold-pressed rapeseed oil, vinegar, salt, pepper, capers and chopped dill.

Heat a frying pan and fry the cod pieces in the standard rapeseed oil for about 1–2 minutes on each side so that they are beautifully golden and crisp on the surface. Season with salt and pepper. Serve the fried cod fillets with the marinated leeks, Carrot and Egg Sauce (see right) and boiled potatoes or grains.

Tip Buy an additional 200g cod, put it in a dish and coat it in 1 tablespoon sea salt flakes and 1 teaspoon sugar. Cover the dish with clingfilm and place it in the refrigerator to cure for 12 hours. Serve the salt and sugar-cured cod with Squash Purée and Chervil Dressing (see page 192) as a starter the following day.

Carrot and egg sauce

1 carrot
2 organic eggs
1 tablespoon prepared mustard
sea salt flakes and freshly ground
   pepper
50ml cider vinegar, plus extra if needed
100ml cold-pressed rapeseed oil

Peel the carrot and cut it into small pieces. Add to a pan of boiling water and boil for 12–15 minutes until completely tender.

Meanwhile, boil the eggs in another pan for 8 minutes. Drain and shell the eggs, then take out the yolks – you won't be using the whites.

Put the egg yolks in the blender along with the carrot and some of its boiling cooking water, the mustard, salt, pepper and the vinegar, and blend it all to a smooth cream. Then slowly add the oil in a thin stream while the blender is still running. The end result should be a thick, creamy sauce. Taste the sauce to see if it needs a bit more salt, pepper or vinegar.

Fried flounder with braised chicory »

Fried flounder
with braised chicory

2 whole flounders (or 8 flounder fillets)
sea salt flakes
4 heads of chicory
3 tablespoons standard rapeseed oil
2 tablespoons unrefined cane sugar
juice of 1 orange
50ml cider vinegar
2 apples
freshly ground pepper
½ handful of parsley

If using whole flounders, rinse and clean them, making sure that they are free of blood and mucus. Cut out the fillets and skin them (or get your fishmonger to do the work for you). Save the bones for making stock, soup or sauce.

Cut the fish fillets in half, place in a dish and sprinkle with salt, then put them in the refrigerator while you make the braised chicory.

Halve the chicory heads, rinse them in cold water and drain them well. Heat 1 tablespoon of the rapeseed oil in a sauteuse. Add the chicory halves, cut side down, and fry for a few minutes so that they have a beautiful golden crust. Flip them over, sprinkle with the sugar and leave to caramelize slightly (watch out that the sugar doesn't burn). Add the orange juice and vinegar and simmer for 4–5 minutes until the chicory has absorbed about half of the liquid.

Wash and core the apples, then cut them into small cubes. Add them to the pan and simmer with the chicory for 30 seconds. Toss around to mix well, and season with salt and pepper. Finely chop the parsley and sprinkle it over the chicory, then round off by drizzling over 1 tablespoon of the rapeseed oil.

Fry the flounder fillets in the remaining tablespoon of oil in a hot frying pan for 1–2 minutes on each side until they have a beautifully golden and crisp crust.

Arrange the chicory on 4 plates – 2 halves on each plate – and serve the fried flounder on top of the chicory. The chicory can also be served by itself as a small dish or as a side to fried poultry.

Pan-fried haddock
with broad bean stew

200g dried broad beans, soaked in cold
**   water for 12 hours**
8 slices of bacon
2 shallots
2 tablespoons standard rapeseed oil
10 thyme sprigs
sea salt flakes and freshly ground pepper
400–500ml water
2 tablespoons cider vinegar
600g haddock fillet, skinned and
**   pin-boned**

Drain the beans, rinse them in fresh cold water and leave in a colander to drain.

Cut the bacon slices into small pieces. Peel the shallots and cut one into small cubes and the other into thin rings (save the rings for the garnish).

Grease a sauteuse with 1 tablespoon of the oil, add the bacon and diced shallot and sauté over a low heat for 2–3 minutes. Add the drained beans, season with the thyme sprigs (save a few for the garnish), salt and pepper and then pour in the measured water.

Bring the vegetables to the boil and then simmer for about 30–35 minutes until the beans are tender and have absorbed the water. Season with the vinegar and possibly some more salt and pepper to taste, then cover with a lid to keep the stew warm.

Make sure that the haddock is fresh and smells of the sea, not of the harbour. Check for any remaining bones and use a knife to scrape off any stray scales, then cut into 4 or 8 pieces.

Heat a frying pan, add the remaining tablespoon of oil and fry the haddock pieces over a high heat for about 2 minutes on each side so that they develop a beautifully golden crust and remain juicy in the centre.

Arrange the haddock on top of a couple of tablespoons of the bean stew and sprinkle with the raw shallot rings and reserved thyme sprigs. Serve with a good bowl of Marinated Beetroot (see page 224) and some good bread, or make a nice crudité and some baked root vegetables.

WILD GARLIC
Along little streams, you'll find the first delicious green shoots of wild garlic.

Home-smoked whiting
with beetroot tartare and horseradish cream

whiting fillets, about 300–400g (or cod)
10 fennel seeds, crushed
2 tablespoons sea salt flakes
1 teaspoon sugar

You will also need
a barbecue charcoal chimney starter
some straw (such as oats) or hay

Day 1
Remove any skin and bones from the whiting fillets (or ask the fishmonger to do the work for you). Put them in a dish and sprinkle both sides with the crushed fennel seeds, salt and sugar. Cover the dish with clingfilm and refrigerate for 12 hours.

Day 2
Take the whiting fillets out of the refrigerator and gently pat dry with kitchen paper. Go outside in the cold and stuff the bottom of a barbecue charcoal chimney starter full of straw or hay, ignite and place it on the ground. Lay the whiting fillets on a barbecue rack and place it on top of the starter so that the smoke goes right through the fillets. Leave to sit in the smoke for 45 seconds–1 minute, then take the fillets off the rack and put in the refrigerator to chill.

Cut the whiting fillets into thin slices and serve with Beetroot Tartare and Horseradish Cream (see right).

• •

TIP If you don't have the courage or the opportunity to smoke fish, you can pre-order it ready-smoked at your fishmonger's. That being said, the process is quite simple, as all you need is an ordinary charcoal starter and some straw or hay. If you don't have a farm nearby that can provide you with the straw or hay, your local pet supplies store will have some.

• •

Beetroot tartare

400g beetroot
2 tablespoons cherry vinegar or other
**   fruit vinegar**
sea salt flakes and freshly ground pepper
1 cooking apple
1 red onion
1 tablespoon cold-pressed rapeseed oil
1 handful of chervil, chopped
1 tablespoon honey
1 tablespoon prepared mustard

Peel 100g of the beetroot and cut it into minuscule cubes. Marinate the beetroot cubes in the vinegar and some salt and pepper.

Wrap the rest of the beetroot in foil and bake in a preheated oven at 200°C/Gas Mark 6 for 1 hour–1 hour 10 minutes until tender.

Take the beetroot out of the oven and leave until cool enough to handle, then rub the skins off.

Wash and core the apple, and peel the red onion. Cut the baked beetroot, apple and onion into tiny cubes to match the raw beetroot cubes and then mix them with the raw beetroot. Add the oil and season with the chopped chervil, honey, mustard, salt and pepper. Toss it all around well and season again – the tartare should be fresh, sweet, sharp but at the same time well-rounded in flavour, to suit the smoked fish.

Horseradish cream

100ml Greek yogurt, 2% fat
finely grated zest and juice of
**   ½ organic lemon**
5–10g freshly grated horseradish,
**   to taste**
1 teaspoon honey
sea salt flakes and freshly ground pepper

Mix all the ingredients together in a bowl. Leave the cream to sit for 5 minutes in the kitchen to allow the flavours to infuse and then season, if necessary, with some extra horseradish before serving.

Light dishes

Roast pork sandwich

SERVES 4

2 tablespoons Greek yogurt
2 tablespoons Homemade Mayonnaise
  (*see* page 68)
1 tablespoon prepared coarsely ground
  mustard
1 teaspoon cider vinegar
1 teaspoon acacia honey
sea salt flakes and freshly ground pepper
2 apples
4 pickled gherkins (preferably
  cornichons)
1 small portion of Warm Red Cabbage
  (*see* page 201)
800g leftover Roast Pork with Crispy
  Skin (*see* page 201)
4 good-quality sandwich rolls

Mix the yogurt, mayonnaise and mustard together in a bowl to make a dressing, and season with the vinegar, honey, salt and pepper. Wash the apples, cut them into quarters and remove the cores, then slice them thinly. Also slice the gherkins.

Heat the red cabbage in a small saucepan. Reheat the pork in a preheated oven at 170°C/Gas Mark 3½ for 10–15 minutes if you wish (reheat before slicing so that it doesn't become too dry).

Split the sandwich rolls and lightly toast them if you like. Spread the mustard dressing on both top and bottom halves. Cut the pork into 8 slices and place 2 slices in each roll. Sprinkle with a little salt and then garnish with the apple slices, warm red cabbage and sliced gherkins. I usually leave the red cabbage to drain in a sieve just before I add it to the rolls to avoid the juice making them wet and soggy too quickly. Sandwich the rolls together and serve. Since the pickled cabbage will eventually seep into the bread, don't make the sandwiches in advance but enjoy them straight away.

The roast pork sandwich has become a classic in my Meyers Deli shops in Denmark,

and we make it every autumn and winter. At Christmas they sell really fast. The roast pork sandwich is lovely for lunch (not least on the day after a 'wet' Christmas party), but would definitely make a nice dinner too.

Open rye bread sandwich with smoked lumpfish and pickled onion
with celeriac purée

1 red onion
1 tablespoon cider vinegar
sea salt flakes and freshly ground pepper
1 teaspoon acacia honey
1 smoked lumpfish or cod
1 apple
1 tablespoon cold-pressed rapeseed oil
Celeriac Purée (*see* below)
4–8 slices of rye bread
2 tablespoons skyr

Peel the red onion, cut it into thin wedges and put in a bowl. Toss with the vinegar, salt, pepper and honey, and leave to marinate for 30 minutes so that the onion softens a little but remains crisp.

Skin the smoked lumpfish and place the flesh in a bowl, discarding any bones. Wash the apple, cut it into quarters and remove the core, then cut it into very thin wedges. Add the apple to the marinated onion and toss with the oil and salt and pepper to taste.

Spread the Celeriac Purée over the bread slices, top with the lumpfish flesh and finally add the marinated onion and apple. Garnish with a spoonful of skyr on top of the rye bread sandwich, and serve immediately.

Celeriac purée

½ celeriac
sea salt flakes
20g butter
finely grated zest and juice of
  ½ organic lemon
freshly ground pepper

Peel the celeriac and roughly cut it into pieces. Put them in a pan, cover with water and add some salt. Bring to the boil and boil for about 20 minutes until it is tender.

Drain the celeriac and blend in a blender or food processor with the butter and lemon zest and juice to a smooth purée. Season to taste with salt and pepper. The consistency of the purée should be smooth and slightly softer than mashed potatoes.

Leave the purée to cool slightly before using it. The purée is brilliant as a spread for rye bread and wheat bread rolls, and will complement both cold meats and fish and seafood.

Salad with smoked cod roe

250g smoked cod roe
1 shallot
100ml Greek yogurt, 2% fat
1 teaspoon honey
1 teaspoon prepared mustard
1 tablespoon cider vinegar, plus extra
  if needed
sea salt flakes and freshly ground pepper

Cut the smoked cod roe into small cubes and place them in a bowl. Peel and chop the shallot finely, then mix it with the yogurt, honey, mustard, vinegar, salt and pepper in another bowl to make a dressing.

Fold the cod roe into the dressing so that it is well incorporated but still keeps its shape and doesn't become mushy. Leave the cod roe salad to rest for 20 minutes in the refrigerator and then season with salt and pepper to taste and, if necessary, a little extra vinegar.

Serve the cod roe salad with crisp bitter salad leaves and some nice bread. This is an obvious choice for a lunch box but it also works well for dinner, supplemented with cold or warm leftovers from the day before – like lentil stew. And if you top it off with a bread roll and a little cheese, you have a cosy snack meal – my kids love these fridge leftover evenings!

Smoked lumpfish salad
with marinated beetroot and apple sauce

SERVES 6

2 smoked lumpfish or cod
1 shallot
100ml soured cream, 18% fat
1 teaspoon prepared mustard, plus
  extra if needed
1 tablespoon cider vinegar, plus extra
  if needed
sea salt flakes and freshly ground pepper
½ handful of chives

Skin the lumpfish, putting all the delicious smoked flesh in a bowl, discarding any bones. Peel and chop the shallot finely, then mix it with the lumpfish flesh.

Add the soured cream, mustard, vinegar, salt and pepper and mix together thoroughly, but make sure that the fish still keeps its shape and doesn't become mushy.

Leave the salad to rest for 20 minutes in the refrigerator before you taste it and season with any additional salt, pepper, vinegar and mustard if needed. At the very last moment, chop the chives and add to give the salad a green finish. Serve the salad with Marinated Beetroot and Tangy Fresh Apple Sauce (see right), and possibly a little fresh apple with a bit of the marinade from the beets. Serve with good bread.

Marinated beetroot

100g beetroot
3 tablespoons cider vinegar
3 tablespoons olive oil
1 tablespoon acacia honey
sea salt flakes and freshly ground pepper
1–2 teaspoons freshly grated
  horseradish

Peel the beetroot and cut into very thin slices using a mandoline or a sharp knife. Place the beetroot slices in a bowl and toss them with the rest of the ingredients. Leave to marinate for at least 2 hours or preferably 12 hours in the refrigerator before serving them, tossing the beetroot slices around a few times so that they are evenly marinated.

The marinated beetroot is also a good supplement to steamed or fried cod.

Tangy fresh apple sauce

3 tart apples, such as Belle de Boskoop
  or Bramley
2 tablespoons unrefined cane sugar
finely grated zest and juice of
  ½ organic lemon
sea salt flakes and freshly ground pepper
1 tablespoon cold-pressed rapeseed oil

Wash the apples, cut them into quarters and remove the cores, but leave the peel on. Save half an apple for garnish, then cut the rest into large cubes, place them in a small saucepan with the sugar and lemon zest and juice and bring to the boil. Simmer the apples, with the lid on, for 4–5 minutes until they are tender and beginning to turn into a compote. Take the pan off the heat and leave the apples to stand, still with the lid on, for 5 minutes

Mash the apples through a coarse colander, then season the mash to taste with salt, pepper and the oil. Leave to cool slightly, then add the reserved raw apple, cut into cubes, and it is ready to be served.

Bruschetta
with squash purée and goat's cheese

8 slices of day-old white bread
½ quantity of Squash Purée
  (see pages 192–3)
100g goat's cheese, thinly sliced from
  a log
2 tablespoons olive oil
1 rosemary sprig, needles picked
sea salt flakes and freshly ground pepper

Place the bread slices on an oven or grill rack, spread the Squash Purée over them and top with the thin slices of goat's cheese. Drizzle with the olive oil and season with the rosemary, salt and pepper.

Bake the bruschetta in a preheated oven at 250°C/Gas Mark 10 (or your highest Gas Mark setting) for 3–4 minutes until the bread is crisp and the cheese is crispy and golden. Serve the bruschetta immediately while they are warm, either as a snack or as a starter with a good salad.

SLOES
Remember to pick these blue-black fruits from the trees before the birds do!

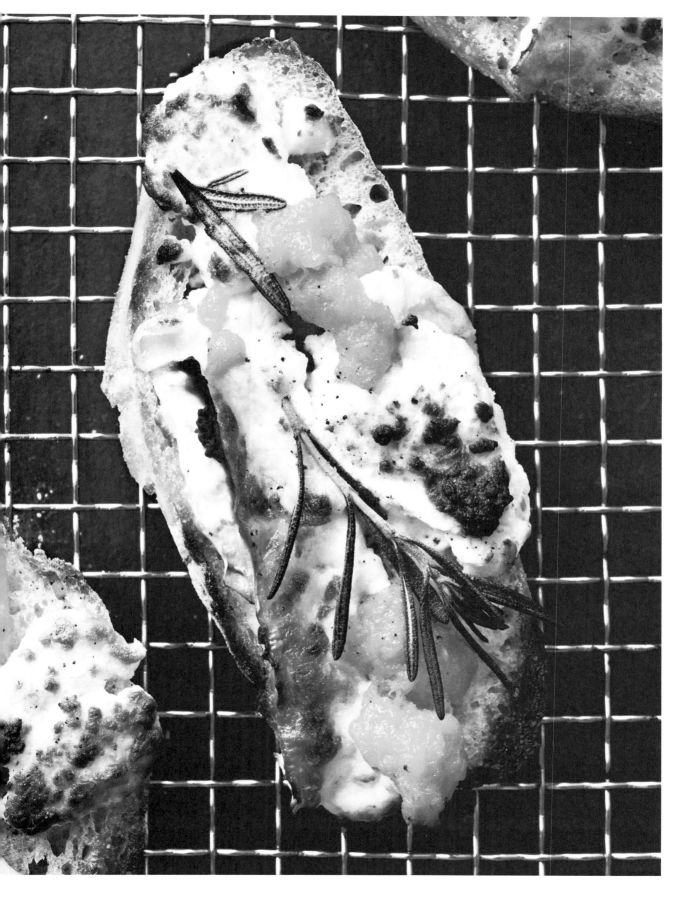

Dandelion leaves

In mild winters, you may in February already be able to pick the first leaves of dandelion from underneath the hedge, in the kitchen garden or in the meadow. The small ribbons of barbed, bright green leaves are easy to spot against the bare soil. The plant is known for the milky sap that seeps out when you pluck a leaf. The taste is pleasantly bitter, as long as the leaves are young; older leaves are stronger in flavour. Dandelions can be very different from plant to plant. In fact, there is not just one but up to 1,000 different species of dandelion with roughly the same appearance.

Harvesting and using dandelion leaves

To harvest, cut off the plant with a sharp knife just below the surface of the soil so that all the leaves are still attached to the root. Wash them free of soil and pick off the smaller leaves. Always discard the old leaves from the previous year. The first dandelion leaves tossed with bread croutons, fried cubes of bacon, walnuts and a nice vinaigrette give a wonderful feeling of spring.

If you 'force' dandelion plants, your leaves will have a less bitter taste. This is an old tradition used, for example, in English kitchen gardens. Cut off the leaves of the growing dandelion and place a box, bucket or flowerpot (remember to cover the hole) over the plant. When the plant shoots, the leaves will be brighter in colour and milder in taste.

You can blanch older leaves and make a stew with them just like you do with spinach. They are also good in a soup and of course on top of mashed potatoes.

Dandelion salad

Try this fantastic dandelion salad. It heralds spring and carries the promise of those piles of fresh salad and vegetables soon to come. You will need 200g small, fresh dandelion shoots, 1 small red onion, 4 radishes, 2 tablespoons cold-pressed rapeseed oil, 2 tablespoons cider vinegar, sea salt and freshly ground pepper.

Wash the dandelion leaves thoroughly in cold water and put them in a colander. Wash them again if necessary to make sure there are no traces of soil left, then leave to drain in the colander. Peel the red onion, nip the tops off the radishes and shred both very finely. Mix the dandelion leaves, onion and radishes together in a bowl, then toss in the oil and vinegar, and season to taste with salt and pepper. Dandelion salad is a lovely breath of fresh air to accompany steamed or braised meats, among other things.

Crispy onion pie

Dough
10g fresh yeast
600ml lukewarm water
700g plain flour
300g wholemeal flour
1 teaspoon fine salt

Topping
3 onions
6 tablespoons olive oil
3 rosemary sprigs, needles picked
**   and chopped**
coarse sea salt, for sprinkling
a little cider vinegar

This pie is not a pie in the traditional sense but more like a pizza – just without the cheese! Start by dissolving the yeast in the measured lukewarm water, then add half the flours and incorporate well. Add the salt and the rest of the flours (save a little flour for rolling the dough out), and knead thoroughly, either in a stand mixer fitted with a dough hook or by hand on a lightly floured surface, until smooth and supple.

Place the dough in a bowl, cover the bowl with a clean tea towel and leave in a warm place for 1–2 hours until it has doubled in size.

Turn the dough out on to a floured surface and roll it out thinly into a circle – the thinner, the better, so that it is more likely to become crisp when baked.

Preheat the oven to 250°C/Gas Mark 10 (or your highest Gas Mark setting) with a baking tray inside the oven so that it is hot when the dough is placed on it. Place the rolled-out dough on a sheet of baking paper for transferring to the hot baking tray. Peel the onions and cut them into very thin rings. Spread the onion rings evenly over the dough, drizzle with the olive oil and sprinkle with the rosemary and some coarse salt.

Take the hot baking tray out of the oven and slip the baking paper with the pie on to the tray. Put the tray back in the oven and bake for 7–9 minutes until completely crisp and dark golden.

Remove the pie from the oven and drizzle a little cider vinegar on top, to balance out the sweetness of the onion. Cut the pie into pieces and eat immediately as a dish on its own with a good salad.

TIP I often make a large portion of the dough, roll it into several small bases, stacking them with baking paper in between, and put them in the refrigerator. That way they are ready to be used the following day, and I have an easy dinner for the family.

Potato omelette
with smoked pork fat and purée of baked garlic

400g potatoes
1 tablespoon olive oil
35g smoked pork fat (lard), cut into
**   small cubes**
2 thyme sprigs
6 organic eggs
150ml semi-skimmed milk
sea salt flakes and freshly ground pepper

Peel the potatoes and cut them into small cubes. Fry the potato cubes in an ovenproof frying pan with the olive oil and the smoked pork fat cubes over a medium heat for 4–5 minutes until the potatoes are tender and slightly golden while the pork fat cubes have become crisp. Pick the leaves from the thyme sprigs and add to the potatoes.

Beat the eggs and milk together in a bowl and season with salt and pepper. Add the egg mixture to the pan and stir lightly so that the potatoes and pork fat cubes are evenly distributed. When the egg mixture has set, transfer the pan to a preheated oven at 250°C/Gas Mark 10 (or your highest Gas Mark setting) and bake for about 5–6 minutes. If necessary, turn on the grill near the end of the cooking time so that the omelette is completely golden on top.

Remove the pan from the oven and slide the omelette gently on to a platter. Eat the omelette warm or cold with rye bread, the Purée of Baked Garlic (see below) and a good salad, such as a beetroot salad with a mustard dressing, which goes well with eggs, smoked pork fat and potatoes.

Purée of baked garlic

2 whole garlic bulbs
2 tablespoons coarse sea salt
sea salt flakes and freshly ground pepper
1 tablespoon cold-pressed rapeseed oil
1 teaspoon cider vinegar

Place the whole garlic bulbs (skin on) in a small ovenproof dish with the coarse salt. Bake in a preheated oven at 170°C/Gas Mark 3½ for 35–40 minutes until the garlic is browned and crisp on the outside and tender inside.

Remove the garlic bulbs from the dish and leave them to cool slightly. Separate the cloves then crush them into a bowl, discarding the skins. Mash the garlic with a fork into a coarse purée and season to taste with salt and pepper and the oil and vinegar. The baked garlic has a unique, almost caramelized sweetness that turns the purée into pure candy. Eat the purée with the omelette; it is also great with roast meats and poultry.

The origins of potato omelette

Before we started feeding chickens, they didn't lay eggs in the winter, only in the summer. Omelettes were therefore a rare but appreciated dish connected with summer, and in the oldest recipes dating back to the first half of the 1800s, they always appeared as a sweet dish. In the middle of the 19th century, a major expansion in poultry farming took place and this was reflected in the cookbooks of that time, which began to include eggs in savoury dishes, first with bread and pork fat, then later with potatoes in place of the bread. Smoked pork fat and potato complement each other perfectly in an omelette.

Crispy onion pie »

Omelette
with cheese and leeks

1 leek
1 tablespoon standard rapeseed oil
1 rosemary sprig, needles picked and
   finely chopped
4 organic eggs
50g hard cheese, such as Høost,
   Vesterhavsost or Præstost, or ripe
   Gouda or Grana Padano, freshly grated
sea salt flakes and freshly ground pepper

Cut off the root and top of the leek, then cut into thin rings and rinse them thoroughly in cold water so that all the soil is washed away. Drain the leek rings thoroughly and then fry them in the oil with the finely chopped rosemary in a hot ovenproof frying pan for 2–3 minutes so that they soften a little.

Beat the eggs and cheese together in a bowl and season with salt and pepper. Add the egg mixture to the pan, place the pan in a preheated oven at 200°C/Gas Mark 6 and bake for about 6–8 minutes until it has set and is completely golden on top. Remove the pan from the oven, turn the omelette on to a plate and serve while it is warm as part of a brunch.

Risotto
with oyster
mushrooms and
spinach

1 litre chicken stock or water, plus
   extra if needed
1 shallot
a little butter, for sautéing
300g pearl barley
100ml white wine
sea salt flakes
100g fresh spinach
150g mixed mushrooms
30g butter, diced
50g Parmesan cheese, freshly grated
freshly ground pepper
finely grated zest and juice of
   ½–1 organic lemon

Bring the stock or water to the boil in a saucepan. Peel and finely chop the shallot, then sauté it in a little butter until it is translucent and tender but without colouring.

Add the pearl barley and sauté for a few minutes, then add the white wine and allow the barley to absorb it. Add the boiling stock or water a little at a time so that the barley is constantly just covered, stirring as you go. Leave the pearl barley to cook for 15–18 minutes until it is soft but still with a little bite to it. It is important to season with salt during the cooking so that it is absorbed by the pearl barley (but not too much if your stock is very salty).

Wash the spinach thoroughly, place the leaves in a colander and leave it to drain. Shred the spinach using a sharp knife.

Clean the mushrooms with a brush or small vegetable knife and cut them into small pieces, then fry them in a little butter in a pan for 3–4 minutes. Season the mushrooms with salt and pepper, then mix them into the pearl barley (saving some for the garnish).

Remove the pearl barley from the heat and stir in the diced butter and grated Parmesan to create a smooth and creamy consistency (you may want to add some extra stock or water to get the right consistency). Add the fresh spinach to the hot risotto so that it softens a little, then season to taste with salt, pepper and the lemon zest and juice.

Serve the risotto with the reserved fried mushrooms on top and eat it straight away while it remains soft in texture and the barley is still al dente.

Pearl barley risotto
with beetroot, goat's
cheese and black
pepper

100g pearl barley
750ml chicken stock or water
1–2 beetroot, about 200g
35g hard cheese, such as Høost,
   Vesterhavsost or Præstost, or ripe
   Gouda or Grana Padano, freshly grated
2 tablespoons fresh goat's cheese
10g butter
1–2 tablespoons cider vinegar
sea salt flakes and freshly ground pepper
½ handful of parsley, chopped

Put the pearl barley and stock or water in a saucepan, bring it to the boil and skim off the foam. Lower the heat and simmer the grains gently for about 30–35 minutes until they are tender and almost all the liquid has been absorbed.

Peel the beetroot and cut them into 5mm cubes. Add the beetroot cubes to the pearl barley 10 minutes from the end of the cooking time so that they also become tender.

Remove the pan from the heat and add the freshly grated hard cheese, goat's cheese and butter to give the barley a creamy consistency à la risotto. Season with the vinegar, salt and pepper so that the balance is just right, and serve straight away topped with the chopped parsley. This can be eaten as a dish on its own or as an accompaniment to meat or fish.

Vegetable accompaniments

Glazed beetroot
with plum vinegar,
apples and juniper

1kg beetroot
sea salt flakes
1 tablespoon honey
100ml plum vinegar or other
    dark fruit vinegar
1 tablespoon juniper berries
2 apples with good acidity, such as
    Belle de Boskoop or Cox
1 tablespoon standard rapeseed oil
freshly ground pepper

Put the whole beetroot in an ovenproof
dish with a little salt and bake in a preheated
oven at 170°C/Gas Mark 3½ for 45 minutes–
1 hour until tender, depending on size.

Take the beetroot out of the oven and
leave until cool enough to handle, then rub
the skins off – a small kitchen knife can be
helpful for this. Cut the peeled beetroot
into chunky cubes.

Pour the honey and vinegar into a small
saucepan, bring to the boil and reduce for
a few minutes until the mixture begins to
thicken and become slightly syrupy.

Crush the juniper berries coarsely – just
give them a heavy push with the flat side
of your kitchen knife – and add them to the
syrup, then add the beetroot cubes to the
pan. Glaze in the syrup for a few minutes,
then take the pan off the heat and tip the
beets into a bowl.

Wash the apples, core them and cut into
cubes a bit smaller than the beetroot,
then add them to the bowl with the
glazed beetroot. Mix well and season with
rapeseed oil, salt and pepper. Serve these
sweet, glazed beetroots alongside rich
meats such as pork cheeks, hare or game.

Celeriac au gratin

1 celeriac
sea salt flakes
200ml full-fat crème fraîche
1 handful of flat leaf parsley
1 tablespoon prepared coarsely
    ground mustard
30g Parmesan cheese, freshly grated
freshly ground pepper
1 tablespoon olive oil

Peel the celeriac and cut it into 2cm cubes.
Bring a saucepan of salted water to the
boil, add the celeriac cubes and cook
for 2–3 minutes until they are tender but
still have some bite. Strain, reserving the
cooking water.

Put the celeriac cubes into a small saucepan
along with the crème fraîche and simmer
for 4–5 minutes so that they are fully cooked
and have integrated with the crème fraîche.

Wash the parsley and pick off the leaves
from the stems, then cook the leaves in the
celeriac cooking water for 30 seconds–
1 minute. Lift the leaves out, squeeze out
all the water and chop roughly. Add the
parsley to the creamy celeriac, take the pan
off the heat and season with the mustard,
Parmesan and salt and pepper to taste.

Grease a gratin dish with the oil and pour
in the celeriac mixture. Bake the gratin in
a preheated oven at 180°C/Gas Mark 4 for
15–20 minutes until it is slightly golden
on top.

Remove the gratin from the oven and
serve warm as a vegetarian dish or as an
accompaniment to fish, roast meat or poultry.

Salt-baked celeriac
and butter

1 celeriac
plenty of coarse salt, about 2–3kg

Wash the celeriac thoroughly with a sponge,
or peel it with a vegetable peeler if it is very
dirty and coarse. Pat it dry with some kitchen
paper, place it in an ovenproof dish and
cover it with the coarse salt.

Bake in a preheated oven at 170°C/Gas
Mark 3½ for 2–2½ hours until it is quite
tender. You can check if it is soft enough by
inserting a thin skewer or very thin knitting
needle into the celeriac.

Remove the dish from the oven and leave
the celeriac to rest for 20 minutes, then
crack the salt shell with the back of a knife
and lift the root out. Brush off the excess
salt and cut the celeriac into chunks.

This way of cooking celeriac will bring you
a taste so delightfully sweet and mild yet
intense, nothing like the way you normally
experience the vegetable. Serve the
celeriac while it is hot with a good dollop
of cold butter. Serve it as a lunch or as an
accompaniment to a main course with some
caramelized onions and bacon, along with
some good bread.

TIP Save the salt from baking and use it
as cooking salt when boiling potatoes or
making stock.

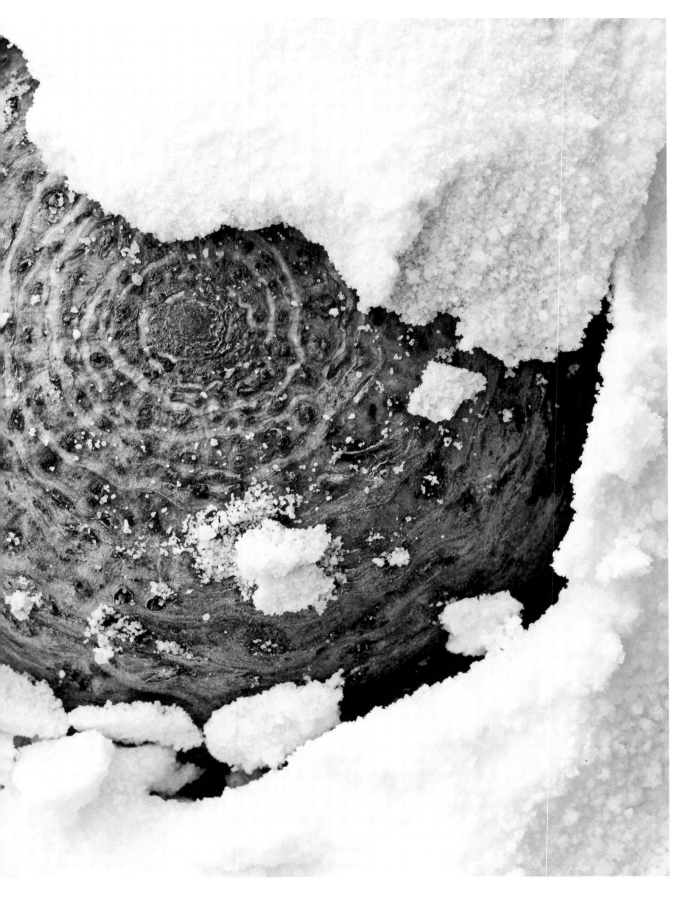

Potatoes fried in duck fat
with apple ketchup

800g baking potatoes
1 tablespoon duck fat
sea salt flakes
5 thyme sprigs, leaves picked
freshly ground pepper

Wash the potatoes thoroughly, leaving the skin on, and cut them into large cubes. Place the potato cubes in a bowl and sit under cold running water for 2–3 minutes – this way you remove the starch so that the potatoes become crispier when you roast them.

Drain the potatoes thoroughly and turn them in the duck fat. Season them with salt and the thyme leaves. Spread them out on a baking sheet lined with baking paper and bake in a preheated oven at 180°C/ Gas Mark 4 for 35–40 minutes until they are perfectly crisp and golden.

Remove the potatoes from the oven and season with pepper and a little extra salt. Eat the potatoes with Apple Ketchup (see below) as part of a Sunday brunch.

Apple ketchup

1 onion
1 garlic clove
2 apples
1 tablespoon olive oil
40g unrefined cane sugar, plus extra to season
2 star anise
10 coriander seeds
sea salt flakes and freshly ground pepper
2 x 400g cans peeled plum tomatoes
50ml cider vinegar, plus extra to season

Peel and chop the onion and garlic – you don't have to worry about how finely, as the ketchup will be blended later on. Wash and core the apples, then cut them into pieces.

Sauté the onion, garlic and apples in the olive oil in a pan for 3–4 minutes without them taking on too much colour. Add the sugar, star anise, coriander seeds, salt and pepper and cook until the onions and apples caramelize in the sugar. Add the tomatoes and vinegar and cook over a low heat for about 45 minutes until reduced and you have a dense compote.

Blend the compote in a blender or with a stick blender to a smooth purée, then pass it through a very fine sieve – use a spoon to press the purée through. Season to taste with sugar, salt and vinegar, and then pour the ketchup into a bowl and leave to cool. If you are not using the ketchup straight away, pour it into a sterilized preserving jar, seal and store it in the refrigerator, where it will stay good for 50–60 days unopened, and 10–15 days once you have opened it.

Baked potatoes
with crisp bacon, mushrooms and crème fraîche

4 large or 8 small baking potatoes, such as Russet
sea salt flakes
100g oyster or button mushrooms
80g bacon
200ml crème fraîche, 18% fat
1 tablespoon prepared mustard
finely grated zest and juice of ½ organic lemon
½ handful of parsley, chopped
freshly ground pepper

Wash the potatoes and pat them dry with kitchen paper. Place the potatoes in an ovenproof dish, sprinkle with salt and bake in a preheated oven at 180°C/Gas Mark 4 for 1 hour until they are fully cooked.

Clean the mushrooms with a brush or a small vegetable knife and cut them into small pieces. Cut the bacon into small pieces and fry them in a dry pan until they have rendered all their fat and are crisp. Pour the fat out of the pan, then add the mushrooms to the crisp bacon.

Mix the remaining ingredients together in a bowl and season with salt and pepper. Make an incision in each potato, squeeze them so that they open out and fill with the bacon and mushrooms and the crème fraîche sauce. Serve the potatoes while they are still warm as a dish in its own right or as an accompaniment to roast poultry or meat.

Kale salad
with carrots and apples

200g curly kale with stalks removed
2 carrots
2 shallots
8 dried figs
2 cooking apples, such as Belle de Boskoop or Bramley
2 tablespoons standard rapeseed oil
2 tablespoons cider vinegar
1 tablespoon unrefined cane sugar
sea salt flakes and freshly ground pepper

Remove any remaining bits of stalk from the kale, wash it thoroughly in cold water and place it in a sieve to drain. Then chop the kale finely and put it in a bowl.

Peel the carrots and shallots, then cut them both into thin slices. Cut the figs into thin slices. Wash the apples, quarter them and remove the cores, then cut them into thin wedges.

Add all the prepared ingredients to the kale, and toss together with the oil, vinegar, sugar and salt and pepper to taste.

Enjoy this salad the day you make it when it is still crisp. Serve it with dried, salted fish, duck, ham or sausages as an alternative to stewed kale on days when you fancy a fresh, green side.

Brussels sprouts

The vegetables of the cabbage family, of which Brussels sprouts are a member, are the rough diamonds of the Nordic kitchen garden. With their ability to withstand winter's snow and cold and their delicate texture, crispness and mildly bitter keynote flavour, they are unlike any other vegetable. They are also possibly the most nutritious vegetables of all that grow in the Nordics.

Brussels sprouts originally came from Belgium and only arrived in Denmark in the late 1800s. At the outset, it was only the uppermost crust of society who consumed the vegetable, and in contrast to its relative the cauliflower, the Brussels sprout had some difficulty making it into our kitchens because of its slightly sharper flavour.

During the cold winters, frost helps to mellow the sharp flavour, and the plant can also survive outdoors all winter, to the great pleasure of the local wildlife from hares to deer. Cut off the stalks and bring them in as you need them, or find a Brussels sprouts producer and buy the stalks directly from the field – they will easily stay fresh on the stalk for two weeks in a cold cellar or in the refrigerator. If you dig them up by the roots during a mild period and plant them in your garden, you will have fresh supplies throughout the winter. But don't worry if you can't eat them all – the small fresh shoots that come up in the spring are one of the most delicious vegetables you can have – just as delectable as green asparagus. Eat them raw or blanch them, then toss them in a good vinaigrette.

The worst thing you can do is to overcook Brussels sprouts. If you give them more than 5–6 minutes, they develop a fusty, bitter taste and lose their beautiful green colour. I prefer sprouts raw and marinated, either cut into thin slices or picked as whole, beautiful leaves. Try blanching sprouts for a few minutes in boiling water and then frying them in butter. Alternatively, glazing them in butter and cider vinegar is really quite amazing. Brussels sprouts also make a luscious purée.

Sliced Brussels sprouts

Wash the sprouts, then remove the outer leaves if they are damaged and cut off the bottom-most part of the root. Slice the sprouts into very fine strips with a sharp knife or a mandoline.

Brussels sprout leaves

Wash and prepare the sprouts as above. Using your fingers or a herb knife, carefully peel off the leaves, as many as possible until you reach the very heart of the sprout. The leaves are great in salads with root vegetables, apples or pears. Take note that the leaves should soak in the marinade for a little longer than with sliced sprouts – about 2–3 minutes in total before serving.

Boiled Brussels sprouts

Wash and prepare the sprouts as before. You can cook them whole or halved; personally, I prefer to halve them because the cooking time is shorter and you can cook them until tender while retaining their beautiful green colour and wonderful juiciness. Bring a pan of salted water to the boil, add the sprouts and cook until tender. As a rule of thumb, cook halved sprouts for 2–3 minutes and whole sprouts for 4–5 minutes. Once done, if they are to be used cold, plunge them directly into cold water so that they keep their colour and crispness. If you want to serve them hot, just take them directly from the pan to the table. Please don't leave sprouts for too long after they are cooked – it will ruin both their smell and their taste.

Brussels sprout salad

You will need about 100g Brussels sprouts, 2 tablespoons cider vinegar, 2 tablespoons cold-pressed rapeseed oil, sea salt flakes and freshly ground pepper and, if necessary, a little sugar.

Wash the sprouts and drain them thoroughly. Prepare them as before and then slice very finely (see left). Dress with the oil and vinegar, then season to taste with salt and pepper. Depending on the cider vinegar you have used, you may want to balance it with a little sugar.

Kale purée
with nutmeg and almonds

sea salt flakes
250g curly kale with stems removed
150g ricotta
30g Parmesan cheese, freshly grated
50g whole blanched almonds
finely grated zest of ½ organic lemon
4 tablespoons cold-pressed rapeseed oil
a little freshly grated nutmeg
freshly ground pepper

Bring a pan of lightly salted water to the boil. Check the kale for any pieces of stalk and discard, then wash it thoroughly in cold water. Add the kale to the boiling water and blanch for about 2 minutes, then immediately plunge it into a bowl of cold water – the kale should be tender but retaining its beautiful green colour and freshness.

Wring all the water out of the kale in a clean tea towel or between your hands, then place it in a food processor along with the ricotta, Parmesan, almonds, lemon zest and oil. Process to a coarse purée and season to taste with nutmeg, salt and pepper.

· ·

TIP This purée is perfect as a spread on toast or for tossing with pasta, or as dip for fried poultry and fish.

· ·

Bitter salad greens
with deep-fried onions and mustard and honey vinaigrette

Deep-fried onions
1 onion
sea salt flakes
1 litre standard rapeseed oil
a little plain flour

Salad
1 head of radicchio
½ frisée lettuce
½ handful of flat leaf parsley

Dressing
1 shallot
50ml apple balsamic vinegar
1 tablespoon prepared mustard
2 tablespoons honey
sea salt flakes and freshly ground pepper
50ml cold-pressed rapeseed oil

First make the deep-fried onions. Peel the onion and cut it into very thin rings. Sprinkle the onion rings with salt and leave to stand in the kitchen for 10–15 minutes until softened.

Pour the oil into a pan and heat it up slowly to about 160–170°C. It is important that the temperature of the oil is just right – check it by dipping the wooden end of a match into the oil, and if it bubbles a little around the match, the temperature is correct.

Dip the onion rings in a little flour and shake off the excess. Add the onion rings to the hot oil, a few at a time, and fry them for 1–2 minutes until golden and crisp. Remove with a slotted spoon and place them on kitchen paper to absorb the oil.

For the salad, tear the salad leaves roughly and rinse them thoroughly in cold water. Dry the leaves in a salad spinner or pat dry with a clean tea towel. Wash the parsley and pick off the leaves from the stems.

Now make the dressing. Peel and chop the shallot, then put it in a blender with the vinegar, mustard, honey, salt and pepper. Blend until the mixture is smooth, then slowly add the oil in a thin stream while the blender is still running to create a thick and smooth dressing.

Toss the salad with the parsley and dressing, and serve with the crispy onion rings on top. This salad is great with fried meat, where it provides a fresh and bitter contrast.

Crispy Brussels sprout salad
with orange, walnuts and pearl barley

SERVES 6

100g pearl barley
800ml water
sea salt flakes and freshly ground pepper
300g Brussels sprouts, rinsed
2 organic oranges
20g walnuts
4–5 flat leaf parsley sprigs
2 tablespoons cider vinegar
4 tablespoons cold-pressed rapeseed oil
1 tablespoon honey

Rinse the pearl barley in cold water, place in a saucepan and add the measurement water. Bring to the boil and cook the barley, with the lid on, for about 20 minutes until it is tender and has absorbed the water. Remove the pan from the heat and leave the barley to stand, still with the lid on, for 5–10 minutes. Now season with salt and pepper and leave the barley to cool completely.

Remove the outer leaves from the Brussels sprouts and discard, then cut off the bottom-most part of the root. Slice the sprouts finely with a sharp knife or a mandoline and place in a bowl. Grate the zest of the oranges finely and add to the sprouts. Peel the oranges, cut the orange flesh into small cubes and add them to the sprouts.

Break the walnuts into small pieces and mix them into the sprout salad, along with the cooked, cooled barley.

Pick the leaves from the parsley stems, wash them well and chop roughly, then toss into the salad. Now add the vinegar, oil, honey, salt and pepper, and mix well. Taste the salad – it might benefit from a little extra vinegar, salt or pepper. Serve the Brussels sprout salad as an accompaniment to Pigs' Cheeks (see page 199) or other main courses, or as a salad for lunch.

Baking and sweet things

Raisin buns

MAKES 15–20

500ml semi-skimmed milk
75g fresh yeast
100g softened butter
75g sugar
10g fine salt
1kg plain flour
2 teaspoons ground cardamom
1 teaspoon vanilla sugar (*see* tip,
    page 246)
3 organic eggs
150g raisins
1 organic egg, lightly beaten

Warm the milk a little (35–40°C) and then pour into a bowl and dissolve the yeast in it. Stir the softened butter, sugar and salt into the milk and mix well, then mix in the flour, cardamom and vanilla sugar. Finally, add the eggs, one at a time, and knead the dough for 10–15 minutes. Don't add the raisins yet – I will come back to those.

Leave the dough to rise in the kitchen, covered with a clean tea towel, for about 1 hour. Meanwhile, soak the raisins in cold water, which will prevent them from scorching when the buns are baked.

Drain the raisins and knead them into the risen dough. Divide the dough into 15–20 pieces and shape into buns. Put the buns on a baking sheet lined with baking paper and leave to rise in the kitchen until doubled in size.

Brush the buns with the beaten egg and bake in a preheated oven at 220°C/ Gas Mark 7 for 6–7 minutes until they are completely golden.

Take the buns out of the oven and leave them to cool slightly on a wire rack. Serve them with a little butter – nothing else. These buns are the best on the day of baking, but if you can't eat them all, they can be frozen and then defrosted and reheated as you need them.

Buns
with grated carrots and sunflower seeds

MAKES 20

700ml lukewarm water
20g fresh yeast
1 tablespoon acacia honey
2 tablespoons standard rapeseed oil
250g wholemeal flour, plus extra
    for dusting
50g sunflower seeds, chopped
3 teaspoons fine salt
150g peeled carrots
800g plain flour

Pour the measured lukewarm water into a bowl and mix in the yeast until dissolved. Add the honey, oil, wholemeal flour, chopped sunflower seeds and, finally, the salt, and stir to mix. Grate the carrots and add them to the dough. Add the flour, little by little, and then knead the dough in the bowl for 10–15 minutes. Cover with clingfilm and leave the dough to rise in the refrigerator for 8 hours.

Remove the dough from the refrigerator and place it on a floured surface.

Divide the dough into 20 pieces and shape them into buns. Place the buns on a baking sheet lined with baking paper and leave to rise in the kitchen for about 20 minutes.

Bake the buns in a preheated oven at 200°C (fan)/Gas Mark 7 for 12–14 minutes – the buns are ready if they sound hollow when you tap them on the bottom.

Take the buns out of the oven and leave to cool slightly on a wire rack. Eat them freshly baked, or use them as your lunch bread.

• •

Tip I often bake a large portion of these buns at the beginning of the week and freeze the few ones that my family haven't devoured while they are freshly baked. It is easy to defrost a single bun or two for packed lunches or for a snack during the week.

• •

St Lucia saffron buns

MAKES 10

1g saffron threads
400ml cold full-fat milk
50g fresh yeast
1 organic egg, lightly beaten,
    plus 1 extra beaten egg for brushing
800g plain flour, plus extra for dusting
15g sea salt flakes
80g sugar
100g butter, melted
raisins or currants, to decorate

Grind the saffron threads finely using a pestle and mortar. Pour the milk into a bowl and stir in the yeast. Add the egg, half the flour, the salt, sugar, ground saffron and melted butter, and knead in the bowl.

Incorporate the rest of the flour, but hold back a little – the dough should not be too firm, so it is up to you to determine whether you need it all. Knead the dough for 5–6 minutes, either in a stand mixer fitted with a dough hook or by hand in the bowl, until you have a supple, smooth dough.

Leave the dough to rest, covered with a clean tea towel, in the kitchen for about 2 hours.

Turn the dough out on a floured surface, divide it into 10 pieces and form each piece into a curved shape: the Lucia classic is a tightly closed 'S', but get creative with curved and plaited crosses, snails, curly 'U's, rams' horns and so on. Place the shapes on a baking sheet lined with baking paper and leave them to rise for 1 hour.

Brush the shapes with beaten egg and decorate them with raisins or currants. Bake them in a preheated oven at 200°C/ Gas Mark 6 for about 10–12 minutes. Take the buns out of the oven and leave to cool slightly on a wire rack. Eat the sweet, yellow bread freshly baked and warm – they taste of a happy childhood just as they are, and quite sinful with butter.

Buttermilk pancakes

MAKES ABOUT 20 PANCAKES

2 organic eggs
2 tablespoons unrefined cane sugar
finely grated zest of 1 organic lemon
½ vanilla pod, split lengthways and
    seeds scraped out
½ teaspoon fine salt
1 teaspoon bicarbonate of soda
1 teaspoon baking powder
300g plain flour
40g butter, melted, plus a little extra
    for frying, if needed
300ml buttermilk
100–150ml semi-skimmed milk

Beat the eggs with the sugar, lemon zest, vanilla seeds and salt in a bowl. Mix the bicarbonate of soda and baking powder with the flour and then sift into the egg mixture. Stir the butter into the batter and then slowly stir in the buttermilk and milk. Leave the batter to rest in the refrigerator for 3–4 hours.

Fry the batter in a small frying pan for 1–2 minutes on each side until golden. There is butter in the dough, but depending on the pan I use, I might also add a little butter to the pan while frying. My old blini pan is so 'saturated', it doesn't require any grease, but with other pans, I sometimes notice that the batter sticks to the pan if I don't add a little butter as I go. Keep the cooked pancakes warm in a dish covered with foil while you cook the rest. Enjoy the warm pancakes with syrup and fresh fruit. You can also bake the pancakes in advance and reheat them before serving.

Tip If you replace half the plain flour with wholemeal flour and remove the sugar, you have a great pancake recipe for savoury dishes – delicious as part of a brunch or in your packed lunch. Sometimes I add a handful of steamed spinach (drain off excess water) or freshly chopped herbs to the batter for a savoury meal.

Danish doughnut holes
with orange and cardamom

450g plain flour
½ teaspoon fine salt
2 teaspoons sugar
1 teaspoon ground cardamom
1 teaspoon bicarbonate of soda
½ teaspoon finely grated orange zest
3 organic eggs
400ml buttermilk
3 tablespoons standard rapeseed oil,
    plus extra for frying
juice of ½ organic orange
icing sugar, for sprinkling

Mix the flour, salt, sugar, cardamom, bicarbonate of soda and orange zest together in a bowl. Separate the eggs into yolks and whites, then beat the yolks with the buttermilk and stir into the dry ingredients. Also add the oil and the orange juice, then leave the batter to rest in the refrigerator for about 30 minutes.

Beat the egg whites until stiff and then fold into the batter – I always stir the first spoonful of the beaten egg whites in very thoroughly, then I can easily fold the rest gently into the batter without losing their airiness.

Warm a doughnut hole or *æbleskive* pan (*see* panel) and pour a little oil into each hole – this is only necessary for cooking the first round of batter, not for the rest because the oil is already added to the batter. Fill each hole three-quarters full with batter. When the doughnut holes begin to stiffen and rise at the edges, use a fork or a skewer to turn them upside down, and continue to turn them several times during cooking to make them perfectly round. Check whether the doughnut holes are done by poking them with the skewer – if any batter is stuck to it, keep cooking a little longer.

You can keep the cooked doughnut holes warm in the oven while you finish cooking the remaining batches of batter, or place them in a dish covered with foil. Serve the doughnut holes with a light sprinkling of icing sugar, and enjoy them with homemade jams and compotes.

Danish doughnut holes or *æbleskive*

Pastries are very regional. This also applies to the Danish æbleskive, literally meaning 'apple slice'. The currently familiar form – cakes baked in a special pan with semicircular indentations – is known only in Sweden, Norway and Denmark, and most evidence indicates that it was originally Danish. The æbleskive, earlier also known as 'monks', probably emerged as slices of apple dipped in a batter and baked in fat. However, the special æbleskive pan has been around since the 1500s, which made it possible to bake the small round cakes with much less fat. The southern Danish islands of Lolland and Falster had their own version known as svupsakker, created by poking a hole in the cake with your thumb and filling it with brandy.

Christmas cookies

MAKES 25–30

80g whole unblanched almonds
250g plain flour
½ teaspoon baking powder
125g icing sugar
1 vanilla pod
250g softened butter
1 organic egg, beaten

Put the almonds in a heatproof bowl, pour boiling water over and leave them to soak for 30 seconds. Drain and then peel off the skins. Dry the almonds with kitchen paper or a clean tea towel and grind them finely in a food processor – check for any remaining large pieces, as they will clog the piping bag later.

Sift the flour, baking powder and icing sugar into a large bowl and mix in the ground almonds. Split the vanilla pod lengthways, scrape out the seeds and mix them thoroughly into the flour mixture – it is easier to do this if you first sprinkle a little flour on the chopping board and mix the vanilla seeds into the flour with the flat side of a chef's knife. Stir the softened butter into the dry ingredients until you have a smooth paste, then mix in the beaten egg to create a supple dough.

Fill a piping bag, fitted with a small star nozzle, with the dough and pipe small rings on to a baking sheet lined with baking paper (you will probably need 3 baking sheets in total). If you find piping all the rings a bit too arduous, you can pipe the dough into long strips, cut these into 8–10cm lengths with a knife and then assemble the rings by hand.

Bake the vanilla cookies in a preheated oven at 170°C (fan)/Gas Mark 3½ for about 8 minutes until they are light golden around the edges. Take the cookies out of the oven and leave them to cool completely on a wire rack before you pack them into airtight cake tins, where they will remain crisp for 1–2 weeks.

Chocolate cream mousse

SERVES 8

6 organic egg yolks
120g unrefined caster sugar
200ml semi-skimmed milk
350ml whipping cream
300g good-quality dark chocolate, such as Valrhona Caraïbe 66%, chopped

Using an electric whisk or a balloon whisk, whisk the egg yolks and sugar together until white and foamy.

Pour the milk and cream into a saucepan and bring to the boil, then pour into the egg mixture and continue whisking. Pour the mixture back into the saucepan and cook over a low heat until thickened slightly, whisking constantly. Don't let it reach boiling point.

Remove the custard from the heat and pour through a sieve into a bowl containing the chopped chocolate. Stir with a spatula from the centre outwards so that you create a supple core of melted chocolate that gets bigger and bigger as you work your way outwards. Stir until all the chocolate is melted as it meets the warm cream. Pour into a bowl and place it in the refrigerator for 3–4 hours until it is firm.

This chocolate cream is a mix between a light truffle and a mousse, and it can be scooped up beautifully with a spoon dipped in hot water. Serve with candied or baked autumn fruit or fruit sauce.

Bread pudding
with apples and sultanas

25g butter
140g unrefined cane sugar
½ loaf of day-old white bread
3–4 apples
100g sultanas

4 organic eggs
300ml whipping cream
300ml semi-skimmed milk
1 vanilla pod
2 tablespoons icing sugar, plus extra for sprinkling

My home is a high bread-baking and bread-consuming household, so we usually have some day-old bread in stock that is a little dry around the edges. I have developed a wide repertoire of use-the-bread-to-the-last-crumb recipes and this easy bread pudding is one of them.

Grease an ovenproof dish with the butter and sprinkle with 2 tablespoons of the cane sugar. Cut the bread into thin slices. Wash and core the apples, then slice them into thin wedges. Arrange the bread and apple slices in alternate layers in the dish, sprinkling the sultanas in between.

Beat the eggs, cream, milk and the rest of the cane sugar together in a bowl. Split the vanilla pod lengthways, scrape the seeds out and add both the seeds and the scraped pod to the egg mixture. Pour the mixture over the bread and apples in the dish, sprinkle with the icing sugar and bake in a preheated oven at 180°C/Gas Mark 4 for about 25 minutes until the pudding is golden and crisp on top.

Sprinkle a little extra icing sugar over the pudding before serving, and enjoy it warm with a little crème fraîche, ice cream or lightly whipped cream.

• •

Tip You can replace the apples with red berries to make a summer pudding. Raspberries, blackcurrants, redcurrants and blackberries are all very well suited to this dish.

• •

Yogurt ice cream
with pomegranate

SERVES 4–6

700ml natural yogurt, 10% fat
200g sugar
1–2 teaspoons vanilla sugar (*see* tip)
2 pasteurized egg whites
1 pomegranate

Pour the yogurt into a bowl and add 50g of the sugar along with the vanilla sugar – the better the quality of vanilla sugar, the richer and more delicious the vanilla taste. Mix well and place in the freezer for about 1–1½ hours, stirring it occasionally.

Pour the egg whites into a clean, dry bowl (this is very important, as any impurities or moisture will prevent the whites from becoming perfectly stiff) and whisk them until stiff using an electric whisk. Add the remaining sugar and whisk again until the whites are dense and shiny.

Take the yogurt out of the freezer, gently fold the egg whites into the ice cream and put it back in the freezer. Freeze the ice cream for about 2–3 hours until it is solid but still has a creamy consistency. The ice cream can stay in the freezer for longer than 2–3 hours, but after several days it will become too hard.

Split the pomegranate and knock the seeds out with the back of a spoon. Serve the ice cream sprinkled with the beautiful fresh pomegranate seeds.

• •

Tip I use the good trick of saving empty vanilla pods in a preserving jar and filling it with light unrefined cane sugar. Every time I have a scraped vanilla pod, I put it in the jar and then top it up with sugar as I use some of the contents – it makes a very nice flavoured sugar.

• •

Crème brûlée
with stout and orange salad

SERVES 6–8

200ml stout
½ vanilla pod
250ml whipping cream
50ml semi-skimmed milk
70g sugar
3 organic egg yolks
finely grated zest of 1 organic lemon
unrefined cane sugar, for sprinkling

Pour the stout into a saucepan and reduce to half its original volume.

Scrape the seeds from the vanilla pod and add the seeds and the pod to a saucepan with the cream, milk and sugar. Bring to the boil, then pour the warm mixture into a bowl with the egg yolks. Add the stout and lemon zest and mix to a smooth mixture. Leave to cool in the refrigerator for 2–4 hours.

Pour the cream into 6–8 ramekins, place on a baking sheet and bake in a preheated oven at 90°C/lowest Gas Mark setting for about 1 hour. The mixture should be firm but won't rise like soufflés. When cooked, leave to cool in the refrigerator. Sprinkle a thin layer of the sugar on top of the cold cream and caramelize with a blowtorch until the surface is crisp. This can also be done under a very hot grill, but make sure the grill is at full temperature beforehand so that you don't also heat the cream. Serve immediately with the Orange Salad (see below).

Orange salad

3 organic oranges
15g whole blanched almonds
2 mint sprigs

Peel the oranges, making sure you remove all the white pith, then cut the orange flesh into small cubes, discarding any seeds. Chop the almonds and mint roughly and then mix with the orange.

White glogg
with fruit brandy and pear

MAKES 6–8 GLASSES

500ml good-quality cold-pressed or
  clear apple juice
300ml water
200ml elderflower concentrate or cordial
juice of ½ lemon, plus extra if needed
2 tablespoons unrefined cane sugar
1 star anise
3 whole black peppercorns
1 cardamom pod
1 slice of fresh root ginger, 5mm thick,
  peeled, plus extra if needed
50–100ml pear or apple brandy
1 pear
30g sultanas

Place all the ingredients, except the brandy, pear and sultanas, in a saucepan and bring to the boil. Take the pan off the heat and leave the glogg to stand for 30 minutes–1 hour for all the spices to infuse.

Strain the glogg through a sieve and slowly heat it up again, taste it and possibly add a little extra lemon juice or ginger – do not let it boil, as this changes the taste from distinctly gingery to intensely burning. When using fresh root ginger, the trick is to grate a little bit on the fine side of a grater and then squeeze the pulp between 2 spoons so that only the pure, strong ginger juice goes into the glogg.

Remove the glogg from the heat and season to taste with the brandy – again, do not allow the drink to boil after the brandy is added.

Wash the pear, cut it into quarters and remove the core, then cut the flesh into small cubes. Divide the pear cubes and sultanas between 6–8 heat-resistant glasses and pour the hot glogg on top. Serve straight away as a refreshing and spicy winter drink that will get the heat back in your cheeks after a walk in the cold.

Index

Manifesto for the New Nordic Cuisine

As Nordic chefs we find that the time has now come for us to create a New Nordic Cuisine, which in virtue of its good taste and special character compares favourably with the standard of the greatest kitchens of the world. The aims of the New Nordic Cuisine are:

*
To express the purity, freshness, simplicity and ethics we wish to associate to our region.

*
To reflect the changes of the seasons in the meals we make.

*
To base our cooking on using ingredients and produce that are characteristically from our own climate, landscape and waters.

*
To combine the demand for good taste with modern knowledge of health and well-being.

*
To promote Nordic products and the variety of Nordic producers, and to spread the word about their underlying cultures.

*
To promote animal welfare and ethical production process in our seas, on our farmland and in the wild.

*
To develop potentially new applications of traditional Nordic food products.

*
To combine the best in Nordic cookery and culinary traditions with influences from abroad.

*
To combine local self-suffiency with regional sharing of high-quality products.

*
To join forces with consumer representatives, other cooking craftsmen, agriculture, fishing, food, retail and wholesales industries, researchers, teachers, politicians and authorities on this project for the benefit and advantage of everyone in the Nordic countries.

Erwin Lauterbach

René Redzepi

Hans Välimäki

Leif Sørensen

Rune Collin

Mathias Dahlgren

Gunndur Fossdal

Roger Malmin

Hákan Örvarsson

Ejvind Hellstrøm

Fredrik Sigurdsson

Michael Björklund

Signed at The Nordic Cuisine Symposium, 18th November, 2004

An Hachette UK Company
www.hachette.co.uk

First published in Great Britain in 2016
by Mitchell Beazley, a division of
Octopus Publishing Group Ltd
Carmelite House
50 Victoria Embankment
London EC4Y 0DZ
www.octopusbooks.co.uk

ISBN 978 1 78472 156 5

A CIP catalogue record for this book is
available from the British Library.

Printed and bound in China

10 9 8 7 6 5 4 3 2 1

Group Publishing Director Denise Bates
Managing Editor Sybella Stephens
Translation DHC Translations
Copyeditor Jo Richardson
Photographer Anders Schønnemann
Creative Director Jonathan Christie
Designer Jack Storey
Senior Production Manager
  Katherine Hockley

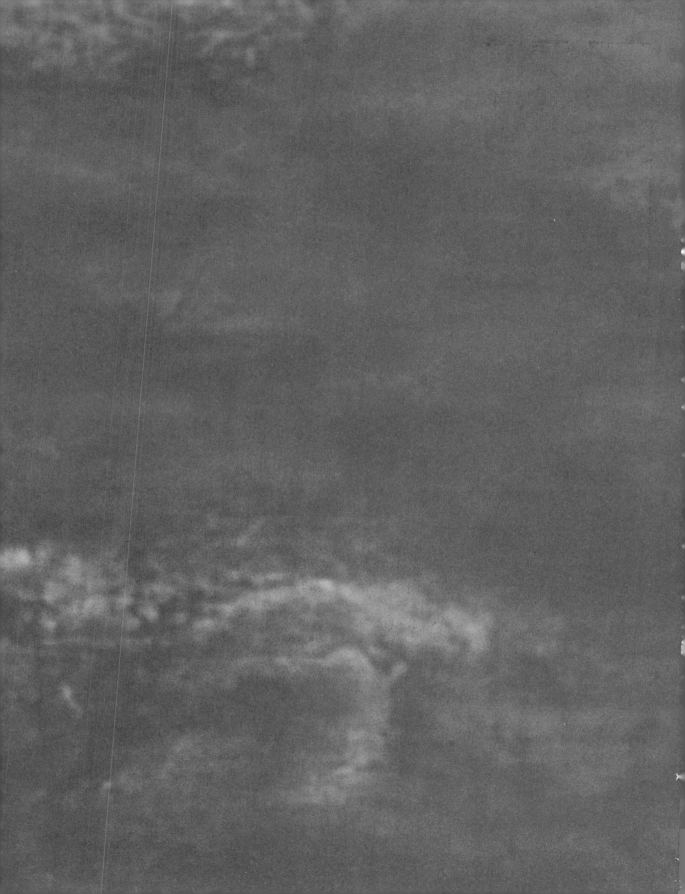